Themes in Comparative History

Editorial Consultants: Alan Milward
Harold Perkin
Gwyn Williams

This series of books provides concise studies on some of the major themes currently arousing academic controversy in the fields of economic and social history. Each author explores a given theme in a comparative context, drawing on material from western societies as well as those in the wider world. The books are introductory and explanatory and are designed for all those following thematic courses in history, cultural European or social studies.

Themes in Comparative History

General Editor: CLIVE EMSLEY

PUBLISHED TITLES

Jane Rendall
  THE ORIGINS OF MODERN FEMINISM: WOMEN IN
  BRITAIN, FRANCE AND THE UNITED STATES,
  1780–1860
R.F. Holland
  EUROPEAN DECOLONIZATION 1918–1980
Dominic Lieven
  THE EUROPEAN ARISTOCRACY 1815–1914
Ken Ward
  MASS COMMUNICATIONS AND THE MODERN WORLD
Pamela Pilbeam
  THE MIDDLE CLASSES IN EUROPE 1789–1914: FRANCE,
  GERMANY, ITALY AND RUSSIA
Ian Inkster
  SCIENCE AND TECHNOLOGY IN HISTORY

FORTHCOMING

David Englander and Tony Mason
  WAR AND POLITICS: THE EXPERIENCE OF THE
  SERVICEMAN IN TWO WORLD WARS
Joe Lee
  PEASANT EUROPE IN THE 18th AND 19th CENTURIES
Rosemary O'Day
  THE FAMILY IN FRANCE, ENGLAND AND THE UNITED
  STATES OF AMERICA, 1600–1850

MASS COMMUNICATIONS AND THE MODERN WORLD

Ken Ward

MACMILLAN

First published 1989 by
THE MACMILLAN PRESS LTD
Houndmills, Basingstoke, Hampshire RG21 2XS
and London
Companies and representatives
throughout the world

ISBN 0–333–37262–X hardcover
ISBN 0–333–37263–8 paperback

Printed in Hong Kong

Reprinted 1990, 1991, 1993

Contents

General Editor's Preface

SINCE the Second World War there has been a massive expansion in the study of economic and social history generating, and fuelled by, new journals, new academic series and societies. The expansion of research has given rise to new debates and ferocious controversies. This series proposes to take up some of the current issues in historical debate and explore them in a comparative framework.

Historians, of course, are principally concerned with unique events, and they can be inclined to wrap themselves in the isolating greatcoats of their 'country' and their 'period'. It is at least arguable, however, that a comparison of events, or a comparison of the way in which different societies coped with a similar problem – war, industrialisation, population growth and so forth – can reveal new perspectives and new questions. The authors of the volumes in this series have each taken an issue to explore in such a comparative framework. The books are not designed to be path-breaking monographs, though most will contain a degree of new research. The intention is, by exploring problems across national boundaries, to encourage students in tertiary education, in sixth-forms, and hopefully also the more general reader, to think critically about aspects of past developments. No author can maintain strict objectivity; nor can he or she provide definitive answers to all the questions which they explore. If the authors generate discussion and increase perception, then their task is well done.

CLIVE EMSLEY

Preface

In 1952 our television set went on fire while we were watching newsfilm of Sergeant Bill Speakman receiving a Victoria Cross for heroic deeds in Korea; since then I have been aware of the danger of studying the media too closely. However, living and working in Northern Ireland over the last twenty years has encouraged the view that such a study is of crucial importance to any understanding of the character of modern society. Furthermore, the view from 'the edge of the Union' has emphasised the importance of placing the British experience within a wider framework, and the necessity for comparative history.

It has been my good fortune to have had heads of department who have encouraged me to study the history of the media: Bill Wallace in the New University of Ulster, and subsequently Peter Roebuck, when it stopped being new. Of my colleagues I must particularly thank Alan Sharp, Gill Coward, Tom Fraser, Steve Ickringill and Des Cranston, who have helped to focus my ideas, not always to their, or my, satisfaction. The contribution of students over the years has been incalculable, not least of those who reminded me that I was a 'Brit'.

This book has been a long time in gestation, and my thanks must go to Clive Emsley for his patience and encouragement: that it is finished at all is due to the belief of Eileen and the boys that it would never happen, and by becoming media stars and winning BBC TV's *Ask the Family* they provided the computer on which it was written.

KEN WARD

University of Ulster at Coleraine

1. Introduction

THE aim of this book is to study the development of three forms of mass media in three countries, between 1870 and 1970: a simple statement which hides fundamental problems of methodology, selection and organisation.

The process of communication may be considered by studying the communicators and the nature of the institutions in which they work, or the character of the audience, or the structure and meaning of the message, or the relationship between all three. Each of these approaches relies upon different academic disciplines; sociology, psychology or linguistics: the choice of approach depends upon the interest and outlook of the investigator. Each individual medium has its own specific institutional organisation, technology, message structure, and relationship to the audience. Any attempt at a comparison of their role in a developing society must emphasise common features while recognising the distinctive characteristics which affect the form and reception of the messages.

The main concern in this book will be the political and institutional frameworks within which forms of mass communication have been located and controlled. This approach has been partly dictated by the greater amount of material available in this area, and my particular interest in the relationship between the mass media and the state. However, there is an underlying assumption in the book that the audience for the products of the mass media should be seen as differentiated and active participants in the communication process. Furthermore, there is an implicit acceptance of the importance of studying the texts as bearers of meanings, encoded by the communicators and decoded by the audience.

One major deficiency in any attempt to discuss a visual or moving medium in print is the impossibility of reproducing the texts in any meaningful way. I am likely myself, in the course of the book, to ascribe particular importance to particular films or programmes without emphasising the ways in which audiences might negotiate with different aspects of the text. It is the result of lack of space rather than a lack of awareness.

The problems of comparing media are compounded by considering their role in three different societies. All forms of mass communication have been sited within technological, industrial and political frameworks but these, in turn, have developed in different ways over the last hundred years. The importance of a comparative study lies in establishing those factors which were common to all societies, and understanding why they arrived at different solutions to common problems. The choice of Great Britain, the United States of America, and Germany is, once more, partly the result of an abundance of material, and partly their contrasting and interlinked experience. They have been three of the greatest contributors to the political and ideological shaping of the contemporary world, and have been in the forefront of all the major developments in mass communications.

The book is chronological in structure, not only to produce a coherent narrative, but also to emphasise the importance of change through time, and the interlinked character of developments in different media and different societies. The work is concerned with the process of modernisation, and how forms of mass communication were connected to changes in the industrial, political and social structure of society after 1870. Although an analysis of the press requires discussion of earlier developments, the starting date is not arbitrary since at this time both the USA and Germany began to consolidate new political structures and commence the path towards industrial supremacy. Britain, too, moved to a new plane of industrial and political maturity, and entered a period of imperial expansion. The growth of political democracy was matched by the concomitant growth of state power, and forms of mass communication would not only reflect these changes, but also be instrumental in creating the means by which the two might be reconciled in the political consciousness of populations.

The study concludes at the point when new technologies once again raise fundamental questions about the role of the media in the state, and the way they might shape the contemporary world. The current debates merely continue those which have been in existence over the last hundred years, and even longer. This book is an attempt to provide an historical framework within which to place present and future controversies.

Throughout the period covered by the book there has been a continuing debate about the function of the mass media in society. It has been conducted within the pages of learned books and journals, in government reports, in court judgements, as well as in the policy-making structures of media institutions and governments. The debate has been centred around fundamental beliefs about the nature of man, society as a whole and the ways in which change is effected and dominance secured. The main aspects of that debate are presented as an opening chapter which while offering a coherent statement is also intended to emphasise the diversity of views, and their often contradictory character.

Those contradictions may well surface in the text which follows, since the discussion is not based upon a strict theoretical framework. Underlying the work is my own belief in active audiences negotiating with media texts, which in themselves emanate from institutions embedded in the political, social and economic infrastructure of society. How these exert influence, as against other institutions and social pressures, I am still in the process of learning. This book is a contribution to my own area of knowledge.

2. Approaches to the Study of the Media

THE last two decades have witnessed a growing awareness among contemporary historians of the importance of mass communications in understanding historical developments over the last hundred years. Assumptions about the influence of propaganda, the escapist character of feature films, the newspaper as a 'Fourth Estate' in the political organisation of Britain, and the neutrality of 'public service broadcasting' have been subjected to rigorous and systematic examination. For many years contemporary historians in Britain, although less so in Europe and the United States, regarded the mass media as peripheral to their main concerns, and considered newspapers and films as unproblematical sources of evidence of public opinion. A wider discussion of the evaluation of historical sources and a greater awareness of the complex character of mass communications in society has provoked a change in outlook which is reflected in this book.

Since historians have only recently entered the continuing debate about the role and function of the mass media, the frameworks of analysis within which this discussion takes place have been set mainly by literary critics and social scientists, and historians follow them with some trepidation. Many are suspicious of theoretical and predictive models which are often the stock in trade and *raison d'être* of social theorists. They are also unwilling to extrapolate from the particular to the general as some empirical social scientists are wont to do. Furthermore, the multiplicity of approaches and complexity of theories sometimes militates against clear exposition.

There is, however, much to be gained from an awareness of the ways in which sociologists have attempted to quantify and analyse the character of the mass communication process since they have been concerned to define the elements and assess the effects of one upon another.

Society, it has been suggested, 'is not only a network of political and economic arrangements, but also a process of learning and communication'. Society is how individual members understand it to be; a perception achieved by assessing and processing the information which is available to them. The most important point is that society is not static, but a continuously changing environment within which individuals orientate themselves to each other, and reflect their response to the changes in the character and content of communication.

Social interactions, acts of communication, define the society by reflecting and reaffirming particular forms of relationship between individuals and institutions. They take place through specific channels, in particular languages and symbolic codings and are particularly associated with the organisation of power in society.

An act of interpersonal communication may be simply described as a communicator sending a message to a receiver. The simplicity of this statement disguises the complexity of the relationship, and at the same time is a reflection of a view of the way in which communication takes place which may be quite erroneous, and would therefore need further qualification.

The communicator may be a single person, or groups of people within an institution; for instance, a government department or a Rotary Club. The linear form of the model suggests that the communicator originates the message to which the receiver, passively, appears to react. However, in most social situations an active choice is made between any number of messages emanating from numerous sources. The receiver, in choosing one message, is 'initiating' a relationship with the communicator.

The message may be considered at three levels. There is the information which it contains, presumably requiring a reaction from the receiver. In order to achieve this response it must be coded in a language, or shared sign system, understandable to both parties. Furthermore, it requires a medium of transmission which is accessible to communicator and receiver.

The concept of a linear relationship between the three elements in the system is clearly inadequate to explore the nature of the communication process. It leaves out the role of 'feedback' which may take many forms, from facial expressions in interpersonal contact to voting preferences at elections. In this way the information provided by the communicator may be modified in the light of information gained from the receiver. Communication is invariably circular, with messages of various kinds moving between groups and individuals, and without the rationality and purposiveness suggested by the linear model.

Communication takes place within a 'shared environment', in that the participants in the process live within social, linguistic, physical and temporal frameworks which hold them together, but which in turn are mediated to the participants through the messages circulating in the system. This is what Williams means by 'the learning' element. Efficient communication depends upon 'shared understandings' of the messages between communicators and receivers, but the very fact of communication alters the relationship between the participants and subsequently their understanding of the society and their part in it. While the linear model suggests that the message is intended to have an immediate effect on the receiver, the actual nature of the changes occurring because of the communication process is much less specific.

In outlining this simplified concept of communication I have been following, in the main, a school of thought which argues that the process of social interaction is how an individual establishes his relationship to the rest of society through an exchange of messages. The emphasis is on the efficiency and accuracy of the communication process, and as far as possible a reduction of 'noise' in the system; that is, obstacles which preclude easy communication, such as different languages or misheard remarks. There is, however, an approach which is more concerned with the content of the message and the construction of meanings which lie within it. The emphasis is on an examination of the text of the message and the way in which a communicator/receiver negotiates with it, so producing the 'shared understandings' which, it has been suggested, are a key element in constructing the commonality of individuals in society.

It is an approach which concentrates on the language, rather than the process, of communication and which has drawn upon the work of linguistic theorists, social anthropologists and psychologists. In looking particularly at the relationship between language and meaning it is concerned with the underlying ideological frameworks of society.

This emphasis upon ideology has proved to be one of the most controversial aspects of the debate about communication. Such an approach seeks to investigate further the way in which 'shared understandings' affect the organisation of society and how they are arrived at. Marxist and post-Marxist analyses of society have been particularly concerned with the importance of ideology as a channel of class dominance and an active constituent in the formation of social frameworks. It is particularly relevant to the discussion of mass communications and we shall return to it at a later stage.

I have identified some of the problems in looking at communication in society as a necessary prelude to examining the specific characteristics of the mass media. While still working within the framework of communicator/message/receiver we must consider in more detail each element, and the importance of the medium of transmission.

Harold Lasswell, an American social scientist, provided a verbal model for mass communication which often serves as a starting point for discussion:

WHO SAYS WHAT, TO WHOM, THROUGH WHAT CHANNEL, WITH WHAT EFFECT

and it can be readily identified with the linear model of communication with which we started. It clearly lays out the areas of enquiry which may be answered in an *ad hoc* fashion but emphasises the role of the medium, and states more specifically the social importance of the effect of the message upon the receiver, in this case an audience. Although subject to much criticism, which we shall examine later, Lasswell's model does direct our attention to each discrete area of the communication process and allow us to examine how they differ from inter-personal communication.

In the case of the communicator (the who) we are not concerned with individuals but groups organised in commercial and bureaucratic structures who produce a message. This may be a newspaper office, broadcasting organisation or film company. Each of these institutions has its own internal form of communication, norms and practices which sets it apart from its audience and within which the message is constructed. Similarly the audience (the whom) is a collectivity of individuals, but without the internal communication structure of the communicating institution.

The content of the message (the what) is susceptible to the semiological approach which we have already discussed, but the medium (the channel) takes on a particular importance in mass communications. The medium is a form of technological apparatus which is capable of reproducing the same message, simultaneously, for large numbers of people; this may be either the large-scale printing press, broadcasting transmitter, or film camera/projector. The media of mass communication are not neutral channels for the flow of information, but determine both the organisation and content of the messages. Furthermore, since the technical apparatus is expensive, access to its use is restricted, either for economic or political reasons, and often situated within and organised by the institutions which produce the message.

The technologies of mass communication produce a uni-directional flow of information with very little opportunity for the audience to respond directly to the communicator, and the speed of diffusion and simultaneous reception does lead to a greater uniformity of selection and interpretation of the message by the audience.

Lasswell's model identifies the four main elements in the communication process and encourages discussion of their main characteristics but his fifth question, to what effect, has produced the most criticism and debate. As Seymour-Ure points out, it appears to be tacked on at the end, with no clear focus of enquiry, and in the absence of this one assumes he means 'effect upon the audience'. Therefore, as in the case of the general communication model, assumptions about the role of mass communications in society underpin Lasswell's formula.

What if one asked the question, 'with what intention?' It would immediately focus on the 'who' rather than the 'whom', which was of lesser concern to Lasswell in the 1940s. He was part of a long tradition which believed in the power of the new forms of communication to influence the beliefs and behaviour of large numbers of people.

It is important to recognise the shifts in outlook among social scientists and theorists about the role of the mass media in society since they reflect popular fears. Early social thinkers, concerned with the development of industrial societies at the end of the nineteenth century, became convinced of the persuasive power of the forms of mass communication which developed in the period. They perceived of urban societies as consisting of individuals, divorced from their roots, who were susceptible to the messages and ideas produced by newspapers and films, and eventually broadcasting. A concept of a 'mass society' created by the products of the mass media was one which dominated critical thinking for well over fifty years, and is still found in public discussions about the mass media in the 1980s.

The concern over the role of mass communications was only one aspect of a generally pessimistic view of the effect of industrialisation upon political and cultural life. To the critics mass society was an amalgam of large-scale factory production, urban conglomerations, the growth of centralised state apparatuses, and new democratic political organisations, mobilising and politicising subordinate groups in society. The apparent breaking down of old values and modes of political and economic organisation posed a threat to elites, and this was symbolised in terms of the tyranny of the 'mass'.

It was a highly romanticised view of society and the nature of man, constructed out of the political and cultural fears of groups of men who found their own position threatened. While some saw a threat in the challenge to an aristocratic, elitist form of government from liberal, bourgeois politicians who appeared to espouse democracy, others saw the threat to their control of democratic practice from the more numerous, but less articulate 'mass'.

Both strands of political pessimism regarded the growth of popular education as essentially detrimental since it appeared to level society to a lowest common denominator, instead of allowing individualism and competition to develop. The growth of mass communications, in their eyes, merely compounded this tendency.

In Britain, cultural pessimists such as T. S. Eliot and F. R. Leavis, in the 1920s and 1930s, bemoaned the undermining of individual cultural experience by the products of the mass media. They harked back to a world in which different cultural traditions co-existed, but where cultural leadership lay with an elite. 'Mass culture', to them, was that produced for the non-discriminating masses by the mass media of film and publishing, concerned with providing a 'divertissement' for a passive public. People, in

Leavis's view, lacked a critical standpoint, as evidenced by the decline in literary standards, and this in turn was one sign of a crisis of values in society. The indigenous culture of the people, moving across barriers of status and class, had been packaged by the commercialised media into a form of 'popular culture' which was both inferior and dangerous in that it undermined and de-humanised a population.

This conservative approach to the changes in society was paralleled and echoed by a similar pessimism from Marxist critics in the same period. The reason lay partly in the fact that there was no body of theory developed by Marx to deal with the development of mass communications, although questions of ideology were central to the Marxist analysis of society. This critique is normally associated with a group called the Frankfurt School.

Theodor Adorno, Max Horkheimer, and Herbert Marcuse were influential members of the Institute of Social Research in Frankfurt, who on the rise to power of the National Socialists in the 1930s, emigrated with others to the United States, and had an important influence on social thinking on both sides of the Atlantic. As convinced Marxists they had experienced and contemplated the failure of socialist revolution in Germany, and the rise of fascist movements; as emigrants they brought their European perceptions to America, and sought to understand how the capitalist societies were able to survive and prosper in a time of revolutionary change.

They recognised the importance of economic and technological changes in affecting older socialising agencies, and in particular, the family. This they saw as one aspect of the demise of the autonomous individual and his subservience to the state, and the mediating organisations, such as the mass media, provided a 'popular culture' which deadened perceptions and created and encouraged passivity. In this way the Frankfurt theorists answered the question of how the working class was deradicalised, but they were as elitist in outlook as the conservative critics of the mass media, seeing the audience as passively accepting its products.

Culture was clearly of importance to the Frankfurt School, although they were divided over the way in which the new technological forms affected art through the nature of reproduction. Whereas in Britain the debate was conducted in the main by cultural theorists, in the United States the sociological theories of the Frankfurt School provoked empirical research in order to test some of their assumptions about the character and organisation of mass society.

The theories of 'mass society' had effectively set the agenda for investigation into the character of mass communication processes. The concept of a uni-directional flow of information, pacifying an audience, produced an image of inoculation, a 'hypodermic' view of mass communication whereby information was injected into the audience and produced an instant response. It was within this context that much empirical scientific research was organised, primarily investigating the audience and the direct effect of mass media messages upon it.

Intellectual critics articulated a general concern about the development of the mass media in some circles. The growth of the mass-circulation popular press and the popularity of the cinema among the lower classes was associated in some peoples' minds with a decline in morality and growth in the levels of crime and violence, particularly among young people. Since the most visible 'new' factors in society were the media of mass communication, philanthropic foundations and government agencies began to provide funds for close observational research of tangible effects upon individuals and groups in society.

Mass media institutions, particularly advertisers, and those who depended upon advertising for their continued existence, were also concerned about the effect of their products upon the public and they funded research. The development of market research and public opinion polls in the 1930s was a direct result of the needs of commercial organisations to discover the tastes and outlooks of the consuming public.

The result of this research, which began to be noted publicly in the 1940s, failed to substantiate the claims advanced by 'mass society' theorists. The mass media, it was now suggested, were only one of a number of variables which acted upon the individual in society, and the effect was generally one of reinforcing previously held attitudes, rather than changing them. Such changes as there were could not be put down solely to the mass media, but to a combination of circumstances at the time. It had also become clear that much more research was required on the nature and performance of the media institution originating the message, and particularly the attitude of the audience towards them.

By focusing attention on the audience, effects research had demonstrated the importance of prior attitudes towards social and political events, as well as placing the information gained from the mass media into the wider context of communication in society. The idea of a passive audience as an undifferentiated mass, although not completely abandoned in the popular mind, and reinforced by the continued use of terms such as 'mass media', began to give way to that of groups of people and individuals actively engaging with the messages provided by the media. Emphasis was placed on the way members of an audience 'used' the products of the mass media for their own social 'gratification'. Research over the last twenty years has suggested that individuals seek out material which will confirm their own social and political outlook, as well as support their status in their own social grouping.

The weakness in this approach lies in estimating the declared aims and needs of the audience, as against those which may be unconscious and unarticulated. Nevertheless, the emphasis on the active character and diversity of the audience was a necessary corrective to some earlier approaches.

Paralleling this approach were others which took as their starting point other elements in the mass communication process. There had been a few studies of mass media institutions in the 1940s and 1950s, but now a more systematic review of the social position, organisation and performance of the 'communicators' was started. Whereas the uni-directional model of mass communication suggested that the primary focus of research should be on the relationship with the audience, the new perspectives concentrated on the internal dynamics of the mass media organisations and their external relationships with other institutions in the state.

The main concern was to investigate how far social and political influence, of a general or specific character, affected the outlook and performance of the individual communicators, and the content and form of the message. It was not an easy task, since it was intimately connected with the wider question of the control and dissemination of knowledge in society and its relationship to the organisation of the power structure. The concept of media institutions as 'neutral' channels of communication in society was seriously challenged, and their interactive role in society was re-emphasised.

The performance and output of all mass media organisations are affected by the work practices, management structures, forms of financial control and marketing operations which are part and parcel of an industrial concern. Empirical observations by sociologists working inside the institutions have focused on the routine procedures in the collection and organisation of news, or the production of entertainment programmes. This, in turn, is linked to the idea of professional standards by which norms and values inside the institution are reinforced. Ideas of what is news, or 'good' programmes, are held in common and receive internal approbation in the form of personal promotion or the allocation of further resources. The allegiance of the individual communicators is as much, if not more, to the institution which employs them as to the audience they seek to serve, since their own work depends on the continuing existence of the organisation.

They also act as representatives of the institution to the world outside, and can affect its relationship with other organisations and individuals who are interested in the general dissemination of information and the performance of the mass media. This will include commercial and financial interests as well as institutions of government. A consideration of the external constraints upon mass media institutions once again raises the question of the way in which the economically powerful might organise and determine their output either through the allocation of capital resources to the institution, or through influence on government apparatus.

The wholly deterministic approach of the Frankfurt School would have found the empirical evidence for their theories in the concentration of ownership in major industrialised societies over the last hundred years. This has included newspapers, film production companies and some broadcasting organisations. Since their main objective is to maximise profits, either through the sale of advertising, or by attracting the largest audience, there are clear policy implications for the mass media institutions and their employees. There is no doubt that commercial pressures are important determinants of the performance of the mass media in any society, but they have particular relevance in democracies where the expression of a diversity of opinions and outlooks is regarded as a necessary element in the organisation of the state.

This perspective emphasises the commercial constraints on the mass media, including those, like the BBC in Britain, which while apparently secure in its financing through a licence fee, must now compete for the largest audience in a commercial environment in order to justify that particular form of funding. Furthermore, if resources become scarce, production becomes restricted to that which is commercially viable, and small-scale operations are liable to be absorbed into larger, well-established groups, restricting still further the possibility of access to the mainstream market of opinions and outlooks which have little economic potential.

Media organisations have been areas of capital diversification for other commercial enterprises, as well as investing, themselves, in non-media operations. This, in turn, has produced an interlinking of interests which have to be taken into account when looking at the performance of the institutions.

At the same time the state, as an organisation concerned with the general welfare and outlook of all its citizens, has a role to play in the mass communications industries. There are legal restraints on the communicators, aimed at preserving the rights and general welfare of the individual, and the existence of the state itself. The extent to which a government avails itself of such powers, and the interpretation it gives to such responsibilities, are directly related to the political and social principles upon which it has been founded and continues to exist. The state may define the legal parameters within which the media may operate, but in democratic societies it would rarely intervene directly in the production process.

The result is a form of self-censorship within media organisations, attempting to define the shifting limits of public taste and political acceptability without incurring the interest and intervention of the government. The routines of production, forms of editorial control, and professional practices act as internal safeguards in media organisations against external interference, whether it be the Hays Office in Hollywood in the 1920s, or the referral upward of contentious news stories in television in the present day.

The general effect of the external constraints, both commercial and governmental, upon the content and form of messages is to produce a stereotyping of individuals and countries, and a patterning of events, leading to a coherent and consistent outlook on the world, of which the communicator and the audience are part. By the means of mass communication we have the provision and selective construction of social knowledge, of social imagery, through which we perceive the 'worlds', the 'lived realities' of others, and imaginarily reconstruct their lives and ours into some intelligible 'world-of-the-whole', some 'lived totality'.

The complexity of modern society is brought into a unified focus within the messages, whether films, newspaper stories or television programmes, produced by the institutions of the mass media. The 'neutrality' of the channel is a fiction, since it is completely bound up with the economic, social and political structures in society. While appearing to reflect consensual values in society the messages are in fact constructing and reinforcing them, acting as a form of social control, not imposed by the state, but subscribing to those values which predominate; allowing an appearance of freedom of opinion while effectively restricting it. Yet the acceptance of the picture of the world presented by the mass media depends upon it 'making sense' to the audience. Clearly, it will have a greater effect where there are no personal bases of knowledge or completely formed views and where trust in the source of information is greatest. However, there is one further approach which suggests that an examination of the message itself is a valid way of examining the communication process.

One form this takes is content analysis, an empirical approach, which is concerned with identifying and counting chosen elements in the message. In this way a verifiable pattern can be established which is based on a number of comparisons in usage within the text. It may be the number and kind of words used to describe someone, or the form in which stereotyping of groups occurs. The problem with this approach lies in its inability to answer the question, why? It can provide the information on which a debate may proceed, but only the most sophisticated analysis can offer anything but the crudest statement about intention and effect. The larger the survey of message content across all the media the more likely it is that significant patterns will recur which may give some clue to how values and norms are presented within the texts. Content analysis studies presume there is a reality to be explored and verified, structural analysis of the texts, or semiology, examines reality as something constructed within the message itself.

While other approaches have utilised the expertise of psychologists, historians and political scientists, the source of this theoretical approach lies in linguistics and social anthropology and revolves around the importance of language as the creator and communicator of meaning in society. Rather than concentrate on the process of communication, it is argued, we should consider how ideas are communicated through sign systems.

The 'sign' is any unit in a verbal or non-verbal language system which is used by people as a form of communication. These in turn are organised into codes which are connected to specific societies and cultures and effectively define them for the participants in the system. The sign must always have an object to which it refers and a user to interpret the sign and the object. It is therefore a key element in the communication process.

The linguist, Ferdinand de Saussure, emphasised much more the importance of the 'sign' itself rather than the object it represented, splitting it into two elements: the signifier, the image of the sign; and the signified, the mental concept to which it refers. To Saussure the important relationship was between the signs themselves and how an image of society was built up through its use of different codes.

The important development of this theory for mass communications lay in the work of Roland Barthes, who considered the way in which the text interacted with the environment in which it was placed, and this has a special significance in understanding the development of ideology, that is the production of meanings and ideas which form a system of belief.

Barthes developed the ideas of Saussure by arguing that there were two orders of signification, and that which was signified and denoted at the first became connotated at the second, and was linked to the idea of myth. This meant that all signs had a commonsense denotation which linked to a specific reality, while the connotation was part of a wider belief system which was confirmed and developed through the second order of signification; as a consequence all forms of texts can be analysed for their ideological construction. Thus unstated assumptions and outlooks are reaffirmed through the organisation of conventional codes used in specific societies and in this way the commonality of a group can be reasserted by the use of common symbols since the recognition and acceptance of particular signs places the individual within a particular group. The structure of the message becomes the crucial element in the communication of ideas and values, but the active nature of the audience has been asserted, since it may, or may not, reject the connotative values embodied in the text, and may produce a totally different reading.

It is at this point that structural analysis as a theoretical tool has made an important contribution to the general theories of mass communication. We have noted that an examination of the component elements in the process of communication does not produce a totally satisfactory explanation of the way in which communication is related to social change in the modern world. The deterministic outlook of many critics has had to be refined, but the problem still lies in understanding how mass communications affect society. By concentrating on the creation of meaning, and explaining how this is organised within the texts, the socially integrative character of mass communication may be examined.

If society is seen as the field in which competition between social and political groups is constantly taking place, then the dominance of one group over others cannot be secured for ever, but must take account of other oppositional and subordinate elements and win them over. One area in which this is continually taking place, it is argued, is within the messages produced by the mass media. There is continual reworking of ideological forms through the production and encoding of texts with which the heterogenous audience engage and decode. The way in which individual elements in the audience react to texts will depend on their own social conditions, but the range of readings available to them will be constrained within a number of dominant ideologies, thus producing a preferred reading of the text. This operates at the connotative level and the texts construct and reaffirm a view of society within which the changes affecting individuals are made 'intelligible'. In this way social change may be mediated through the texts produced within the mass media and a cognitive world constructed in which the tensions in society may be played out and resolved.

Whether this is in fact the case is still a matter of speculation. By arguing against the determinism of the early Marxist theorists it avoids the idea of a passive audience and the simplistic view of the creation of a false consciousness. It takes account of the complex organisation of media institutions, and gives no primacy to any one form of message. It is, however, based on a clear view of the economic and political organisation of power in society revolving around the importance of class relationships, and for this reason is rejected by critics who argue that the mass media merely reflect an achieved consensus within a pluralist society. They, however, still have to explain how the consensus is reached, and recognised.

There are still two areas of discussion which need to be explored: the first is the importance of technology in the mass communication process; the second, the specific characteristics and interaction between different forms of the mass media. Both cases affect our understanding of the relationship between the mass media and the modern world.

The ability to reproduce and disseminate texts simultaneously, and in some cases, immediately, to a large audience depended upon a sequence of scientific developments which were often unconnected. Our main consideration must be how the particular forms of technology were used and developed within specific institutions for particular purposes, and how far they determined the content and form of the messages conveyed in the process of communication.

The expansion of the large-circulation newspaper press would have been impossible without separate developments in the fields of paper-making, printing and distribution. However, the form and content were the result of improvements in news collection through telegraphy and telephony, and the introduction of photography. How each of these elements was used depended on the aims and outlook of newspaper proprietors, and how much capital was required.

Improvements in photography and experiments in producing moving images were the important first stage in the technical development of film as a medium of communication. The organisation of an entertainment industry did not follow automatically, but resulted from the use of film equipment by individuals and groups already involved in some form of entrepreneurial activity. Improvements in the technology offered further scope for development, but how quickly, and in what way this took place depended on the outlook, and financial means, of those who used it.

Similarly, radio, which was made possible by any number of

improvements in electrical engineering, was first conceived as a more sophisticated version of wired telegraphy. The potential for widespread, simultaneous dissemination of messages was not developed until radio equipment manufacturers began experiments in order to expand their markets. Broadcasting was subsequently organised within institutions which aimed to realise the potential for economic, social, and educational purposes, all of which had clear political and cultural connotations.

The technology for two new forms of social communication was available before it was clear how it might be used. However, the need for new forms was clear in societies in which the role of the state was growing while new forms of political organisation were developing. While offering the opportunity for the wider dissemination of information in society, the nature of the technology and the institutions in which it was placed restricted access and offered the possibility of centralised control. Further development was dependent upon the sources of capital which already dominated industrial societies, and the form of future technology was dictated as much by commercial as well as social and political needs. It then becomes clear that we are not merely concerned with communication systems, but with new social institutions in which the technology is placed. Once more the uni-directional model must be revised, and the channel linked specifically to the communicator since they are invariably part of the same institutional framework.

The technology also determines the specific character of the channel of information and consequently the form of the message. This clearly affects the relationship of the audience to the message. The newspaper press requires an audience to have a modicum of literacy since it is composed of the printed word and pictures. The medium itself, the newspaper, normally becomes the property of the buyer. It can be read, and re-read at leisure, and depending upon the number of pages in the issue can contain information on a wide range of issues. In the light of this, the form and content of the paper reflects the need of the communicator to engage the attention of the audience by headlines, pictures and the general lay-out.

In the case of film the audience normally buy the right to see a film within a specific environment, but not to own it, so emphasising their role as spectators and consumers of a controlled experience, which takes place within an allotted time span, determined by the producer of the film, and within a social environment, the cinema. The director, using a combination of picture and sound within a narrative structure, uses a number of cinematic devices, developed over many years, to engage the interest of the audience, who need no prior educational experience.

This would also be true of the audience for broadcasting, particularly in the early days of radio. In order to receive the messages they needed only to buy the necessary equipment, but the nature of the technology determined the form and content. Much less information could be provided than in newspapers, but it could be disseminated with more immediacy, and simultaneously from a central source. At the same time it could call on other accepted forms of entertainment, such as classical music or vaudeville artists, and relay them to the homes of the audience. The experience was private, and yet shared with many other people.

The further development of television, the combination of picture and sound, emphasised its essential parasitism, since the means to transmit and receive was established well ahead of considered decisions on content. This has had important repercussions on other forms of mass communication, which in turn have had to adapt to a new social role, although the advent of television has only been one factor in that process. Yet, as television adopted other forms the character of their presentation changed, partly because of the nature of the technology and the expectations of the audience, and also because of the financial and institutional framework in which the technology had developed. From this perspective it is clear that the message structure is partly determined by the technical organisation of the medium. The extent to which this is the case is one of the many questions around which the continuing debate revolves.

3. The Development of the Mass Media in the Nineteenth Century

THE NEWSPAPER PRESS

In the nineteenth century the press became the first medium capable of reaching a mass audience through a combination of technological improvements in the production and distribution of newspapers and fundamental developments in their financial organisation. It was a capability that was not fully realised until after the First World War when other forms of social communication, particularly broadcasting, began to challenge the predominant position of the press as the main channel of information in society.

The extent, rapidity and form of this expansion had three principal determinants: the economic and political conditions obtaining in any country; the outlook of those in power towards the potential political influence of the press; and the flair of individual entrepreneurs.

Increases in population, expansion of industry and urbanisation affected Britain, the United States and Germany to varying degrees, and engendered different political responses to the social and economic problems which arose in their wake. Newspapers reflected the changing character of society in their own organisation and presentation of issues and events. Daily and evening papers appeared combining a number of functions, as presenters of news, entertainers, and sources of commercial information, specifically for the expanding urban populations. Through the selection of stories and presentation of news they created intellectual and ideological frameworks within which readers were able to come to terms with their local, national and international environment.

Newspapers had always performed this function for specific commercial or political groupings whose common outlook was mobilised through the organisation of information. The expansion of the press clearly affected this function, as did the political philosophy that argued for freedom of the press from any governmental control. In the liberal democratic climate that developed out of the twin revolutions in industry and politics, the idea of the press as a neutral channel of information for the political education of the electorate began to take hold.

The liberal concept of the press as an independent political institution in the state was highly developed where democratic structures were most in evidence. It was believed that the expansion of the number of newspapers would create a free market in ideas. In practice, the expansion of the press led to a contraction of opinion, with newspapers becoming commodities, adapting to the needs of the consumer, and abjuring a distinctly party-political role. This was not, however, an accomplished fact in any industrialised society before 1914.

In Britain, the lifting of economic restrictions on the press in mid century coincided with a reorganisation and consolidation of party politics and with the extension of the franchise. London was becoming not only the political and commercial centre of the United Kingdom, but also the focus of a world-wide empire. The press would develop within a context of continuous but peaceful political change and economic progress.

This may be contrasted with the experience of other countries for which the 1860s were watershed years. The United States underwent the trauma of the Civil War and its immediate aftermath. Political affiliations had been disturbed, and although the question of states' rights had been settled, the political and territorial consolidation of the nation had yet to take place. At the beginning of the 1870s uncertainty about the future political structure of central Europe was ended with the establishment of the German Empire, based upon the economic and military power of Prussia. Relationships between the individual German states were fundamentally changed, but not the economic and political structures inside the states.

In the case of both the United States and Germany the trauma of war and political change was the prelude to rapid economic expansion. This, in turn, put further pressure on the reconstituted political institutions in the 1870s. It is within this context that we need to consider the changing function of the press, as the readership expanded. From being the means of communication between the government and important groups in society, or between members of the same groups challenging for political power, newspapers increasingly became commercial properties addressing the largest possible audiences on behalf of advertisers who provided the wherewithal for their continued existence. The changes were dependent on newspapers taking advantage of new production technologies, on the pattern of population distribution, on the character and extent of commercial undertakings, and on how far the purely political press could survive in an unpropitious economic climate.

The important development after the 1860s was the proliferation of relatively cheap newspapers of all kinds, offering differing views of society to increasingly larger numbers of people. However, the major innovations in form and content occurred in the urban, large-circulation newspapers, and it was these which dominated discussion about the role of the press and its function in society.

The style and scale of the large-circulation press depended on the technology of newspaper production. In the period before the 1850s the flatbed printing press was quite adequate for the majority of newspapers, with production merely being increased by the use of steam power. The introduction of locked type on a cylinder led to Richard Hoe's rotary press of 1846, which when linked to other cylinders could produce up to 20,000 newspapers per hour. The use of *papier mâché* moulds, instead of type, subsequently led to the development of 'stereotypes', metal plate impressions of the type to be fitted on the cylinder. When added to the continuous feeding of paper to the machines, a process inhibited in Britain before 1855 by the Stamp Duty on individual sheets, the only bar, theoretically, to increased circulation was the number of machines available.

From the 1890s the introduction of 'Linotype' machines allowed page composition by the use of a keyboard. Other typographical improvements, and the widespread use of photo-engravure for illustrations, allowed more freedom in lay-out and picture presentation.

A fundamental element in the development of the cheap press was cheap paper. Before the 1860s no satisfactory substitute for rags in the paper-making process had been found, although esparto grass and straw were tried as the supply of rags diminished and demands for paper grew. By the 1880s a process using woodpulp had revolutionised paper-making, and prices dropped to new levels.

Newspapers which sought a large circulation required the technology to sustain it, and faced a progressive rise in the cost of newsprint. Those which continued to serve small communities were able to survive as long as the penetration of the larger, commercial papers was restricted. In Germany, the political and social framework of the country certainly retarded this development, and the size of the United States allowed small papers to exist, although there was some development of chain ownership. This had also begun to occur in Britain before 1914, but was less significant than the development of the heavily capitalised metropolitan newspapers.

The expansion of circulation was linked to the problem of distribution. In Germany and the United States the bulk of newspapers founded before the 1880s relied upon subscribers, and distribution through an efficient rail system and postal service. Newspapers used the communications network to reach larger numbers of people, but the distance to be covered was one factor which militated against the creation of a national press. Even in Britain, the wide-scale penetration of the London daily press into the provinces was accomplished, from the turn of the century, as much by simultaneous publication in different centres as distribution from the capital.

Changes in the technology of news collection and transmission were most important to the organisation of the cheap, daily press. The spread of the telegraph across Europe and America in the 1850s, and the connection of the two continents by an underwater cable in the 1860s produced an efficient form of transmission. Agencies were established to collect and distribute news to subscribers, and this in turn affected the style and content of news presentation, since the range of possible customers led to an emphasis on 'hard facts', apparently divorced from opinion, and the cost of using the telegraph encouraged conciseness. News agencies became pre-selectors and pre-processors of news, creating a conformity, which while apparently apolitical, had important ramifications for the transmission of information in society and the understanding of political messages.

The press had always been recognised by politicians, and others active in public life, as an important organiser of opinion among elite groups. Throughout the nineteenth century newspapers still appeared which performed this function. In the main, newspapers continued to be local and regional in outlook. The fragmented, dispersed, and essentially agricultural nature of life was represented in many of the smaller newspapers, and this continued well into the twentieth century.

However, in the changed political climate after 1870, and the growth of democratic national political life, the opinions and attitudes of larger groups in society were seen to have importance to decision-makers and those who sought political power. The growth of the large-circulation press offered scope for communication with these groups, but it was a press dependent for its profits upon commercial advertising rather than political subvention or a high cover price, and this had an important effect upon the presentation of politics and the relationship of editors and proprietors to politicians and parties.

As the news content of papers became more varied in order to capture larger groups of potential readers, less space was available for the coverage of debates and speeches by politicians. By the 1890s in Britain the shortened third-person versions transmitted by news agencies were most acceptable to the majority of newspapers. Political figures who had achieved, or sought, national or local prominence depended upon extensive coverage in the press, and viewed this development with concern.

Politics, although the staple of most daily papers, began to be treated as other news stories, with a change of style to a personalised 'human interest' outlook, and individual interviews, both of which were associated with the new form of commercial journalism. Journalists sought out new angles which would continue to interest a readership which was less concerned with civic enlightenment than with daily entertainment.

Much of the newspaper press which had emerged by the turn of the century was 'popular' in the sense that it was bought by a large number of people. It did not necessarily represent their views, and certainly was not produced by them. The press was not an arena of debate, as those who argued for the freedom of the press had hoped, but the means whereby constructed images of society were presented to a public of consumers in a form that was least capable of offence to the largest number. In this way a popular newspaper sought, and constructed, areas of agreement, rather than differences, between individuals in its readership. Such a newspaper was beginning to create the ideas of 'the mass', rather than serving the individual

groups of people already in existence. Through symbols and stereotypes the language of politics was simplified, and the governing
groups in the three societies we are concerned with found that the
popular press propounded those values which brought a society
together. The press became an important factor in the popular
expression of nationalism before 1914. To explore these issues in
more detail we need to consider the specific experience of each
society as the newspaper press began to develop during the nineteenth century.

On the eve of the Civil War there were 387 newspapers published
daily in the United States, representing about 10 per cent of the
total newspaper press and reflecting the growth in population,
urbanisation and literacy among the white population since the turn
of the century. There were many which still had only three-figure
circulations, addressing clearly defined commercial and political
subscribers, and costing anything up to $10 per week for six issues.
However, in the 1830s the wider audience for news was recognised
in the establishment of 'penny papers', which were aimed specifically
at the large urban populations, and were sold on the streets for one
cent.

The foundation of the New York *Sun* by Benjamin Day in
September 1833 is generally recognised as the first successful venture
in modern daily journalism. The paper laid no claim to literary
excellence, mixing news of crime, scandal and sensational happen-
ings in the urban area with clipped reports from other papers.
Within four months it had a circulation over 5000, justifying Day's
belief that a market existed for a paper which supported no political
party, and which treated all news as of equal importance. The
emphasis on the least savoury aspects of society may have been
anathema to the 'respectable' members of New York society, but it
provided amusement for a growing newspaper-buying public.
Popular success, in turn, attracted advertising, until by 1837, with
a circulation of 30,000, it comprised three-quarters of the paper.

The *Sun* represented the future character of the American daily
press, and popular journalism. Commercial profitability was to
become the keystone of existence and lay in attracting readers
through cheapness and advertisers through circulation. New printing
and paper technology allowed for such growth but became increasingly expensive. The news itself became a commodity, packaged

in forms which would be acceptable to the widest readership, emphasising aspects of personal life and relationships, whether within a political or a domestic framework.

The development of the press in this form was a long-drawn-out process, and only slowly impinged on newspapers which sought neither large circulations nor general readership. However, Day's example quickly spurred on competitors in New York, with 34 daily papers appearing at any one time.

In 1835, James Gordon Bennett established the New York *Herald* as the main rival of the *Sun*, at the same price, using similar contents, but with better quality features and presentation. While Day soon tired of journalism, Bennett began to establish himself as a major public figure, aided by his blatant use of self-advertisement. He combined entreprenurial skill with crusading vigour, a combination that many found unconvincing. While emphasising human degradation in news stories, the *Herald* called for reform of a society in which crime and corruption were endemic. Although leaning towards the Democrats, it had no party political affiliations, but argued that as a popular newspaper it spoke directly to, and for, the people above the divisions of party. It was an outlook, with its reflection of Jacksonian democracy, which provoked downright hostility from established groups in New York society, but by 1860, with a circulation of 77,000, the *Herald* was the world's largest daily newspaper.

It was not necessary to emphasise scandal to achieve success. Horace Greeley, who founded the New York *Tribune* in 1840, was unhappy with the sensationalism of Bennett, and sought an audience concerned about social issues but wanting a cheap paper. While never capturing the daily audience to the same degree, the weekly edition, with a circulation of 200,000 in 1860, gave Greeley a national reputation as a crusading editor/publisher, and further emphasised the social role of the press. Henry Raymond, in founding the New York *Daily Times* in 1851, emphasised the informational role of newspapers, directing its coverage towards factual news reporting, and not seeking to compete with the moral crusades of other papers. He too, had recognised a clear market, and by 1857 the *Times* had a circulation of 40,000.

The success of these New York papers needs to be put into perspective. There were many in the city which failed within months, and others which did not try to emulate the cheap papers, preferring to carry out their traditional roles as channels of commercial intelligence, or party political opinion. New papers were founded specifically for non-English language groups, particularly Germans, among the immigrant population and never sought a larger audience. Such diversity was reflected in the country as a whole, but the influence of the cheap press of New York began to impinge at a number of levels. Cheap daily papers modelled on those of Day and Bennett began to appear in other major cities in the 1830s and 1840s, taking advantage of the spread of the telegraph and other means of news transmission. This, in turn, began a gradual shift in the presentation of 'news', with the emphasis on local events, often depicted in a sensational and personalised form.

A more direct influence lay in the collection of foreign news coming from European steamships arriving in eastern seaboard ports. By an agreement of 1848 the six main New York papers, including the *Times* after 1851, formed the New York Associated Press in order to secure one telegraphic transmission of foreign news from an agent in Boston. It not only represented a saving of money for individual papers, but by an arrangement with European news agencies secured a monopoly for those papers inside the cartel. Through agreements with the Western Union Telegraph Company in 1855, regional and local newspapers secured a franchise to use this service and no other, so creating a monopoly controlled by the New York papers. This was one factor leading to the decline of special interest newspapers which were effectively cut off from a source of foreign news.

New York had become the centre of news gathering and news transmission in the United States by the 1860s, but two major factors militated against a national daily press distributed from the city. It was impossible to distribute papers speedily and economically to other urban centres to compete with dailies using the telegraphic news service. Also, while there was a diversity of local papers, their commercial success came to depend on the scale of their news reporting, which was determined by access to agency reports. There was a resultant uniformity in style and content and an emphasis on straight factual reporting.

The growth of daily papers reflected the developing urbanisation of the United States, but in 1860 nearly 80 per cent of all published titles were weeklies or periodicals distributed cheaply by the Post Office to all areas of the country by various means, particularly the new railroads. The bulk of the rural population gained news of the world outside their immediate vicinity in this form well into the twentieth century, but the growth of urban populations, linked to a new commercial world of heavy industry and trade, was the basis for the development of the press as an industry in its own right. The convulsive and rapid changes in American life in the last third of the nineteenth century were chronicled by a medium which had been in continuous evolution since the 1830s; and, as was the case elsewhere in American society, the Civil War acted as a catalyst, emphasising and accelerating those changes.

In 1861, the year in which the British government removed the last pre-publication constraint upon the press, the United States government under the pressure of war 'had to adapt to the dilemma of the organisation of opinion in a free press tradition'. Previous Presidents had not always respected this tradition. In the 1830s Andrew Jackson had built his own political position on the manipulation of the political press and allocation of government printing contracts, but by 1861 no such influence was available to the President. The number and range of newspapers had grown, and Lincoln patronised no one editor or reporter, recognising the need to set out his position before the widest public in the North. He faced editorial opposition from many newspapers, particularly in New York, and the government was not averse to restricting access to the mails to those papers which were too openly antagonistic to the Federal position. It might be added that newspapers in the Confederate area were as susceptible to pressure from government and mob alike.

In the North, the publishers of the large-circulation papers were more responsive to the desires of their readers than to the needs of the government in Washington, even when these were clear. Some New York papers devoted over a third of their news columns to war reports and they required up-to-date news, ahead of their competitors. For this they were willing to sacrifice accuracy for speed and sensationalism and they were well served by a new kind of reporter, the war correspondent, whose main concern was personal and professional survival. Many of these men had little newspaper experience and competing pressures from publishers, generals and government censors together with the physical privations shared with the armies, led to reports which bore little relationship to reality. However, they satisfied a public anxious for news, since they displayed the authenticity of the 'eyewitness' account.

Correspondents on both sides of the lines were important in the boosting of morale, and organisation of opinion about the enemy. This was achieved, in the main, through small-circulation news-papers which could not afford their own reporters and relied on news agency bulletins and syndicated features from the war correspondents. As the war progressed these became more inflamma-tory, emphasising the division between the parties, and the righteous-ness of each side. One result was that few newspapers dispassionately dealt with the wider implications of the war for American society, since changes in news transmission, newspaper finance and journali-stic practice militated against calm reflection.

The Civil War, which devastated the Southern states, set out the framework within which the United States would develop in the following decades. Economically, it accelerated the industrialisation in the North as the demands of a war economy promoted expansion in all areas of heavy industry. It destroyed the slave economy of the South, and set in train the period of reconstruction in which social and racial tensions continued to be unresolved by a new economic and political leadership. The political issue of states' rights had been settled, and the stage was set for the consolidation of the country under a Federal leadership responsive to the declared needs of the different areas of the nation.

In the two decades following the Civil War the press in the United States began to assume the form with which it would enter the twentieth century. Changes in the technology of news gathering and transmission clearly reinforced the growing emphasis on factual reporting, but there were wider changes associated with the more complex character of newspaper operations, particularly the personal role of the editor in determining the character of the paper. The political instability resulting from the Civil War, the death of Abraham Lincoln in 1865, and splits in the Republican Party gave newspaper editors an opportunity to support individual factions, culminating in the nomination of Horace Greeley, editor of the New York *Tribune*, as a presidential candidate against Ulysses Grant in the 1872 election. Greeley's failure was followed by his death a few months later. Editors, it appeared, were safer behind desks. Nevertheless, a larger number of newspapers were critical of both major parties, a good example being the New York *Sun* from 1868 to 1897, under the editorship of Charles A. Dana.

Dana put his individual stamp upon the newspaper which continued as a four-page, two-cent edition throughout much of this period. This restricted the amount of news which could be carried, but not the style, which was invariably personal and interesting. It was Dana who coined the term 'human-interest' story for reports which were of significance only in detailing the 'poetry of life'. They sold papers. By 1876 the *Sun* had achieved a circulation of over 170,000.

Dana's contribution to journalism was in the sphere of news presentation, while that of Edwin Godkin was in editorial activity. The New York *Evening Post*, which Godkin edited throughout the 1880s and 1890s, became the epitome of moderate liberal opinion, and a model of the non-sensational activist newspaper beloved of liberals everywhere. It never sold more than 20,000 copies, but usually made a profit. Godkin was one of the last of the old-style editors; less concerned about lay-out and circulation than issues and politics. There were others in the 1880s, but the configuration of American life was changing around them and with it their function, and the character of the American press.

Between 1880 and 1900 the number of towns above 8000 inhabitants doubled, and the population of these urban areas went from 11 million to 25 million in the same period. By 1890 there were 58 cities with populations over 50,000, over half of which were concentrated in five states in the East. Between 1880 and 1900 national wealth doubled, and the bulk of that industrial wealth was organised in trusts which guarded against over-production and excessive competition. Great individual fortunes were accumulated, some of which were ploughed back for the good of the community in the form of educational establishments and libraries. Overall there was a rise in the general level of literacy, offering the newspapers a wider audience.

It was in this context that a new group of owners and editors came to the fore in the main cities and towns of the United States. Two-thirds of the daily papers founded after 1880 were evening editions, taking advantage of the telegraph, time differences between different areas of the US, and adapting to an urban audience with new habits and new lifestyles. They were important vehicles for local retail and national brand advertising and struck an even more independent political stance.

Newspapers reflected the many conflicting aspects of American society, particularly the debate concerning the interventionist role of government. Old-style liberals, like Godkin, with a *laissez-faire* outlook, argued for individual initiative and little government interference. The challenge to this outlook came from editors and journalists who sought to communicate directly with a population who were experiencing the worst aspects of uncontrolled economic life. Factual reporting, which was of increasing importance, provided the evidence for scandals which not only produced good copy, but the basis of campaigns and crusades conducted on behalf of the common man. It was one example of good social principles being good business practice.

The New York press in the 1890s was dominated by three figures (Pulitzer, Hearst and Ochs) who represented the cosmopolitan character of American life, and the opportunities which existed for an individual with flair, courage in economic affairs, and an intuitive journalistic and business sense. To succeed in this period the last two had to go together.

Joseph Pulitzer was originally an Austrian citizen, born in Hungary in 1847, who emigrated to join the Union Army in the 1860s and through working in German-language papers became interested in journalism in the Mid-West. In 1878 he became a newspaper proprietor in St Louis, amalgamating two papers into the *Post-Dispatch*, with the aim of representing within the paper the ideas 'of a true genuine, real Democracy'. Irrespective of his success in this, he had accrued enough resources by 1883 to feel confident enough to enter the New York newspaper market in which his brother Albert already had an interest, owning the *Morning Journal*, and in which Charles Dana's *Sun* was pre-eminent in journalism and advertising power. Joseph Pulitzer's acquisition of the *World* put pressure on the whole New York press. Within eighteen months the circulation of his paper had risen to 100,000, and by 1892 the combined circulation of his daily and Sunday editions, 374,000, was greater than that of any two other New York papers.

The key to Pulitzer's success lay in developing the ideas and techniques which Bennett had pioneered in the period before the Civil War. He employed first-class journalists who established a style of reporting which appealed to large numbers of people. While in the early years sensationalism seemed to predominate over the more serious aspects of the newspaper, a balance was established which, allied to local and national crusades, including a fund to build a pedestal for the Statue of Liberty, kept the *World* continually in the public eye. It gave value for money in the number of pages published for the price of two cents, as well as the large numbers of illustrations; and it promoted its own excellence in the 'ears', the advertising spaces, on each side of the title.

Pulitzer saw the commercial success of the 'new journalism' as merely capturing a wider audience for his editorials in which he pronounced upon important issues in American life. The idealism of the *St Louis Post-Dispatch* was transferred to New York, but inside packaging which caused 'responsible' journalists and politicians much offence. Other New York papers soon followed the example of the *World* in exploiting crime and scandal, and emphasising the worst aspects of human behaviour. In other areas of the United States the reasons for the success of the New York *World* were studied and copied by editors and proprietors alike, not least by a young man in California, William Randolph Hearst.

Whereas Pulitzer represented the older generation of immigrants, Hearst was the product of the frontier. Born in 1863, he was sired by a silver-mine prospector whose dreams had come true on the Comstoke Lode four years earlier. The result was a Harvard education for his son, and a paternal indulgence of his interest in journalism.

George Hearst's acquisition of the San Francisco *Examiner* to further his own career in Californian politics had been a mistake, but it offered Willie the opportunity to try out his skills as journalist and entrepreneur. He took over in 1887, modelling the paper on the worst excesses of the *World*, and soon increased circulation and advertising figures.

The opportunity to 'invade' New York came from the settlement of his father's will in 1895 leaving Willie Hearst with a $7.5 million fortune. With it he bought the ailing New York *Morning Journal* and set in train a circulation war with Pulitzer, the effect of which was the eradication of other, weaker, New York papers, and a development in newspaper content and presentation which was given the soubriquet 'yellow journalism'. This was merely a further extension of the techniques perfected in the previous ten years; and the worst excesses of yellow journalism lasted little more than a decade.

Hearst followed Pulitzer's own example in buying in the best journalists, in this case those who edited and wrote the *World* Sunday edition with its colour comic section. One popular comic favourite, 'The Yellow Kid', was part of the package, and began to stand in popular thought for the type of journalism perpetrated for the sake of profit. It was a heady mix of sensational stories, accompanied by emotional headlines which often dominated the page. Artists' pictures abounded, often illustrating crusades and campaigns, the most famous of which was the pressure for war against Spain over Cuba in 1897.

Whether Hearst did in fact send the apocryphal message to his reporter/artist Remington in Havana, 'Please remain. You furnish the pictures and I'll furnish the war. – W. R. Hearst' is still in doubt, but it adequately sums up the importance Hearst and Pulitzer felt towards the possible effect of a war on circulations. American xenophobia was encouraged, anti-Spanish stories abounded in both papers, and with the outbreak of war the loss of the American warship *Maine* led to coverage in Hearst's paper which has been called 'the orgasmic acme of ruthless, truthless newspaper jingoism'. Circulations of both papers rose to over a million a day during the war period, but the cost of reporting the war was enormous, and no one made a profit. The victory for Hearst lay in beating the *World* in circulation, whatever the cost.

The importance of this internecine war lies in the general effect on the American press, and attitudes towards it in the United States and elsewhere. Many papers across the continent carried wire stories which merely reiterated the reports of the pro-war New York papers. More than that, many of the large city papers took on the 'yellow' format, suggesting to some observers that the standard of American journalism had reached its nadir.

They needed only to look at the New York *Times* to be reassured. While the Pulitzer and Hearst papers were selling millions the *Times* sold only 25,000, but this was nearly treble the circulation of the paper when Adolph Ochs bought it in 1896. He was the son of German–Jewish immigrants who had a desire to assimilate himself into American society, and after experience in Tennessee in Knoxville and Chatanooga, he felt ready to take over the New York *Times* and challenge the other proprietors with a different kind of newspaper. His aim was accuracy, comprehensiveness, and propriety, character-ised by the slogan 'All the news that's fit to print'.

The commercial decision to cut the cover price from three cents to one, undercutting the *Journal* and *World*, was Ochs's masterstroke.

Cheapness in this case did not mean a recourse to sensation, merely a recognition by Ochs that once the machinery was installed and type set up it was as cheap to print 100,000 copies as 40,000. Within a year the circulation of the *Times* had reached 75,000.

The end of the Spanish–American War, and the implication that the *Journal* had been responsible for encouraging the assassination of President McKinley in 1901, marked the beginning of the decline of 'yellow journalism'. It represented the end of the circulation war in New York, with Pulitzer bruised but unbowed, Hearst bloody but uncowed, and other proprietors, apart from Ochs, counting the cost of attempting to challenge the giants.

Meanwhile, in the smaller American cities a newspaper business was being built upon cheap afternoon dailies by E. W. Scripps and his associates, who would advance $25,000, appoint a manager, and encourage him to achieve a profit before the investment ran out. If he succeeded Scripps took 51 per cent of the stock; if not, Scripps bore the loss. By 1910 he owned twenty-two dailies, and in 1897 started his own news agency, United Press, to challenge the mighty Associated Press and service the numerous papers in his chain. There were few other chains in existence before 1900, and between them they controlled only 1 per cent of the total number of dailies published in the United States, but it was a pointer to the future when economies of scale could be applied to a number of local newspapers within a wider umbrella organisation.

The example of Scripps did demonstrate how cheap it was to start a newspaper enterprise outside the larger cities. However, the experience in New York showed that large-circulation newspapers had become industrial enterprises in their own right. Proprietors sought a profit on their investment, and editors became managers rather than journalists. They needed to hold circulation in order to secure vital advertising income while satisfying the individual needs of groups contributing to the paper whether journalists, printers or newsboys.

The populist stance of many newspapers, with campaigns against corruption in public and business life, was one way to attract and maintain readership. It also demonstrated that while some newspapers were becoming financially conservative institutions they were still willing to investigate and criticise many aspects of life in the United States. Newspapers were the only channel where the worst excesses of rapid industrialisation and change could be brought to wider attention. Yet by 1914 the 'muckraking' of the weeklies such as *Collier's* or *McClure's*, and the crusades of the daily press were subsiding as circulation levels peaked and the public looked for something new from the newspaper press.

It is clearly impossible to give a complete picture of the press in the United States before the First World War. The experience of the New York papers must not be allowed to distort the picture, and yet they had an important effect upon the character and outlook of the press in general through their experiments in style and content, and overall control of the news agencies servicing the majority of the papers. They also served as a pattern for other countries, not least Great Britain where the influence of London and the metropolitan newspapers was greater than that of New York.

One of the issues which sparked off the American Revolution was the attempted imposition of taxes upon newspapers in the American colonies by the government in London. Although one of a number of measures to raise revenue, it was seen as another example of the attempt by governments in the eighteenth century to undermine opposition by restricting the free flow of opinion. As the rebellion developed, spurred on by radical journalists, freedom of the individual was inextricably linked to freedom of opinion, and that of the organs which disseminated them. The first Amendment to the Federal Constitution, ratified in 1789–91, stated that 'Congress shall make no law . . . abridging the freedom of speech or of the press.'

This recognised the clear link between the development of political democracy and the concept of freedom of the press. The argument, developed out of the 'self-evident' truths of the Founding Fathers of the United States, was that democracy is unobtainable without, and only sustained by, press freedom. The extension of political power to a wide body of people required the means to give them knowledge of political affairs: in the nineteenth century this meant a newspaper press untrammelled by governmental control.

It was, however, to be another seventy years before the British Parliament accepted this principle, and only in 1919 did the Weimar Constitution state that 'every German has the right, within the bounds of the general laws, to express his opinion freely in word, writing, print, picture or in any other manner. . . . There is no censorship.'

It is unlikely that the Founding Fathers foresaw more than the possibility of small-scale newspapers catering for the numerous interests of their society. To British governments in the late eighteenth century, faced with incipient revolution liable to be spread by an uncontrolled press, the principle of freedom carried little weight. They increased the burden of taxation which had been introduced earlier in the century to combat scurrility, as well as using the time-honoured policy of subsidising papers which followed a government line. Taxes on newspapers took the form of a stamp on each copy, a duty on each advertisement and on paper itself. These were progressively raised throughout the eighteenth century and this factor, combined with poor distribution and fear of prosecution for libel had the effect of restricting production and circulation. London dailies and provincial weeklies, the two main forms of newspaper, often had sales below 1000 copies, but the readership could be multiplied thirty to fifty times as they were lent and borrowed in inns, coffee-houses and clubs. Legislation prohibiting the hiring of papers, passed in 1789, was ineffective in stopping the practice.

The period of the Revolutionary and Napoleonic Wars witnessed a growing demand for news, and the foundation of papers to meet it, including new categories of Sundays and evening dailies. The number of newspapers and periodicals published in England and Wales more than trebled in the four decades after 1780, rising from 76 to 267. It was a growth which continued throughout the first half of the nineteenth century, with newspapers alone rising to 563 by 1851. Just under half of these were published in the provinces.

The reason for expansion was predominantly economic rather than political. Newspapers offered a source of profit to owners, who were often printers with spare capacity on their machinery. Revenue came from a wide range of advertisements, irrespective of the tax, reflecting the growth of trade and industry, and contributing to its continued expansion. Papers with a circulation under 2000 could still make a profit. In political terms they represented a 'respectable' press, which although capable of an independent political stance was owned and read by those with a clear stake in society as it was constituted.

After 1815 a more overtly political press developed which had neither the financial infrastructure nor the distribution facilities available to the 'respectable' papers. There had always been newspapers and periodicals which ignored the punitive taxation, and printers and publishers willing to risk fines and imprisonment.

However, the government felt sufficiently threatened in the years of political ferment after 1815 to extend the Stamp Duty and seditious libel law in 1819–20. These measures did not eradicate the un-stamped press since, even under the pressure of confiscation and fines, it managed to develop a widespread national distribution system based on the unemployed. Prosecutions for seditious libel became rarer, mainly because juries, empowered under Fox's Libel Act of 1792 to rule on the libellous intention of the publisher, were less willing to convict than judges.

The burgeoning of the radical press and the apparent failure of the repressive legislation was one area in which liberals could mount an attack on the whole structure of oligarchic government in the 1820s and 1830s. It was directly connected to the campaign for suffrage reform, and the wider representation of commercial interests in the legislature and government. Fiscal repression, the argument ran, was counter-productive, in that it had not allowed 'respectable' newspapers to extend their range of readership, while allowing their cheap radical equivalents to offer 'dangerous ideas' to the 'dangerous classes'. Only with a free market in opinion, and an extended electorate, it was argued, would the possibility of incipient revolt among the growing working class be obviated.

In fact, the first tentative step towards reform of the suffrage in 1832 preceded the first major reduction of the cost of the newspaper stamp by four years. The measure, cutting the duty from 4d. to 1d., pointed in the direction of total repeal, but was also accompanied by more effective action against the 'great unstamped'. An apparent concession, tempered by coercion, succeeded in its purpose, mainly, it has been suggested, because 'expediency triumphed over ideology'. It was simpler to pay the stamp, raise the price, and still undercut other papers. A radical press, capable of making a profit, continued to exist, and was crucially important in the political crusades of the late 1830s and 1840s as a unifying force and source of propaganda. The Chartist *Northern Star* with a weekly national sale of 48,000 in 1839, at $4\frac{1}{2}$d. per copy, was the main organ, but it was complemented by dozens of other papers, stamped and unstamped. The Anti-Corn Law League, less radical, but critical of government policy, recognised the importance of the press as an organiser of opinion among all classes. The success of this movement in 1846, and the failure of the Chartists to secure universal suffrage in 1848, opened the way to the demise of taxation of the press in the next decade for two reasons.

Firstly, the danger from the revolutionary aspects of Chartism disappeared, and the fears of those contemplating the effect of inflammatory radical papers were lessened. Secondly, the concept of freedom in economic and intellectual affairs began to predominate in governing circles, and the imposition of 'taxes on knowledge', as the duties were emotively called, began to seem highly inappropriate. The campaign for the abolition of duties was led by men like Richard Cobden and John Bright, who had been successful in the repeal of the Corn Laws in 1846. By 1853, the Advertisement Duty, lowered in 1833 from 3s. 6d. to 1s. 6d., was finally abolished. In 1855, the stamp went, and the campaign was concluded with a flourish in 1861 when the paper duties were repealed.

It has been suggested that the history of the popular press in nineteenth-century England must be centred around the development of Sunday newspapers. From the beginning of the century they had had circulations well ahead of the daily press, reaching a combined total of 275,000 against 60,000 in 1850, climbing to nearly 2 million by 1900. The two main Sundays, *Lloyd's Weekly News* and the *News of the World* were founded in the 1840s, before the repeal of newspaper taxes, and found their main audience among the working class in London. They were commercial papers, relying on a staple of crime, sport and entertainment to gain an audience; they succeeded admirably. They gained substantially from repeal, and were in the forefront of all the major technical developments. Their content harked back to earlier ballads and broadsheets, but their organisation as commercial entities with little concern for party politics, especially after mid century, was the pattern for the future.

The new cheap daily press which began to be established after 1855 sought to distance itself from the Sundays. The first successful metropolitan morning newspaper, the *Daily Telegraph*, was first published on the day the Stamp Duty was repealed; and by 1860 had a circulation of 141,000, rising to 300,000 by 1890. Its price, 1d., became standard for other dailies published in the next few years. The new cheap press was essentially urban in outlook, whether making use of the railways to extend distribution out of London or centred in provincial towns.

Although metropolitan newspapers had the largest individual circulations, the main expansion of the press after 1855 was in the

English provinces. The number of dailies published rose from 15 in 1856 to 171 in 1900, of which 101 were evening newspapers, benefiting from the foundation of the Press Association (PA) by provincial proprietors in 1868, and cheap telegraph rates following nationalisation of the system under the Post Office in 1870. The PA collected and distributed news throughout the British Isles, and concluded an arrangement with Reuters for an exchange of foreign and domestic intelligence. By this means the provincial press had access to comprehensive coverage of international and national affairs while carrying large amounts of local news.

Evening papers were usually started by publishers of morning dailies who were able to use existing plant. Costing $\frac{1}{2}$d. they represented a further extension of the cheap press, and reached a wider social mix than the morning editions. Their popularity lay in their content, continuously up-dated news and sports results, as much as their price.

With the proliferation of newspapers, growth in circulation and the fall in the modal price, the cost of starting and maintaining newspapers continued to rise. In 1870 the establishment of a London daily might cost £100,000; and while the initial sum advanced for Harmsworth's *Daily Mail* in 1896 was less than £25,000, the paper actually required an investment of £500,000 over a number of years, and this does not appear to take account of plant already available from other newspaper ventures.

Inevitably, the success of a newspaper became dependent on the amount of advertising it attracted. This in turn became linked to the size and nature of the audience for the paper. The so-called 'Northcliffe Revolution' in the British press was the recognition of this fact embodied in the day-to-day organisation of a newspaper.

Alfred Harmsworth, the future Lord Northcliffe, was no revolutionary, but a first-class entrepreneur, publicist and coordinator who, utilising the business acumen of his brother Harold, the future Lord Rothermere, was able to construct a newspaper and magazine empire based upon sound commercial principles.

The real innovators were men like George Newnes, who in 1881, started *Tit-bits*, a weekly miscellany of clipped news items, costing 1d. It had no pretensions to offer serious information, but was enormously successful both with readers and advertisers. In 1886 Harmsworth started *Answers* which was an exact copy of Newnes's magazine, and he used every means possible to publicise and distribute it throughout the country. Over the next eight years, with his brothers, he identified specific markets for small magazines, and continued to build upon the commercial success of *Answers*. The acquisition of the London *Evening News* in 1894, for the paltry sum of £23,000, was the entry point into daily journalism for a company which had gone public in 1893 with a capital of £1,000,000. Within a year it was making a profit, and Harmsworth prepared to challenge the *Daily Telegraph*, still costing 1d. and with a circulation of 300,000, by founding 'A Penny Newspaper for One Halfpenny', the *Daily Mail*.

It was a direct but calculated challenge, and was brilliantly successful. There was little that was innovatory in lay-out or style. The 'new journalism', with its emphasis on human-interest stories and use of short paragraphs and headlines, had become well established by the 1890s. If anything the *Daily Mail* was rather conservative, but it attracted readers by its own publicity and price, and advertisers by continually announcing the scale and nature of its readership. An understanding of the interaction between circulation and advertising, linked to efficient production and distribution, and a generally populist political outlook, was the basis of the *Mail*'s success.

It was a formula which secured a circulation of a million by the turn of the century, and provided the Harmsworth brothers with further capital to invest in other publishing ventures, including the successful foundation of the *Daily Mirror* as a picture paper, and the development of interests in provincial newspapers. Meanwhile, the original periodical and magazine interests continued to provide substantial profits. In 1908 Northcliffe acquired the 'glittering prize' of *The Times*, which by that stage in its history had become somewhat tarnished.

The fortunes of *The Times* were inextricably linked to the fundamental changes in newspaper funding and organisation. In its heyday in the middle of the nineteenth century, under the editorship of John Thadeus Delane, and before the repeal of the Stamp Duty, the paper dominated metropolitan, and thus, British newspapers. In 1850 it sold four times as many copies as its main rivals together, as a result of an astute commercial policy and editorial flair. 'The Thunderer', as it had come to be known, had the confidence to challenge statesmen while being privy to secrets of state. The crusading reputation of the newspaper was established under Delane, particularly over the conduct of the Crimean War between 1854 and 1856. However, the apparent power of *The Times* engendered antagonism among politicians and other journalists.

The advent of cheaper newspapers, the growth of the provincial press, and the loss of political patrons, particularly Palmerston, began the decline. It was hastened by a falling circulation and the catastrophe of the paper publishing forged letters, allegedly written by Charles Stewart Parnell, the Irish Nationalist leader. The moral leadership of *The Times* evaporated, as did the economic position of the Walter family which had owned the paper through three generations and had continually subdivided the inheritance.

Rumours abounded about possible changes in ownership before complicated negotiations secured Northcliffe the paper, and its problems. The vocal opposition, both inside the paper and in society at large, to this state of affairs, reflected the parvenu status of Northcliffe, and fears of what he might do to a paper which was seen as a national institution. The fears were unjustified, and under a strong proprietor, involved in the machinations of domestic politics over the next decade or so, the paper became an important voice in public affairs.

The acquisition of *The Times* was only one aspect of Northcliffe's developing influence. More generally the concentration of ownership was one further aspect of the 'Northcliffe Revolution' in the British press, and heralded a fundamental change in the relationship between the London newspaper industry and the provincial press.

It was clear by 1913 that a 'nationalising of the London press' was taking place, with easier penetration into the provinces, and in some cases, simultaneous publication in London, Manchester and Glasgow. Provincial morning dailies were already finding the competition too great as advertising revenue fell away. By 1914, the greater part of the press in Britain had become a major industry, integrated into the economic system through its reliance on advertising. Freedom from governmental control had led to the proliferation of newspapers and an increase in the number of purchasers, but the large-circulation popular press which developed around 1900 did not arise out of the needs of a new reading public, a result of the Education Act of 1870, but from the recognition by entrepreneurs of a market which was profitable, and the technical means to enter and organise it.

Liberal opinion at the time, and subsequently, has bemoaned the structure, content and influence of the new popular press. It appeared to pander to the lowest common denominator in the readership, had subsumed its function to educate in the search for profit, and individual voices were lost in the concentration of ownership.

More radically it has been argued that the industrialisation of the press in the late nineteenth century not only stifled opposition voices of all kinds, but positively encouraged a particular, integrationist, socially cohesive, view of British society. It had therefore taken on a political function which was in the interests of the economically and socially dominant groups in society, and to the detriment of the mass of the population. What taxation had failed to achieve, the argument runs, the constraints of commercialism had brought about.

It is very difficult to estimate the influence of newspapers on society at any time, but particularly before the First World War. Irrespective of the rise in circulations, newspapers still reached only a small proportion of the population in any country. This did not detract from the view held by politicians in all three countries under review that the press was of immense importance in the organisation of political influence in the community.

The development of the press in the German states after 1815 was affected by the political and economic character of the region. Particularism was entrenched in the autocratic structure of the 39 states which made up the German Confederation. This urge towards territorial integrity was combined with a general fear of revolution among the absolutist rulers and the nobility, particularly in Austria and Prussia, the two dominant states. The activity of newspapers in openly and critically discussing political affairs presented a clear challenge to governments, since constitutional reform was invariably linked to the question of German unity.

In 1819, the Confederation reasserted the principles of press control, fearful of a widespread challenge to authoritarian rule throughout its member states. This decree, enacted at Karslbad, became one focus of liberal opposition in the 1830s and 1840s since it represented the repressive character of the post-1815 settlement in the German area, and restricted attempts to challenge it. Yet these decrees really only reinforced the measures generally available in the German states, and through taxation, confiscation and censorship, the authorities were able to exercise control over newspapers which offered the limited reading public a critical view of political society. When there was some relaxation of censorship, as in Prussia in the 1840s, there was little the Confederation could do.

The German states were predominantly agricultural, but in the second quarter of the nineteenth century some, and Prussia in particular, began to experience both rapid population growth and industrialisation, notably in the western provinces, contiguous to France. The larger towns began to expand, and new social groupings started to challenge accepted economic and political practices. The growing industrial bourgeoisie began to assume a predominant position in economic life, but they were excluded from political decision-making inside the German states.

Many saw the solution to the economic and political backwardness of the German area in the creation of a unified political and economic structure. They were influenced by the theories of Friedrich List, and the success of the Prussian-dominated customs union, the *Zollverein*, which had been established in 1834. What was required was the mobilisation of opinion across the German states, but newspapers were quite incapable of performing this function. They were locally orientated, and although by 1866 there were over 1500 papers in the German states, only 300 appeared daily. Circulations were often below 2000. As in Britain and the United States, this must be multiplied by at least five to get some idea of the overall readership since newspapers were passed from hand to hand and read in social groups.

The importance of the press lay in the organisation of local opinion, and the continuous pressure exerted on the authorities to deal with apparent breaches of censorship regulations. As changes occurred in German society before 1848 there was less assurance in state governments, and the revolutions of that year in the German states led to freedom of the press for the first time.

The liberal argument, that a free press was the key to a progressive, democratic society was embodied in Article 4, paragraph 143 of the Constitution promulgated by the Frankfurt Parliament in 1849. The inability of the representatives to create a nation against the wishes of the major German states represented a defeat for liberal principles of all kinds, and under the reformed Confederation press controls were reimposed.

The experiences of the March Revolution and Frankfurt Parliament were important in the development of the German press.

Freedom from control had existed for a short period, and the statement of principle was a benchmark for the future. The granting of constitutions, however narrow in scope, eventually led to the emergence of political parties, and the press would be a key factor in their formation. This was particularly true in Prussia, but it was a slow process. It was not until the 1860s that the Progressive Party daily, the *Volks-Zeitung*, achieved a circulation of 36,000, double that of the *Vossische Zeitung*, its nearest liberal rival, and four times that of the main conservative newspaper in Berlin, the *Neue Preussische Zeitung*, or *Kreuzzeitung*, as it was better known. It is clear from these figures that the political opinion addressed by the newspapers was very narrow, and confined to those with education, money and social standing. It was within this relatively small group of politically active citizens that the main issues of the 1860s, constitutional reform in Prussia and the unification of Germany, were to be decided.

Otto von Bismarck, the future German Chancellor, had recognised this fact on his appointment as Prussian delegate to the Frankfurt Diet of the reformed German Confederation in 1851. He never underestimated the importance of the press throughout his political career. He shared the contempt of many politicians for journalists, having had experience with *Kreuzzeitung* after its foundation in 1848, but unlike many conservatives he did not fear the press, rather he saw it as a necessary tool of political influence and control.

Censorship was too blunt a weapon in the heightened political atmosphere of the 1850s, particularly when Prussia's position in the Confederation was threatened by Austrian policies rather than internal critics. Bismarck was able to 'place' stories in newspapers, not only in the German states, but in other European countries as well, in order to counter opinion favourable to Austria.

The management of news was only one of the devices he employed after becoming Minister President of Prussia at the height of the constitutional crisis in 1862. The full resources of the state were used to discipline opposition papers, either through economic sanctions imposed by the Post Office, court proceedings, or outright suspension. Papers which followed the government line prospered.

The cultivation of the press was an essential part of government policy. In his struggle with the liberal factions in the Landtag, with Austria in the Confederation, and with France in Europe Bismarck had the means to present the nature of the issues to the politically important groups in the German states on his terms.

This was only possible through the use of the telegraph and news agencies, particularly that founded by Bernhard Wolff to transmit commercial news from Berlin to the Rhineland in 1849. Wolff rapidly achieved a monopoly in Central Europe, and secured reciprocal arrangements for the exchange of market prices with Havas, the main French agency, and Julius Reuter in London. In 1859 these arrangements were extended to political news. The attempt by Reuter to expand into Europe by concluding separate telegraph agreements with individual German states threatened Wolff's position, and an offer from Havas to buy him out, in 1865, provoked a response in Berlin.

Wolff sought Prussian government backing, arguing that telegraph transmission of news would soon be in the hands of foreigners. Through the offices of Bleichröder, the banker friend of Bismarck, the Continental Telegraph Company (CTC) was founded to provide substantial capital for the *Wolffsches Telegraphenbureau* (*WTB*). Further attempts were made by Reuter and Havas to undermine Wolff, leading in 1869 to a secret agreement between the CTC and the Prussian State Ministry whereby the government gave the political despatches of Wolff precedence over private telegrams, offered loans to the company, and in return received news direct from *WTB*.

This mutually acceptable arrangement gave Wolff a monopolistic position in the German Empire after 1871, and led to a series of 'Agency Treaties' between Reuter, Havas and *WTB* allocating to each 'spheres of interest' in the collection and transmission of world news outside the United States. Wolff reported exclusively from Central Europe, Scandinavia and Russia: Reuter developed links in the British Empire and the Far East, while Havas concentrated on the French Empire and South America.

To the agencies, news, whether commercial, political or social, was a commodity like coal or iron. To governments it was, like those commodities, a source of power to be exploited. As the main national news agency, with a semi-official status after 1871, *WTB* offered not only the possibility of government exploitation of news in Germany, but through the external arrangements, favourable coverage throughout the world.

Reuters and Associated Press, in the United States, were essentially private companies, satisfying the commercial requirements of their shareholders and customers. The burgeoning number of newspapers and the wider market for general news increased their importance, as well as their profits. However, the position in Germany was different. Here the press primarily had a polemical function, which was to increase as political parties began to crystallise out of factions in the new constitutional structure of the empire. The government itself stood above party and the organisation of party newspapers but was concerned with the presentation of its policies in the press. The relationship with *WTB* offered scope for the continued management of news. So too did the use of the *Welfen-Fonds*, money confiscated from the king of Hanover, and supposedly to be used against any possible subversion from that source. The soubriquet 'reptiles' by which Bismarck had described the subversives was used by the liberal press to describe the funds, since they were the means whereby Bismarck encouraged journalists and editors to produce copy favourable to the government.

Freedom of the press was anathema to him, since it offered licence to those who sought to undermine the fragile state structure erected between 1867 and 1871. However, the Press Law, enacted by the Reichstag in 1874, did establish the press as a legal entity throughout the empire, and removed many of the controls established in previous years in individual German states. It was still possible for the government to act against newspapers, which in its view were politically dangerous. Bismarck had no compunction in using this emergency clause against the Catholic press during the Kulturkampf, and the Socialist press throughout the rest of his period in office, as well as other legislation specifically aimed at *staatsfeindlich* movements; those deemed by Bismarck to be inimical to the best interests of the state.

His attitude dominated the development of the political press until 1890, and was based firstly upon an assumption which could not be proved, but was strongly believed by many people in Germany and elsewhere, that newspapers moulded public opinion. He recognised, secondly, the role of the party press in mobilising support between elections.

The conservative, autocratic, constitutional structure which had been established in 1871 allowed for the growth of political parties, but separated them from the government of the state. The Reichstag, the national assembly elected by universal male suffrage, represented a nod to mass democracy, but no more. Its existence was a recognition of the need to involve the population in the political organisation of the state, but not the right of the people to rule themselves. Until that principle was accepted the liberal concept of press freedom as a complementary aspect of democracy had no meaning, but was merely another weapon in the armoury of opposition groups with which to attack the government.

The period after political unification witnessed an enormous increase in the newspaper press throughout Germany. By 1914 over 4200 titles were published, a total nearly three times that of 1866. Of these, half appeared at least six times a week. The press continued to be decentralised, reflecting the regional differences upon which unification had hardly impinged. The form which newspapers took was not only determined by the needs of political parties, but the involvement of economic entrepreneurs, who like their counterparts in Britain and America, saw the press as a source of profit.

This was possible because of the dramatic growth in industry and urbanisation in the years after unification. Nearly half the new titles published between 1871 and 1916 were 'non-political' newspapers of the type dubbed *General-Anzeiger*. They were comparable with the 'penny papers' in American cities, having a low subscription price, and being dependent upon advertising for their profitability and existence. Their success can be measured by the fact that in 1900 only 3.5 per cent of all newspapers published in Germany had circulations over 15,000, and this included the *General-Anzeiger* group, who were averaging between 20,000 and 100,000 Marks in advertising revenue each year in the same period.

The *Boulevardblatt* took the *General-Anzeiger* form a stage further, since it was designed for street sales in the larger cities and aimed to catch the reader's eye through sensational headlines. News was presented simply, with a large number of pictures, and without political comment.

They were not typical of the bulk of the German press, including many *Anzeiger* newspapers, which still had an interpretative reporting role, and addressed relatively small groups of people. It was only in the larger cities, particularly Berlin, that popular, liberal-orientated, large-circulation dailies could flourish. They were invariably part of larger publishing enterprises which invested heavily in the technology required to meet increased demand. Ullstein's *Berliner Morgenpost*, founded in 1898, achieved a sale of nearly 400,000 by 1914, but it was only one of a number of papers and magazines developed by the firm. Rudolf Mosse, whose *Berliner Tageblatt* was more traditional in style, but almost as successful as Ullstein's paper, bought up and founded other papers in the Berlin area.

The papers of both firms were atypical in the context of the German press, in that they presented the view of an interested but concerned observer, subservient to no economic or political grouping. While lively in tone, they clearly expressed a liberal belief in the role of newspapers as objective commentators on society, rather than as vehicles of polemicists, or uncontentious upholders of the status quo. As in Britain and the United States the changing character of the German press reflected the economic and social tensions inside society, and the growth of an agency which sought to channel and resolve them primarily for commercial reasons.

THE EMERGENCE OF THE CINEMA

It is often pointed out that the first publication of the *Daily Mail*, on 4 May 1896, took place three months after the first performance, in London, before a paying public of a new phenomenon, the cinematograph. It is as if two forms of mass communication, the popular press and the cinema, in appearing simultaneously in Britain, represent a watershed in social and political life.

Cinema film represented the connection of science to popular culture. Experiments in the nature of visual perception had been carried out since the eighteenth century. Photography, which was itself the result of scientific experiment, became not only an important and popular form of recording reality, but also the means whereby the nature of motion could be investigated. Edweard Muybridge in the United States, and Etienne Marey in France were the pioneers in this field, taking sequences of photographs by elaborate arrangements of cameras, or a form of revolving disc. They were unconcerned with the commercial possibilities of the work they were pursuing, but others were not.

Thomas Edison, commercial inventor *par excellence* in the United States, had the imagination and resources to develop the 'kinetoscope' by 1893, a peep-show machine which ran a continuous fifty-foot loop of film past a light source. It had limited potential in penny arcades, but a means of large-scale projection was sought, and eventually discovered, by the Lumière brothers in France, the Skladanowsky brothers in Germany, and Armat and Jenkins in the United States. It was still not clear to what purpose the new facility to portray a world in motion could be put. The places in which films began to be projected determined the purpose; to create a new form of commercial entertainment which drew upon popular forms already in existence.

In Britain and the United States films were projected in vaudeville and music halls. Interspersed between the acts, they were very short, and were presented as novelties. They could be portrayals of recent events, actual or staged, or short sketches for the interest and amusement of the urban working-class audience. Films were popular in fairs and travelling shows where they quickly replaced the magic lantern slide presentation, and offered particularly good value to the owner and projectionist since the same stock of films could be used in different locations until they wore out.

The alternative to taking films around the country to maximise the audience was to site a centre for the exclusive showing of films in the area of greatest population. Penny arcade proprietors in large American cities curtained off an area and had continuous shows. Soon whole arcades were converted into small theatres. The nickelodeon, a centre of cheap entertainment, had been established, and storefront theatres proliferated throughout urban America. By 1908 there were more than 600 nickel theatres in greater New York with an estimated daily attendance of between 300,000 and 400,000. In Britain and Germany shops were also converted and new, larger theatres built to cater for the different social groups who were now going to see films. In 1914 the weekly audience in Britain was estimated at seven to eight million, and in Germany the number of cinemas rose from two in 1900 to 2446 in 1914, providing one million seats.

Exhibitors demanded increasing numbers of films for audiences who soon became weary of the local scenes and short slapstick comedies which were usually available. For the first decade after 1896 producers, in the main, were merely concerned with making a product which was sold, rather like elastic, by the foot. Film production was international, since there were no language barriers; the market grew rapidly but the product was scarce. There were some innovations, particularly the illusionist films of Méliès in France, which were copied elsewhere, but the general uniformity in style and content reflected lack of capital, and some insecurity about the long-term prospects for the new medium.

In the period after 1903 a number of factors combined to stabilise the economic structure of the nascent industry and point film content and structure in a particular direction. Within ten years the United States had achieved a predominant position in world cinema, a position which has never been relinquished.

In 1903 Edwin S. Porter, an electrician and cameraman in Edison's company, made a film which was to have an important influence on the future shape of the product. *The Great Train Robbery* was 600 feet long, and made up of over twenty separate shots, from different locations and with a variation in use which produced enormous enthusiasm in American audiences. Narrative film, using techniques applicable only to that medium, could offer audiences entertainment which they could find nowhere else. But while the future of the industry might lie in story films, greater financial risks were involved for producers and exhibitors alike, as well as the newly formed distribution agencies.

Originally, exhibitors bought copies of films which they continued to own. With the greater number of permanent cinemas and the larger turnover, film exchanges began to appear and slowly began to take on the role of renters, buying films directly from producers and hiring them to exhibitors. It was a significant pointer to the future organisation of the industry. A different form of control began to develop in Germany after 1907 as the Projektions-A.G. Union attempted to group cinemas throughout the country together in a distribution network.

Since exhibitors and renters were more generally aware of the needs of the public and had the finance available from dealing in films to invest in the product they eventually began to become involved in film-making. In Germany and Britain it was on a very small scale, but in the United States it brought into the business a number of entrepreneurs who, while totally divorced from the practical problems of film-making, were very aware of the commercial aspects of selling the product. Their entry into film-making followed a battle for control of production which reflected the general character of large-scale American industry in the period.

It was believed by Edison that monopoly control of the industry was possible by using the patent laws to restrict film production to those companies using his equipment, or working with licensed products. By 1907 all the main producers had fallen into line, except Biograph, who nevertheless found it impossible to cope with the financial pressure. In 1908 the company joined with eight others, including Méliès and Pathé Frères, in the Motion Picture Patents Trust (MPPT), the first attempt to restrict and control the market in films to the advantage of the main producers.

The monopoly stretched throughout the industry, since an agreement on film stock was made with the main manufacturer, Eastman Kodak, and distribution agents and exhibitors were only allowed to trade in licensed films. If they went outside the MPPT they were totally excluded from handling any Trust films. By 1912 Edison's organisation had virtually taken control of the whole distribution organisation of Trust films by establishing the General Film Company, its own rental organisation.

The Trust was eventually declared illegal under anti-Trust legislation in 1915, but by then the competition which it had intended to stop had mushroomed as independent producers took advantage of gaps in Trust control, particularly developing the nickel theatres, which had been considered uneconomic and of little importance by the MPPT. The owners of these theatres were willing to support the efforts of Carl Laemmle, who from a base in Chicago had built a large distribution business, and who had fallen out with the Trust in 1909. He could offer a large number of outlets for producers who were willing to risk the business wrath, and occasional strongarm tactics, of Trust employees.

Few of the seventy-odd production companies established between 1910 and 1914 survived into the 1920s, but those which did had men behind them with a keen eye for what was popular. New York producers such as William Fox and Adolph Zukor, through ownership of cinemas, also had the financial resources to attract credit. With the added ingredient of 'chutzpah', a Yiddish expression representing resourcefulness and cheek, the new breed of independent producers began to influence American and world cinema.

One feature was the development of the 'star' system, the process of selling a picture through a recognisable name and personality. Another was the production of longer films, with the intention of attracting a more sophisticated audience. Simultaneously, exhibitor/producers began to construct larger and more opulent cinema theatres in the large cities to cope with the new audience.

There was mobility in the film industry during this period represented in the men, mostly first- or second-generation immigrants, who began to dominate it, as well as the experimentation with film form and the organisation of distribution. The movement of production to California was one further aspect of change, not only in the film industry but in American society in general.

Commercial and social factors directed the industry towards the environs of Los Angeles. In 1913 there was only one production company in that area, while there were twenty in the major cities in the east. The move was not, as is often assumed, to escape the attentions of the Trust, but to take advantage of the natural environment for all-year-round shooting, the space to expand operations, a pool of non-union craft labour in the fast expanding population, and a civic commitment to individual initiative and business activity.

Laemmle and Zukor were the first of the independents to centre their production activity in Southern California, and soon others began to follow, as did the numerous ancillary staff required to service the growing industry. They shared a frontier outlook, divorced from the constraints of urban America, forming a community divorced from, and yet through its product intimately related to, the realities of life experienced by the audiences.

The main audiences for films in penny arcades and 'storefront' nickelodeons had been the poor working class, particularly the large immigrant communities, who had little money, time or understanding of the society of which they were now part. Silent films, portraying aspects of American life, both factual and comical, at the turn of the century, offered the illiterate citizen a glimpse into the manners and customs of American life. The early producers were unconcerned about the moral value of their products, but as the success of the nickelodeons became more widely noticed, a movement gathered force, which saw in the cinemas and the films, a source of moral danger to society at large.

Nickelodeons were easy targets for control since licences could be revoked by city authorities, but any closure of these outlets would have an important effect on the industry as a whole, and producers, who were beginning to consolidate their interests in the MPPT, recognised the need to come to terms with religious and political groupings arguing for some control of content.

In Chicago and New York the mobilisation of 'responsible' opinion against the nickelodeons, and the supposed surfeit of immoral films shown in them led to the establishment of the National Board of Review of Motion Pictures in 1909. Based in New York, middle-class ladies used the facilities of the Trust to view films voluntarily submitted to them by Trust producers. They acted as moral arbiters, hoping to create a medium which would be a positive force for good, and social order, in the community. The MPPT certainly gained respectability, but the activities of the Board of Review depended on the acquiescence of all sections of the industry. The rise of the independents, representative of the immigrant groups who were most feared by the moralists, offered no hope of this. Hollywood, in its early years, signified a distinct rejection of outside censorship, but in searching for a wider audience, producers had to exercise constraint in their selection of topics and treatments. Cinema would increasingly reflect the more positive aspects of American life, particularly in the work of David Wark Griffith.

In emphasising positive American values the reformers were also concerned about the number of French and Italian films entering the market which appeared to be based on a morality, not only different, but inferior to their own. The MPPT were not averse to this outlook, since their own position would be strengthened by a reduction of imports. In 1908 over half the films came from abroad, but with the proliferation of production companies this had dropped to 10 per cent by 1913.

The nativists in America had their parallels in European countries who recognised in the growth of the cinema a challenge to political culture and social cohesion. The German film industry was very small, and as the number of cinemas grew they depended increasingly on imports from France and Denmark, as well as the United States. Not only did the cinema lack respectability through its origins and by catering for the lower classes but, critics argued, the films were un-German and morally demeaning by catering for the lusts of the flesh, which was particularly dangerous for young people. One solution put forward was for the cinema industry to be supported by the state. However, the idea came to nothing, and by 1914 imports from America, France, Italy and Denmark made up 85 per cent of films shown in Germany.

The figure for imports into Britain was very similar, of which the bulk was shared by France and the United States. Individual film-makers such as Cecil Hepworth and George Pearson experimented with the new narrative form after 1912, influenced by the early films of D. W. Griffith; but British film production suffered from under-capitalisation. Whereas in France 'freedom from cultural ties and intellectual prejudices' had allowed film to develop, it has been argued that before the First World War, in Britain, the cinema had not been accepted as a respectable art form. It could attract neither finance nor talent. However, the distribution and exhibition sides of the industry were highly profitable while there was a consistent supply of popular films from abroad.

As in the United States and Germany, the new phenomenon of the cinema found its critics among those who feared for its effect upon the young and the impressionable. Parliament took a hand in regulating the licensing of cinemas in 1909, but local authorities appeared to have the right to censor films, a fact which worried the industry enough to set up the British Board of Film Censors in 1911. It had no official status, but its work in vetting films and issuing certificates of suitability was acceptable to the majority of local authorities in the country. In this it satisfied its original aim, while giving the film industry a veneer of respectability.

The cinema as a popular form of entertainment developed in a period of social and political ferment. In the industrialised societies of Europe and the United States the lower classes of society were mobilising politically, and challenging the predominant position of those who had held power for generations. The problem which faces the historian is how far the growing film industry influenced the process of change affecting society during this period.

Contemporary observers often used a moral argument to cover a political fear. The calls for censorship of film material, arising simultaneously in all three countries, ostensibly arose from a fear of the effect of this powerful visual medium upon young people. However, since the bulk of the audience for films came from the working-class population there was a wider issue of the influence over large groups of people who were potentially dangerous unless given the right views of society, in other words, the views of the dominant groups.

What reformers were unaware of was that the changing structure of the industry, and the development of feature-length narrative films was pushing producers towards a more 'responsible' and positive view of their function in society.

Cinema film was initially a parasitic medium, drawing upon the popular cultural institutions, music-hall and fairground, and forms, sketches and magic shows, as well as the audiences for those forms. In the period after 1910 the industry in all three countries moved towards the legitimate theatre since it could capitalise on the plays, actors and even the audiences. If, at first, films merely reproduced plays, it was not long before the nature of film as a medium of suspense and emotion in its own right was being explored. This coincided with increased production costs, and the building of larger and more sumptuous cinemas.

While still a medium of entertainment for the working class, the industry, particularly in America, became clearer about the potential of film as an artistic form, and also as a commercial product, creating a market rather than satisfying an existing demand. Early exponents of the cinema had recognised its potential for capturing the real world, and many of the earliest films were merely reproductions of everyday life. It was clear by the second decade of the twentieth century that the real world was capable of manipulation through film. Time could be elided, locations changed, and problems solved within the space of one short feature. Most crucially, the cinema could 'offer private solutions to public issues' through the representation by screen personalities of common problems and resolving the issues raised in a way which was satisfying, fulfilling, and ultimately reassuring.

The moral panics of reformers defined, for film producers, stories and presentations which would be acceptable to those who still dominated the political and cultural life of society. The box-office returns reflected the interests and outlook of the film-goers. The immediate pressures fell upon exhibitor and distributors, but ultimately they were reflected in how producers solved the twin problems of social acceptance and commercial viability.

This was most important in the United States where the control of the industry was slowly being taken over by men who had yet to prove their credentials as Americans. Many of the new entrepreneurs were Jews from Eastern Europe; outsiders in their original countries they had yet to be assimilated into the host nation. The new cinema industry offered commercial success, but it also offered a medium through which they could explain their outlook on the new American society. They exemplified the virtues of individualism and group solidarity, yet at the same time they recognised the character of cultural assimilation taking place in the cities, and sought to encourage it and, of course, make money out of it. The movie-makers represented the new face of America, but harked back to the values and outlooks of the American past.

The potential was clearly there for the American cinema to become an important element in the integration of society, not under pressure from government, but from the commercial requirements of an industry which had to be heavily capitalised, selling a product to the largest possible public. In 1914 the potential size and influence of Hollywood had yet to be appreciated, and the character of the film industries in Britain and Germany gave little hint of their social and political importance, except in a possibly negative form. The First World War would demonstrate to governments and leaders in both countries the potential of the film medium for the positive construction of attitudes.

4. Propaganda 1914–1918

THE First World War has been seen as a catalyst which brought together the social, economic and political forces which were to dominate the first half of the twentieth century. There was an acceleration of government intervention in the liberal democracies, a greater awareness of the importance of public opinion in the political process, a disruption of traditional trade patterns, and a test of the political, social and military leadership of the ruling groups in all societies. For the first time the populations of all belligerent countries were actively involved in the long-drawn-out conflict. War, to use a famous adjective, became 'total'.

For the first time the large-scale control and presentation of information became an important factor in a country's war effort. Internal censorship became a common feature of life, while attempts were made by government agencies to influence opinion in both neutral and enemy countries. As the war progressed expertise in this area became greater, but the overall effect of these efforts to control and manipulate opinion is difficult to judge.

The causes of the First World War are complex, and the subject of continuing debate, not least the problem of evaluating the role of newspapers in preparing public opinion for war. Sydney Fay, one of the earliest analysts of the origins of the war, was convinced that an underlying factor was the 'poisoning of public opinion by the newspaper press in all of the great countries'. He pre-supposed that large-circulation newspapers organised the outlook of the general public, and that statesmen were affected by the attitudes of the public as expressed in the popular press.

It is clear that newspapers in Britain, particularly the *Daily Mail* and *Daily Express*, did capitalise on general fears of the German menace in the decade before the war. In some cases, particularly spy scares, reporters showed a febrile imagination. In others, such as the naval scare of 1909, they reflected divisions in the government, and were used by factions to present a particular point of view in a personalised and sensational fashion. Decision-makers could not disregard the presentation of such attitudes, but it rarely affected their judgement, since there was a widespread belief among the elite that the popular press represented 'unenlightened opinion', something which they did not understand and rather feared.

The popular newspapers set the agenda of debate about foreign affairs, and occasionally, by their overt hostility, restricted the terms upon which it could proceed. Foreign policy decision-makers were divorced from the mass of the people, and in the face of uninformed and unhelpful stories were inclined to secrecy.

If the popular newspapers did reflect a general feeling of uneasiness with the foreigner, it was constructed into a more positive outlook on Britain and her role in the world. Any recognition of the social divisions in British society, reflected in the increasing number of strikes and the growth of a labour movement, were subordinated, in the large-circulation press, to the expression of imperial and national values. Personal and commercial reasons were equally responsible for this development. Northcliffe's papers accurately reflected his own patriotic outlook, and genuine fears of the growing strength of Germany and her preparations for war. Furthermore, the largely lower-middle-class readership of the popular newspapers were largely sympathetic to news presentation which exaggerated the threats, both internal and external, to Britain while emphasising those aspects of British life which represented a united and strong nation: the monarchy and a strong navy.

The effects may have been to over-emphasise the danger from Germany, and a failure to explore the internal weaknesses in Britain. However, no press proprietor, particularly Northcliffe, could view with equanimity the possibility of war. Wars might 'make the papers sell', according to the music-hall song, but they also led to paper shortages, rising costs, and a fall in advertising revenue.

The organisation of the *Daily Mail*'s own foreign news service after 1896 was one further reason for the wider and more sensational coverage of international affairs. When he bought *The Times* in 1908 Northcliffe gained another excellent foreign news organisation which could provide the angles to stories which Reuters, with their emphasis on fact and attribution, were unwilling and unable to do.

Popular journalism, with its emphasis on personalities, human-interest stories and simplistic representation of events, determined the scope and outlook of foreign news coverage in the British popular press. It was not a major factor in the decision for war in 1914, but made the decision, once taken, acceptable to a large part of the British people.

Similarly in Germany, the popular urban 'boulevard press' with its simple declamatory prose style offered a Germano-centric outlook on international affairs. It was not typical of the bulk of German papers, but the role of the semi-official Wolff bureau in distributing news throughout Germany is important in recognising the possibility of news management in periods of international crisis.

From the creation of the Second Reich in 1871 an important facet of government policy had been to isolate the politically dangerous elements in the state. After 1900 the Kaiser and his government not only had to reckon with the growth of Social Democracy as a political force, but also the threat to Germany as an international power. The concept of *Sammlungspolitik*, the coming together of the nation against the twin threats of internal disorder and external destruction, was taken up by much of the conservative press, and the 'apolitical' commercial papers which argued for a strong and stable German society.

Oppositional voices in the German press, from the liberal left or Social Democrat papers, did no more than confirm their readers' attitudes towards the regime. The bulk of the dispersed, small-circulation press presented a view of Germany and the position of the Reich in world affairs which conformed to the outlook of the government.

Mass public opinion had little influence over the decision for peace or war in Britain and Germany in 1914, and the bulk of either public had little knowledge of or interest in the problems of Europe since the majority never saw a newspaper. The urban population, and the popular press which served them, may have exercised some influence by their proximity to centres of government, but it is a question which still defies a complete answer.

Critics like Fay had a belief in the social responsibility of the press, and any paper which fell below a certain standard, in their view, had a pernicious effect on the people who read it. Popular newspapers before the First World War had a different concept of social responsibility; it consisted of being a medium of information, entertainment, and advertising for the largest available public. In Britain they stood above party politics, in Germany support of the *Sammlungspolitik* signified the same thing.. That to them was being socially responsible, but it had an important political effect which made the acceptance of war in 1914 more understandable.

The nationalism which was a feature of the large-scale press before 1914 was intensified still further after the outbreak of war when governments had the responsibility for the direction of all resources towards the war effort. In Britain and Germany this meant control of information which might be of help to the enemy. The war was expected to be a short affair, possibly of weeks, certainly no more than a few months, and this goes to explain the lack of interest in the more positive aspects of propaganda in the early part of the war. Popular newspapers could be relied upon to continue in euphoric mood while the armies were mobile.

The pre-war spy scares in Britain had led to the government reframing the Official Secrets Act in 1911 in order to restrict the possible leakage of information. Through a voluntary arrangement between the service departments and the press, restrictions on the publication of possibly dangerous material were agreed before 1914, but with the outbreak of war a Press Bureau was set up which monitored all telegrams and despatches, effectively acting as a censoring and delaying body.

More importantly, the Defence of the Realm Act (DORA), gave the government the right to impose limits on the freedom of the press. This could be, and was, used against any publication deemed dissident by the authorities. The use of such powers posed problems for a government which argued it was fighting for democratic freedom, and they were rarely necessary since there were a greater number of papers which patriotically argued for the war and encouraged the population to deal harshly with pacifists and others of like tendencies.

The problem for patriotic newspapers was the supply of news from the Front. No correspondents were given access to the

British lines in France before May 1915; until then information had come from official communiqués, routed through the Press Bureau. When permission had been granted war correspondents were subject to censorship at the Front, and treated with great suspicion by senior officers. There was little opportunity, or willingness, to report the hardship and anxiety experienced by officers and men alike. Despatches gloried in patriotic fervour and optimism, partly because it cast the army leadership in a good light and secured better treatment from them, and encouraged recruiting. After the introduction of conscription in 1916 war correspondents had an even greater duty, it was argued, to keep up morale at home.

As the war bogged down in the mud of the Western Front the German government also became more concerned about the presentation of news to the domestic population. In October 1915 freedom to state opinions in printed or other forms was suspended, a measure which merely reinforced the system of censorship built up from the outbreak of war. Clearly, as in Britain, military security was a foremost consideration, but as the war proceeded, and the military situation deteriorated, the question of control of information, and reporting of opposition viewpoints, became one aspect of the wider divisions between the civilian government and the military authorities.

The focus of this antagonism was the War Press Office, which had been established in October 1915 in order to set out guidelines and avoid the arguments which still continued to occur. An attempt by Bethmann-Hollweg's successor, Michaelis, to bring all censorship under the control of the Chancellor was unsuccessful in the face of military opposition, but the High Command was itself unable to stop the publication of full reports from Allied newspapers appearing in the German press.

There was little positive cooperation between government departments apart from a press conference two or three times a week for the Berlin press which had been started in August 1914. Through the admission of provincial journalists and use of news agencies it was hoped that some direction could be given to the reporting of domestic conditions without recourse to censorship.

The Berlin press conference was the carrot, aimed at softening the stick of the censors, and encouraging a responsible attitude among the press, particularly over the discussion of war aims in

November 1916. It was hoped that the opening up of debate would mobilise opinion for the continuation of the war, and it was left to the press to reflect this as part of their national duty.

Given the conflicting outlooks of the authorities and the deteriorating military situation after 1916 it was impossible to construct a clear propaganda outlook for domestic consumption, and increasingly counter-productive abroad as the Allied information services began to operate more efficiently and the Central Powers faced defeat.

The experience of Matthias Erzberger, the Catholic Centre Party deputy, illustrates the character of German propaganda work. In 1911 he had been one of the politicians involved in the appropriation by the Foreign Ministry of 300,000 Marks for the dissemination of German news abroad, and in the light of his interest was asked to set up a propaganda office in the Navy Ministry concerned specifically with information for neutral countries. He had virtually no foreign experience, few contacts, and immediate opposition from the High Command of the Army. Nevertheless, he persisted, and working mainly through Catholic interests sought to influence informed opinion by means of scholarly literature or, in the case of the Vatican, economic subvention.

A convinced expansionist in 1914, he began to doubt that Germany could hope for anything but a negotiated peace three years later, but found, as Epstein suggests, that 'to serve as a propagandist for a nationalist, militarist and semi-autocratic country . . . was to assume a task where great successes could not be expected.' By November 1918 he had become responsible for all German propaganda, at home and abroad, and could be made a scapegoat for its failure. As a signatory of the Armistice he was more obviously guilty of failure and treachery to those German nationalists who still believed the illusions fed to the press by the Army High Command at the end of the war. In August 1921 he paid the price of failure at the hands of two assassins.

The recruitment of Erzberger demonstrated the paucity of expert opinion on propaganda work, but also the recognition by all belligerent countries at the beginning of the war of the importance of neutral opinion, especially that in the United States. Within days of the outbreak of war the cable connection between Germany and the US had been cut by the British, restricting telegraphic communication, but the German authorities had already prepared a range of leaflets and posters for distribution in all neutral countries outlining in emotive terms their reasons for going to war. This approach relied on blanket coverage without clear targets for their information. The British counter, when it came, was very much more specific.

A War Propaganda Bureau was established in the autumn of 1914 to prepare materials for dissemination abroad. The director, Charles Masterman, concentrated on literate, reasoned discussion of issues, aimed at specific leaders of opinion in neutral countries. He recruited experts to write pamphlets, and encouraged personal links between individuals as a way of transmitting information and gaining an understanding of opinion in other countries.

Wellington House, as the Bureau was better known, was particularly effective in the United States in countering German arguments, but found itself continually under pressure from the Foreign Office, the department of State with responsibility for relations with other countries. Whereas the News Department of the Foreign Office passed information to accredited representatives in Allied and neutral countries the work of Wellington House was less overt but complementary. Both worked on the principle of factual accuracy and the belief that it was enough to tell the truth for people to believe it.

They continued to be the basis upon which the activities of a coordinated structure was established in the spring of 1916. As in Germany, the prolongation of the war led to a discussion about the effectiveness and organisation of propaganda and the literary activities of Wellington House were placed under the general direction of the Foreign Office. This arrangement lasted for little more than nine months. Lloyd George, who became Prime Minister in December 1916, was personally interested in propaganda, and set in motion an enquiry which recommended a separate Department of State responsible for the information services. John Buchan, the novelist, was appointed head of the new department in January 1917, directly responsible to the Prime Minister. In effect the position of the Foreign Office had been strengthened still further, since Buchan looked to that area for advice, and Sir Edward Carson, the Cabinet minister nominally in charge, lacked interest and enthusiasm for his work.

Carson's resignation in January 1918 gave Lloyd George the

opportunity to recast not only the structure but also the attitude towards propaganda abroad. He brought in his confidant, Lord Beaverbrook, owner of the *Daily Express*, as a Minister of Information, and made Lord Northcliffe responsible for propaganda to enemy countries; both were given direct access to the Prime Minister, thus satisfying the individual jealousies of competing press lords.

Beaverbrook and Northcliffe were outsiders in British politics, engendering as much loathing as praise for their activities. Both had already been actively involved in propaganda of one kind or another. Beaverbrook, as a Canadian, had been instrumental in organising information about the war in the Dominion, commissioning war artists and using films; an example of enterprise tardily followed in Britain. He bought the *Daily Express* in 1916, and was immediately bracketed with Northcliffe as a man seeking power through the manipulation of opinion.

In the spring of 1917 Northcliffe, himself, had become head of the British War Mission in the United States, responsible for acquiring the necessary war supplies and working with the new ally. Although it was not part of his brief, he had recognised the importance of publicity for the British war effort, and fallen foul of a suspicious British Ambassador, who was concerned about the niceties and proprieties of diplomacy. It was an attitude which Beaverbrook and Northcliffe would experience throughout the life of the Ministry of Information.

The Foreign Office found its position threatened on a number of fronts, not least that of making policy, as Crewe House, the centre of Northcliffe's activities, argued for a statement of war aims which could be used to propagandise the subject populations in Austria–Hungary into rejecting their rulers and breaking up the empire. This was a direct appeal to 'public opinion' in its widest sense, an approach which had been continuously rejected within British government circles from 1914. The restrained appeal to informed opinion had been focused on neutral and Allied countries when the progress of the war had been less fluid. However, the entry of the United States on the side of the Allies, and the effect of the Russian Revolution in psychological and material terms, produced a wholly new set of circumstances which the Foreign Office were least able to exploit. The organisation of the Ministry of Information under Beaverbrook was the recognition of the expertise which existed in the popular press, an area not normally associated with the machinery of government.

In undermining the morale of the enemy the Ministry of Information were pushing against an open door. As the Germans well knew, even the most efficient propaganda organisation would be hard-put to explain away defeat on the battlefield, whereas success brought its own propaganda rewards. It is difficult to measure the effect of the activities of Crewe House, particularly since many Germans were anxious to excuse their own political and military failures by emphasising the effectiveness of the work of Northcliffe and his associates.

Whatever may have been intended by Lloyd George and Beaverbrook, the Ministry of Information never gained control of home publicity. From the start of the war, government departments with responsibility in the domestic sector, as well as *ad hoc* bodies, had organised campaigns to inform the public and encourage recruiting. There was no attempt at central direction until the recognition in 1916 of the changing character of the war, and the need to boost morale once conscription had been introduced and pacifist voices became more insistent.

Buchan's unwillingness to work in the domestic field led to the foundation in August 1917 of the National War Aims Committee (NWAC), which was linked to the Department of Information while Carson was in office, but refused to work under Beaverbrook, preferring to appear to have a private status, while, in reality, being funded by the government. NWAC reflected the ambiguity which invested British attitudes towards propaganda during the war. These arose from a mixture of entrenched positions and a fear of political personalities, as well as the confidence which could be placed in the press.

Members of NWAC argued that the government should not appear to be trying to influence domestic opinion, since Britain, as a democracy, was fighting against that kind of autocratic control. The structure of local committees to work for NWAC represented the decentralised aspect, which was certainly preferable in many eyes to the direction of one minister, especially someone as politically adventurous as Beaverbrook, who might use a centralised apparatus for his own ends.

As in Germany, attitudes towards the control of information reflected the wider internal battle for political power. In Britain this was less conflict between civilians and the military, although this certainly existed, than the question of prime ministerial control. Lloyd George, in his employment of the 'Press Gang', was not only utilising expertise in national publicity, but also recognising the importance of these men in creating political support in the country.

While newspapers in all countries were vulnerable to the economic effects of the war with shortages of newsprint, the loss of advertising and higher costs resulting from inflation, the smaller German papers were particularly open to outside influence. This came not from the government, but from a combination of Rhineland businessmen and heavy-industrialists who were anxious to publicise their own view of an expansionist Germany as a means to encourage the mass of the German people to work towards victory.

Under the management of Alfred Hugenberg, a director of Krupps, the group had already formed the *Ausland GmbH* in March 1914 as a holding company for the coordination of investments in newspapers. This clandestine operation set the pattern of activities of the group during the war. The main aim of the group was to counter opinion in the country which they considered inimical to their best interests, which included a vastly expanded German Empire. They were one of the first of the economic lobbies to recognise the importance of the new media, and actively attempt to control the channels of communication to the mass of the people.

During the war an estimated 29 million Marks were invested in various areas of publishing. The acquisition of the *August Scherl GmbH* in 1916 not only secured control of two major Berlin dailies, *Der Tag*, which catered for intellectual circles, and the *Berliner Lokal-Anzeiger*, a popular large-circulation paper, but also a number of weeklies and periodicals. The Scherl publishing house had experienced difficulties in 1914 and been rescued by a group of business men with some government prompting. Further financial problems gave Hugenberg the opportunity to secure the company as a vehicle for right-wing views in a capital dominated by the democratically orientated papers of the Mosse and Ullstein publishing groups, the *Berliner Tageblatt* and *Vossische Zeitung*.

Through the *Vera Verlaganstalt*, which was formed in 1917, economically distressed provincial newspapers were offered financial advice, while in the same year the interest in advertising led to the formation of the *Allegemeine Anzeigen GmbH*, a nationalist-orientated agency which was able to channel adverts to specific newspapers. The group were also able to influence the collection and distribution of news by amalgamating a number of small news agencies under the larger auspices of the *Telegraphen-Union* which was controlled financially by Hugenberg.

Intervention in the newspaper industry was only one facet of the financial activity of the Rhineland industrialists, and by no means the most effective, but it was to have important repercussions in the post-war period when Hugenberg was able to build still further upon the investments made during the conflict. Unlike Northcliffe or Beaverbrook, he had, at this stage, no personal political ambition; while they were publicists, his forte lay in covert operations. Their personal fortunes were bound up with the commercial success of their publishing ventures, whereas Hugenberg was the manager of other peoples' money. A career in the Prussian civil service, experience in banking, and ten years on the Krupp's board had produced a man with clear administrative abilities but little flair.

In a sense, Hugenberg represented the future, since the creation and consolidation of a publishing and communications empire in the twentieth century would increasingly take place within a highly diversified economic context. He also recognised the importance of film as a potentially influential medium and susceptible to control, since vertical and horizontal integration were easier to accomplish there than in the fragmented and diversified newspaper industry. His aims, though, were politically retrogressive. There was no tradition of freedom of opinion in Germany, and Hugenberg shared the conservative abhorrence of democratic structures and institutions, while recognising the need to mobilise the allegiance of the large majority of the population behind the conservative leadership. He believed in the manipulative capability of newspapers and films, but had little interest in the content of the media.

Here he differed from Northcliffe, who was at the peak of his publishing career during the war. From his earliest work with *Answers* Alfred Harmsworth's main interest had been in journalism, and he had been an active proprietor, intervening in the day-to-day running of his papers. Beaverbrook, while more remote, was also interested in more than financial management. Successful newspaper proprietors in Britain recognised the importance of selling the paper, and its advertisers, to the reader.

Yet, such was the suspicion in political circles of the power of such figures that they were only recruited into government service to propagandise abroad. To Lloyd George, Northcliffe was safer addressing the enemy than criticising the government. However, unlike Hugenberg, Northcliffe did not represent the economic interests of a privileged group opposing the general outlook of the government. There was a community of interest in Britain, which was lacking in Germany during the war, and which had found expression in the work of propagandists in America earlier in the war.

The effectiveness of that British propaganda in the United States before 1917 is difficult to judge. When, in April of that year, President Wilson took the country into war as an Associated Power, not a full ally, the work of Wellington House appeared to have come to fruition. It is likely that the continuous appeals to informed American opinion reinforced pro-British sentiments among American decision-makers in Washington and elsewhere, but the key factor appears to have been the cutting of the telegraphic cable between Germany and the United States on 5 August 1914. By this measure the immediate communication of war news from Europe had to be routed through London, making it subject to censorship under the DORA regulations, and producing a British slant on the progress of the war. Furthermore, Reuters' own special relationship with the British government, and its links with Associated Press, contributed further to the control of the content and tone of news flowing into the United States.

While the bulk of the newspaper press was neutral, there was a group of important papers which displayed an anti-British bias. The most famous were those owned by William Randolph Hearst, but they also included the Washington *Post*, the Los Angeles *Times*, the Chicago *Tribune*, and, as might be expected, German-language newspapers. Hearst was essentially isolationist, fearful of the greater menace from Japan, and disturbed by the imperialist designs of Britain. His views were disregarded by 'respectable' opinion, particularly after the sinking of the *Lusitania* in May 1915 with the loss of nearly 1200 lives, many of whom were American.

It was a propaganda gift to the British, reinforcing stories of German atrocities in Europe, and propelling previously neutral papers into an anti-German stance. It was an event which galvanised opinion, and continued to act upon the public imagination as an episode in numerous films, possibly proving 'how a single, symbolic act, once dramatised, can carry far stronger impact than a massive battle with hundreds of thousands of casualties.'

When the United States did enter the war against Germany in April 1917 it was not as a result of insistent propaganda, but as a considered response to the German policy of unrestricted submarine warfare, and the unwillingness to allow Germany, an unknown quantity in power politics, to replace Britain as the arbiter in European affairs.

The United States was not prepared for war, nor were the population enthusiastic. The task of informing and persuading the American people was entrusted to a Committee on Public Information (CPI), a euphemism for propaganda, under the chairmanship of George Creel. This was set up by presidential decree within a week of the declaration of war, and in Creel's words, had to 'sell' the war to America. The positive role of the salesman was backed up, as in Britain and Germany, by coercive censorship legislation which tried to make sure his was the only foot in the door.

An Espionage Act of June 1917 reinforced a presidential proclamation that any publisher producing material helpful to the enemy was liable to prosecution for treason. Further measures included a Trading-with-the-Enemy Act in October which authorised censorship of all communications moving in or out of the United States and the requirement of foreign-language newspapers to provide sworn translations of their contents for the local postmaster. The *coup-de-grâce* came in May 1918 with the passage of the Sedition Act which provided for action against any 'disloyal, profane, scurrilous or abusive language about the form of government of the United States or the Constitution . . .'

The restriction on freedom of the press embodied in these measures was widely recognised as necessary, but the newspapers mainly affected by the legislation were the foreign-language press and socialist papers which took a generally pacifist line. In the main, the draconian laws were unnecessary since newspapers supported the government, and willingly carried the information provided by the News Division of the CPI, in its carefully prepared *Official Bulletin*.

The main thrust of Creel's domestic propaganda was the presentation of the barbaric Hun which, combined with the legislative response of the government, legitimised a wave of war hysteria which continued through 1917. Fanatical jingoism was anathema to many liberals who saw the war as a necessary battle for democracy, but were concerned about the undemocratic measures, and the xenophobic outlook of the censors, in prosecuting such a war.

Emotional propaganda was also found in the products of the American cinema industry after April 1917, adding to the war hysteria, but forcing observers to admit to the importance of film as a key element in propaganda. Yet it had only slowly been recognised as such by the organisations set up to organise information in Britain and Germany.

The domestic industries in both countries were relatively small, but the war affected each one differently. Production was stimulated in Germany by the loss of films from France which had supplied over 35 per cent of the market before 1914. Small production companies mushroomed and the number of cinemas increased from 2446 to 3130 over three years, as the industry began to satisfy the entertainment needs of a population thrown back on itself.

The British cinema, in comparison, began to stagnate in the face of superior products coming from America. In the first two years of the war the number of films in production increased, but the disruption caused by conscription of personnel after 1916 and the rejection by audiences of a patently inferior product led to a crisis in the industry. The imposition of an Entertainments Tax on seat prices in 1916 was one further burden, although there was a general increase in cinema-going during the war.

In the first year of the war the interest of the military authorities of both countries lay in restricting the amount of factual war footage appearing in the cinemas. Weekly newsreels of fighting at the front appeared in Germany, having been strictly censored by the military authorities. They were also distributed abroad, a fact which caused great dismay to Wellington House, whose own activities in this area were constrained by the unwillingness of the military authorities to sanction filming on the British front line because of fears over security.

This ban was reversed in 1915, as in the case of war correspondents, because the war had become bogged down and the authorities were alerted to the need for more extensive publicity at home and abroad.

After working with newsreel companies for a year the War Office set up its own Cinematograph Committee in October 1916 under the chairmanship of Sir Max Aitken, who within two months would become Lord Beaverbrook. Subsequently the War Office became responsible for the production and distribution of all films from the front, sending out its own newsreel, the *War Office Topical News*. The Committee worked closely with the Department of Information under Buchan, and in June 1918 was absorbed into the Ministry of Information. The British cinema-going public were presented with a coherent and controlled view of the war by virtue of this arrangement, which was intended to give the impression of a purely commercial operation.

By 1916 the German High Command were also aware of the importance of film in propagating the right patriotic sentiments, and encouraged the commercial organisation of the cinema to achieve its aims both in the domestic market and abroad. The restructuring of the German film industry which ensued was to have a fundamental influence on the development of the German film industry in the post-war period. It also demonstrates a different outlook in Germany towards state intervention, and the inter-relationship of commercial and state interests.

A number of small production companies were amalgamated into the *Deutsche Lichtbild Gesellschaft* (*Deulig*) in November 1916 at the suggestion of the government in order to make films mainly for distribution to neutral countries. Capital for the project came from the funds appropriated by Rhineland industrialists and managed by Hugenberg, his first intervention in the film industry. Within three months the German High Command had reorganised its own film propaganda in a *Bild-und Film amt* (*Bufa*), an agency purely concerned with the presentation of military propaganda. The creation of two organisations reflected the civilian/military tension we have already noted in German propaganda activities. It was resolved, in December 1917, with the creation of the *Universum-Film-Aktiengesellschaft* (*Ufa*) on the orders of General Ludendorff. Capital for the new company came from a variety of sources, including the acquisition, in exchange for shares, of the holdings in Germany, of Nordisk, a Danish film company which owned a major studio complex at Babelsberg on the outskirts of Berlin. The government contributed a third of the 25 million Marks, with the remainder coming from private firms and banks. The chairman, Dr Emil von Stauss, was president of the

Deutsche Bank. Within a few months the *Projektions-Union* chain of cinemas had been merged into the organisation, and vertical and horizontal integration of the industry was being started.

The creation of *Ufa* was a conscious attempt to create a financial and artistic structure capable of competing on a commercial level with the film industry of the United States, even though in those terms it was comparatively small. Its propaganda objectives were unable to be realised as the war drew to a close, although in the eyes of the government this aspect of its work was intended to be paramount. For the first time in a non-revolutionary society, a government had not only recognised the importance of cinema, but also had the political will to intervene in its financial organisation on grounds of state necessity. In the Weimar period, although devoid of government finance, as we shall see, *Ufa* became the key element in an attempt to construct a commercially viable, nationally orientated cinema.

The government in Britain were not unaware of the fact that by 1918 eighteen times as much footage came from abroad as was produced in Britain itself. The division of responsibilities for propaganda between the government-sponsored bodies such as Wellington House and subsequently the Ministry of Information, localised War Aims Committees and a number of *ad hoc* groups meant that there was never a clear policy on how the trade might contribute to the war effort. There were successes, including the distribution abroad of *Britain Prepared* under the auspices of Wellington House in 1915.

The one attempt to utilise popular cinema for propaganda purposes was initiated in May 1917 by Beaverbrook as head of the War Office Cinematograph Committee when D. W. Griffith was invited to make a film. The choice of the American reflected his international reputation after completing *Birth of a Nation* and *Intolerance*, and it is likely that Beaverbrook visualised an epic on the scale of those films, something clearly impossible for a British film-maker. *Hearts of the World*, which was released in 1918, was in fact a melodramatic love story, prompting the comment that: 'Griffith, who had made so many excellent wars before the camera in the hills of California, made a war picture in France with the war left out.' It was an uneasy mixture of anti-German propaganda and anti-war sentiment, and Griffith had three versions prepared, for the United States, Britain and France, as well as one in case of an armistice. 'In the peacetime version, the Germans' behaviour improved', offering an interesting illustration of the belief in the manipulative quality of film.

The employment of Griffith was an early indication of the movement towards 'mass persuasion' which resulted from the involvement of the populist politicians and journalists in the organisation of British propaganda. It was costly, and appeared too late in the war to have any discernible effect upon opinion either in Britain or abroad. It was a recognition of superior American production techniques and the lead which the United States had taken in the development of narrative film.

Yet Griffith's own stock had declined in the United States' film industry by the time he made *Hearts of the World*, as critical incomprehension of *Intolerance* followed controversy over his presentation of racial issues in *Birth of a Nation*. Both films signal the high-water mark of experiments in film-making pioneered by Griffith with the space and resources available in the developing area of Southern California. The box-office failure of *Intolerance*, and the hostility he aroused in moral reformers by his portrayal of their hypocrisy in the film signalled the decline of his predominant position in Hollywood.

The future lay with personalities who began to dominate the star system by the middle of the decade. The three most celebrated figures were Mary Pickford, Douglas Fairbanks and Charlie Chaplin, who represented a decided shift in style and outlook in Hollywood films. They produced an image of youth, adventure and scepticism which was at odds with the picture of family life presented by Griffith. The feature drama, or developed comedy, became the vehicle for stars who related more clearly to the new audience for films, in the middle-class areas of America and elsewhere.

The war in Europe did not affect this development but did impinge upon some aspects of the industry. The majority of films for export were destined for Britain, which meant that any with a war theme had a pro-Allied outlook. However, given the range of feelings in the domestic audience before 1917, the construction of stories attempted to appease all points of view.

Some films tapped an isolationist feeling; others that of pacificism, particularly *Civilisation*, made by Thomas Ince, and shown in 1916. It apparently had an enormous effect upon its audiences, possibly because it suggested that only divine intervention could solve the problems afflicting society, a millenial message which, given the state of the war at that time, was possibly the only rational solution. Other films explored the problem of the preparedness of the United States for war, indeed any war. Hearst's fixation with the danger from Mexico and Japan figured in the serial *Patria*, which he helped to finance. It was not a great success.

The revolutionary war in Mexico had greater relevance to an American audience which had been well provided with factual reporting from its outbreak in 1911. Pancho Villa, the rebel leader, recognised the value of publicity by signing an agreement with a major US film company for exclusive coverage of his exploits. There was no such cooperation in Europe.

As we have noted, in the case of film, the demands of security outweighed those of propaganda in military minds before 1915. The film *Britain Prepared* was the first attempt by Wellington House to demonstrate the character of the war to foreign audiences, and was particularly well received in the United States. Although some American cameramen infiltrated the front lines, the bulk of factual material in American cinemas, as in Europe, was that prepared specifically for the propaganda needs of the European countries.

The blurred and confusing picture of war in Europe presented in the picture houses of the United States before 1917 came slightly into focus with America's entry into the war. This had little to do with the industry based in Hollywood, but resulted from the activities of the Army Signal Corps, stiffened by Hollywood cameramen, which produced footage used, after March 1918, by the CPI for its propaganda work in the United States. Given that 600 cameramen were involved, the results were disappointing, owing to hostility from the military authorities, poor equipment, lack of experience, and the rigorous censorship of the CPI.

Neither Woodrow Wilson as an intellectual, nor George Creel as a journalist, were enthusiastic about the cinema as a propaganda medium, and the delay of nearly a year before the Films Division of the CPI was formed to distribute factual material demonstrates this. So too does the unwillingness to utilise the expertise of the film business which was not declared a vital industry until August 1918. Before this date Hollywood and its stars had demonstrated their patriotism by the release of innumerable anti-German films, and publicity work for Liberty Bonds.

'America's Sweetheart', Mary Pickford, and her dashing beau, Doug Fairbanks, brought their screen personalities out of the cinema. They personified the nation at war, more so possibly than the political leadership. Clearly, they also publicised themselves in a most acceptable fashion. The industry, barely twenty years old, and increasingly in the hands of European expatriates, had an opportunity to show how truly American it was, and how indigenous they were. Stories castigated the slackers, pacifists and enemy sympathisers at home, while more particularly showing the brutality of the enemy abroad.

They clearly contributed to the war hysteria, and did little for the economic prosperity of the industry which was affected by taxation and disruption of the population. Hollywood was not mobilised for war, but made use of the war to present itself to America as the epitome of all the national virtues.

5. Consolidation

THE inter-war period is familiar to us through the images which have been preserved: the Hollywood movie, the propaganda output of National Socialist Germany, newsreels and documentaries illustrating aspects of British life. Personalities, fashions and values may be examined through the vicarious medium of film, and yet our knowledge of the period is incomplete without an awareness of the role which that medium had, among others, in creating frameworks of social reality within which individuals placed themselves, or were, in turn, placed. The function of the mass media in society became an issue of public debate as the political and cultural effects of film and broadcasting were assessed and related to that of the role of the press.

We have already discussed the origins of the debate in the late nineteenth century as Europe and America experienced the effects of industrialisation; the subsequent development was precipitated by the effect of the First World War upon western societies. The war had accelerated the interventionist activity of many governments in social and economic affairs as well as bringing to fruition the principle of popular sovereignty as a practical form of government. In wartime, concepts of press freedom had been undermined in favour of national interest. Presentation of news to the home front, in particular, became part of the war effort in every country, and men with journalistic experience were employed as propagandists.

Walter Lippmann was one such journalist, whose book, *Public Opinion*, published in 1922, represents an early contribution to the debate on the role of the press. Lippmann argued that, far from informing the citizen in objective terms about his society, the press created a 'pseudo-environment', a constructed reality, which produced patterns of understanding, but not the truth. How, he asked, could a citizen make an objective assessment, or rational choice, on the basis of the information he was normally given in a newspaper? The conclusion he drew was that a stable democracy based upon the principles of popular sovereignty was impossible. The answer lay in the training of a group of specialists untainted by the false environment, who would be able to advise governments without reference to the mass. This concept of an informed, bureaucratic technocracy, apparently ideologically uncommitted except to the needs of the state, was to capture the imagination of many people outside the United States in the inter-war period.

The further extension of Lippmann's ideas was for a medium of mass communications to act as a form of social control; as a way of creating order out of chaos in the minds of citizens. In 1925 his views on the role of the mass media were clearer as his pessimism increased.

> The public must be put in its place so that it may exercise its powers, but no less and perhaps even more, so that each of us may live free of the trampling and roar of the bewildered herd.

A similar conclusion was reached by another American, this time a social scientist, Harold Lasswell, who in his study of propaganda techniques in the First World War wrote of 'the collapse of the traditional species of democratic romanticism . . . [because] . . . familiarity with the ruling public had bred contempt.' A government would in the future, he suggested, have to

> inform, cajole, bamboozle and seduce in the name of the public good. Preserve the majority convention but dictate to the majority.

The war had demonstrated to both men the opportunities and dangers which lay in the use of mass communication. A democratic government had channels through which it could not only reach the majority of the population, but also the means to determine the content which went into those channels. However, in peacetime, how could a democratic government determine the circumstances in which it would use its powers, even though, in Lippmann's view, the very survival of the state might depend upon the continuous monitoring of channels and information?

Adolf Hitler, languishing in prison in 1924, and cogitating on the same problems, recognised the opportunities, but as a hostile opponent of democracy saw no dangers. The future dictator of

Germany laid out in *Mein Kampf* his views on the use of propaganda both to win and preserve power in the state. The challenge to democracy inherent in the organisation of mass communications posed no threat, but was the means towards an end which was abhorrent to Lippmann.

They all drew a similar lesson from the experience of wartime; that control of information was the key to political control in the future. Public opinion could not now be assumed to be the opinion of the elite, but the amalgam of the ideas and values of the mass of the population which had, increasingly, to be reflected in the outlook and actions of governments. Newspapers, films and, subsequently, broadcasting offered channels through which general values might be communicated to large numbers of the population. The integrative character of the mass media appeared to have been demonstrated in wartime to the satisfaction of many observers, but future developments were contemplated by some critics with some dismay.

Many moderate conservatives felt that the press, and eventually radio and film, were part of the wider industrial process which had de-humanised people and was producing a collective culture of mediocrity. It was an amplification of the criticisms which greeted the emergence of the 'yellow press' in Britain and Germany at the turn of the century. Their ideal was an hierarchic, pre-industrial, elitist society and the emergence of mass democracy was merely another symptom of a general malaise which in cultural terms was represented by the products of the film industry and the popular press. In the inter-war period such conservative thinking was reflected in the statements of the radical right which in its turn sought to gain power by using the integrative character of the media.

There was, at the same time, a group of left-wing critics who were equally pessimistic about the effects of mass communications. They believed that the industrial environment should throw up a revolutionary working class, but instead, by means of control of the press and other media, it was becoming quiescent, since the class divisions had been obliterated within a uniform, consumer-orientated society. They argued that 'democratisation' of culture was one form of control of the masses.

The common element in all the discussions was a belief in the manipulative capacity of the press and film and the willingness of the mass of the people to be manipulated. Some of the criticism was inspired by fear, some by despair, but it was an intellectual reflection of the real social and economic crisis which characterised the western industrial world in the inter-war period. It had become clear that the modern means of mass communication were inextricably linked to the economic and political structures of society, and were of vital importance in determining the way in which the world around them was interpreted.

In Britain, Germany and the United States the press had become an established social institution by 1918, and the developments of the inter-war period tended to follow the pre-war pattern of consolidation. The newer forms of mass communication, wireless and the cinema, would be seen in the context of the press as well as other forms of entertainment. Their status would have to be defined, and their development would take place within a period of crisis about which they would be organisers of opinion. Broadcasting came under the greatest scrutiny because from its inception state institutions had been involved in the technical aspects of its development. In technological terms it was the product of the war, in institutional terms a product of the peace.

As we have seen, the technology of wireless telegraphy and telephony was well advanced by the end of the First World War. The two-way form of communication had been an important element in the successful prosecution of the war, and it was recognised within government circles that, as in the case of postal communication, the state should be intimately involved in any peacetime operation. The future scale and form of intervention would result from the complicated relationship between the expectations of a prospective audience, the aims of governments and the commercial perspectives of the equipment manufacturers.

Wartime experience had confirmed many government officials in Europe and the United States in the belief that wireless, as a form of communication, was an important national resource, and the ownership of technical facilities should not lie outside national boundaries. The preponderant position of Britain in wired telegraph communication before the First World War had alerted governments to the possibilities of wireless as a way of by-passing British control, but the monopolistic tendencies of the Marconi Company led many to fear a similar development in wireless telegraphy and telephony, particularly in the United States.

The US Department of Commerce had taken responsibility for

the licensing of wireless transmission facilities under the Radio Act of 1912, but many of them were owned by the American Marconi Company, which was a subsidiary of the main British company. During the war they had been taken over by the government, and in 1919 the Naval Department argued that they should not be returned. While anxious not to intervene directly in the commercial organisation of the industry the government approached the problem of control by suggesting the creation of a new company, the Radio Corporation of America (RCA), which was established in October 1919. Initially, American Marconi was asked to transfer stock and assets to the new company, and recognised that there was really no alternative. The government had set the direction for the future in the creation of a private monopoly of which the stockholders were the major wireless equipment manufacturers and cable-owners in the US: General Electric, American Telephone and Telegraph Company, United Fruit and Westinghouse. They held, between them, the majority of US patents for the development of radio. The main aim of the US government had been achieved, and the future pattern of broadcasting in the United States would be dictated almost exclusively by the needs of commercial entrepreneurs.

In 1919 general expansion of wireless as a medium of communication to the mass of the people was hardly anticipated, and certainly not in the immediate future. The main centres of interest in industrialised countries were in the armed services, particularly the naval personnel, and the government agencies concerned with internal communication, although as we have noted, responsibility in the US lay in the Department of Commerce. In Britain the General Post Office (GPO) had responsibility for licensing all telegraphic and telephonic activity, a position paralleled in the Weimar Republic by the Reich Ministry of Posts.

It was in Germany that the question of immediate government intervention in the organisation of wireless activities became most acute. The political instability of the post-war period required the authorities to use all means available to secure internal communications. The Ministry of the Interior became particularly interested in the potential use of radio as a means of communicating efficiently and accurately with different parts of the state. While there was no intention, or possibility, of general dissemination of information, the control of communication would have ramifications for newspapers and their supply of news.

While the potential possibilities of radio as a medium of mass communication were implicit in its technology, the needs of government were still adequately served by the press. Wireless and wired telegraphy and telephony were seen, in the main, as means of inter-personal communication. The impetus for the development of broadcasting came not from those who occupied the seats of political power, but from two specific groups who had different but inter-related reasons for their abiding interest in the medium – wireless enthusiasts, and more particularly, wireless manufacturers.

The war had led to an expansion of interest in the technical aspects of radio among members of the armed services, and this continued into civilian life. They shared a camaraderie in experimenting, building equipment, and communicating with each other, forming a 'lobby' of enthusiastic amateurs. This development was particularly marked in Britain, leading to the creation of a number of Wireless Societies which were influential in supporting the public experiments of the manufacturers.

In the industrialised countries the major wireless component firms had expanded during the war to meet the needs of the armed forces. As with many other industries, the post-war period appeared to offer little more than a decline unless new markets could be secured, or the firms themselves were able to diversify. Westinghouse, the major manufacturer of receivers in the United States, recognised the potential audience among committed radio enthusiasts as well as the general public who had no interest in transmitting, but might buy receivers if there was something to hear. With a transmitting licence, and the call sign KDKA, the company relayed the results of the presidential election of November 1920 from its factory in Pittsburgh. The experiment was considered successful enough for Westinghouse to set up three other stations in quick succession at other company plants. The concept of general broadcasting had been established, and the ramifications were not lost on other RCA stockholders, who immediately set up stations, often joining up with less economically powerful interests who had taken out licences, and were engaged in the activity of broadcasting.

The KDKA experiment arose out of the commercial needs of a major company, but it is interesting that the early broadcast had political content. It also raised a number of important issues which were not immediately recognised. One problem was the question of future financing. While the initial experiments had provided a free service to the listener, any developments in technology or the content of broadcasting would require capital and recurrent finance. Manufacturers were unlikely to be willing, or indeed able, to shoulder such a burden for very long.

On another level, the separation of the transmitter from the receiver had implications for the future development of the medium. The two-way process of communication was unavailable to the general public who merely bought a receiving device in order to hear specific messages emanating from a number of sources. Access to and control of those sources had political and social implications in all societies, and was clearly related to the overall financial structure in the future. It would appear that at the time when Lippmann voiced his fears for the future of the state, an instrument of control was being created, not by the US government, but through the commercial decisions of wireless manufacturers.

All the early experiments had an important scientific dimension. Equipment was continually being tested and developed as part of a wider research programme. The impetus towards broadcasting in Britain came from this source rather than purely commercial motives.

By the autumn of 1920 tests conducted by the Marconi Company from a 6Kw transmitter at Writtle, 40 miles from London, had received favourable reports from enthusiasts across the country. However, any increase in wireless activity was frowned on by the services, and the GPO as the licensing authority recognised the need for further regulation. It was pressure from the wireless lobby which secured for the Marconi Company the right to broadcast, weekly, a half-hour 'programme' for amateur radio enthusiasts from February 1922. There is no doubt that other manufacturers took notice of what was happening in the United States, but government attitudes were less likely to countenance the widespread growth of broadcasting to the general public.

The German government was more positive in its approach, but there was no conception of 'broadcasting' in its original thinking. The body which had been set up to define the role of the new technology in the state recommended a network of news and economic intelligence between centres of population. In this view, radio merely offered an alternative to wired telephony and telegraphy. Access could easily be controlled, and the needs of the state predominated over any other interests. It was, however, the manufacturers who challenged this conception. The two main companies, *Telefunken* and *Lorenz*, sought permission, in May 1922, from the Ministry of Posts to erect transmitters in German towns to provide a general service which would encourage the sale of receivers. At the same time another group of entrepreneurs applied to the Reich Finance Ministry for permission to form a company, *Deutsche Stunde*, in order to transmit concerts and talks to subscribers.

In rejecting both schemes, German government departments did not throw out the idea of broadcasting. A plan was formulated in government circles which would create a new social use for radio. It envisaged a national transmitter, broadcasting from Berlin to receiver sets placed in large halls. It is not difficult to understand the thinking which lay behind such a plan in the early 1920s. The particularist character of German political and social life was still predominant, and control from Berlin of the means of transmission had clear political advantages. Why a 'salon-radio' was contemplated is less clear. The example of cinema, with films projected to a large audience, may have led to such ideas. The plan never materialised since the technical quality of transmission was too poor, and the success of wireless manufacturing companies lay in the development of privatised receiving sets.

There was no *one* way in which broadcasting would develop, but the experience of the US provided a model which other states were able to accept or reject. In Britain and Germany the response was mainly hostile, a feeling largely inspired by seeing the consequences of the 'radio boom' which followed the success of the Westinghouse experiment. As the number of radio stations mushroomed, so too did the problems of wavelength clashes, since there was no regulatory body in existence to allocate frequencies. Although two conferences were convened in Washington to consider the problem the Federal government was loathe to act against the principle of economic freedom. The chaos was further complicated by the large number of enthusiasts who had assembled their own transmitters and receivers, cutting across the monopoly of RCA stockholders whose position had already raised some interest at the Federal Trade Commission. This interest was fuelled by the amateur lobby, who resented the position of the government-backed RCA. Of even greater importance to the Corporation's position was the conduct of a major stockholder, American Telephone and Telegraph (AT&T).

By the 1920s AT&T held a monopoly on telephone lines in the

United States and had formulated the idea of linking a number of
selected radio stations into a network allowing any member of the
public, or organisation, making the requisite payment, to make use
of the system. 'Toll broadcasting', which brought together wireless
and wired distribution of messages, raised important questions of
finance, access to the medium, the content, and the attitude towards
the audience.

The commercial potential of radio had been recognised from 1920
when many stores took part in the setting up of stations as a way of
advertising their own services. The difference with the AT&T
scheme was that the owners of the stations let out time, and left it
to future sponsors to organise content. A network of independent
stations would increase the size of the potential market for an
advertiser, but other members of RCA were prevented from developing a similar system because AT&T claimed exclusive rights to
cables under its telephone monopoly. The same company argued
that 'toll broadcasting' was radio telephony, and thus distinct from
other forms of broadcasting. In 1923 it was the basis of the claim,
fiercely contested by other stockholders, that receivers produced by
Western Electric, a subsidiary of AT&T, were telephone equipment.
This development cut across the agreement of RCA stockholders to
work in specific technical areas, and Westinghouse made wireless
receivers.

Therefore, both inside and outside the industry there were calls
for the government to regulate the growth of broadcasting. The
cacophony of sound emanating from over 600 stations on scarce
wavelengths affronted many Americans as well as Europeans who
feared similar 'chaos in the ether' if developments were unregulated
in their own states. The question was how to balance commercial
interests with the needs of the state, as defined by the government.

Pressure in Britain for an extension of broadcasting came on the
GPO as the licensing authority for the allocation of wavelengths.
Its response was to call together the main wireless manufacturers
who had been seeking the right to transmit. Discussions continued
throughout 1922 until the British Broadcasting Company (BBC)
officially came into existence in January 1923. Under this arrangement the six main companies were to coordinate their resources in
making BBC sets, and provide the bulk of the capital on which they
were restricted to a 7.5 per cent return. The BBC secured revenue
from duty charged on the sale of sets, as well as a percentage of the

receiving licence, which was collected by the GPO. By 1924, it relied on licence fees alone. The new company was responsible both for the provision of programmes on the new medium and the organisation of transmitting facilities and stations in the United Kingdom.

The BBC was a compromise solution to the immediate problem of reconciling the demands of commerce and government in 1922. A monopoly had been created which would require support from government, the industry and the general public to work. There would be no proliferation of competing stations, but also, no choice. The American experience had been rejected at the administrative and philosophical level, but a more positive statement about the aims of the BBC had yet to be made.

It was fortunate that as first managing director the BBC had a Scotsman, John Reith, who had clear ideas about the future of broadcasting, and a capability in arguing the case in public meetings and private discussions. He steered the company between the Scylla of manufacturing interests and the Charybdis of government intervention, continually arguing the case for 'public service'. It was, and is, a nebulous concept, not far removed from Lippmann's idea of a body of informed individuals who can recognise and articulate the general needs of society. Reith's aim was to place the BBC above partisan politics, emphasising the important character-istics of national institutions and culture. He built a small organis-ation which conformed to his views, and between 1922 and 1926 proselytised ceaselessly, aware of many hostile parties, both in commerce and politics, who disliked his outlook and style.

Reith's main aim was to secure financial viability and indepen-dence. The licence fee was not an ideal way of obtaining revenue since it was always open to parliamentary scrutiny, but it was preferable, in Reith's view, to dependence on the whims of the advertiser or the consumer public. Reith considered that the mon-opoly position of the BBC was the key to effective broadcasting. One organisation could identify and serve the national interest as well as plan the expansion of the service in an efficient and cost-effective way. He was successful in appealing, not only to the general public, but to a wide body of informed opinion. The Crawford Committee, which investigated the future of British broadcasting in 1926, accepted his arguments. It recommended a single publicly financed organisation, constituted by Royal Charter, and licensed to broadcast by the GPO, to be responsible for the provision of broadcasting in the United Kingdom.

The British Broadcasting Company had established its independence from government in the crisis surrounding the General Strike of May 1926. Attempts by Winston Churchill to take over the BBC and use it as a source of government information were successfully resisted by Reith. It was the biggest test, to date, of the public service argument, and the provision of news and comment during a period in which rumours abounded and newspapers were scarce impressed politicians and public alike. The BBC had identified itself with the wider national interest, but had been important in constructing for the listening public what form that interest took. The BBC had taken on a responsibility to the state, and its reliability as a state institution was always subject to review since the licence to transmit was not granted in perpetuity, and the level of receiving licence revenue was decided by Parliament. The foundation of the British Broadcasting Corporation in January 1927, the month that Reith received his knighthood, was an experiment in public ownership unparalleled in Britain, or indeed, the rest of the world.

As we have noted, the idea of centralised broadcasting had clearly been envisaged in some German government circles in the early 1920s. Irrespective of the technical problems, there had been opposition from the regions, particularly Bavaria. The government was faced with the need to overcome separatist tendencies while at the same time recognising the legitimate rights of the regions, a particularly acute problem in 1922 and 1923. After a year or so of debate cultural devolution was eventually thought preferable to political separation and by 1924 the Republic had been divided into nine regions, each with its own transmitter. Private companies were formed to provide programmes in the regions, and listeners paid a monthly subscription for the right to use receiving equipment. The dispersal of authority was not total, however, for in 1925 the Ministry of Posts set up a *Reichs Rundfunk Gesellschaft* (RRG) (Reich Radio Company) in which all the regional companies held stock. Its role was to act as an intermediary between the Ministry and the regions as well as the co-ordinating agency for the companies. With a civil servant, Hans Bredow, as its guiding force, the RRG became the national focus for broadcasting, monitoring the performance of the companies and laying down some guidelines in political and cultural matters.

By the middle of the decade the main lines of the future development of broadcasting had been laid down in the three countries which had most exploited the new medium. The solutions to common problems reflected the balance of interests in each country as well as the specific outlook of individual groups. Whereas broadcasting in the United States had developed as a reflection of the needs of commercial groups, the wider political and social needs were given greater prominence in those societies which had a longer tradition of government intervention. Even in Britain and Germany the form of intervention reflected the unwillingness of politicians to become involved in the organisation of a medium whose potential was still unknown. The direction of policy was left to those concerned with the day-to-day problems of constructing a broadcasting service. It is one explanation for the predominant position of Reith and Bredow, although there is no doubt that the circumstances found individuals who were well equipped, both intellectually and politically, to make use of the opportunities available to them.

The complex relationships within RCA had militated against a similar development in the United States until David Sarnoff began to exercise an influence in general policy-making in the period after 1924. An old employee of the Marconi Company, he had been involved in all facets of the radio industry since the first decade of the century. The problems of adjusting to the challenge posed by AT&T gave Sarnoff the opportunity to act for RCA in putting its house in order.

In 1926, while internal negotiations were proceeding, the right of Herbert Hoover, the Secretary of Commerce, to produce restrictions in the allocation of licences, under the Radio Act of 1912, was rejected by an Illinois District Court. It was a major setback in Hoover's attempt, through existing legislation, to cope with the 'chaos' of competing stations on the same wavelengths. Hoover went to Congress, arguing that the present situation required some regulation, and in January 1927 a new Radio Act was passed with the licensing authority vested for one year in a five-man, bi-partisan Federal Radio Commission (FRC). Although the Commission was theoretically neutral, it was heavily lobbied in its early days and the first adjudications of the FRC seemed to bear out the criticism that it was in the pockets of commercial radio activists. Despite this, the effect of the FRC on the advent of toll broadcasting was negligible. The greatest influence on the future form and financial organisation of broadcasting in the USA arose from the need to pre-empt both internal commercial competition among the radio manufacturers, and government interest in the industry.

The Corporation had not only to face the internal pressure from AT&T but also the likelihood of an examination of its possible commercial monopoly by the Federal Trade Commission. Discussions, orchestrated by Sarnoff, lasted into 1926, and resulted in a compromise which appeared to satisfy all parties. RCA, General Electric and Westinghouse were to take over the AT&T broadcasting facilities, but to use its land lines to create a network of stations, to be called the National Broadcasting Company (NBC). Incorporated in September 1926, the NBC network was made up of little more than a seventh of the 732 stations then licensed, and offered no immediate solution to the problems which faced Congress in discussion of the Radio Act. It was a pointer to the future organisation of broadcasting in the United States. NBC was, claimed the founders, an institution of public service for the 'national distribution of national programmes'. The public service aspect had yet to be defined, and it had no national constituency, and yet the sentiments expressed a willingness to use broadcasting for something wider than the interests of RCA and its associated companies.

The financial basis of the network organisation was the selling of time to advertisers who made or sponsored programmes. The larger the potential audience, the greater the advertising rate. The growth of the network depended upon attracting stations which were not controlled by RCA stockholders, and offering to these affiliates programmes which would capture the largest audience. While stations continued to have a local outlook, to remain profitable they increasingly found it necessary to belong to part of either the NBC, or after 1928, the Columbia Broadcasting System (CBS) networks. Out of diversity had come conformity, not by government regulation, but out of economic necessity, of both the manufacturing companies and the local stations. Network programming could be developed on a national basis, and the United States conceived as one market place for advertisers, and in the future, for politicians.

It was easier for Sir John Reith to present the BBC in a national role with administration and programme-making increasingly centred in London and, after 1932, housed in custom-built premises which translated the image of the institution, as a ship, into the shape of the building. The arguments for centralised control complemented the idea of public service. Standards could be upheld in times of financial crisis, and the BBC would continue to be the standard bearer of values, both national and moral.

The apparent stability of society which the BBC sought to present to the British public was clearly absent in Germany towards the end of the decade. Broadcasting companies were ill equipped to deal with the political and economic storms which would buffet them after 1929. It was quickly realised that financing the operation by subscriptions was unworkable. Too many people failed to pay, and the quality of programmes quickly deteriorated. When the financial crisis in 1929, and subsequent years, put an even greater strain on their resources, the government-backed coordinating agency, the RRG, stepped in to advise on amalgamations, pooling of programmes, and financial restructuring. By 1931, six of the regional companies had merged into two separate entities using their transmitters for relaying the same programmes. The RRG also provided the regions with guidelines for news and comment in the politically polarised environment of the early 1930s. The government, under Brüning, recognised the importance of radio as a channel for the communication of its policies, and the RRG offered a convenient centre for the reorganisation of broadcasting. Under severe financial pressure there was little the companies could do to withstand political pressures, and the Ministry of the Interior began to prepare plans for the total centralised control of broadcasting in Germany, with longwave transmitters now available for national coverage from Berlin.

During the political crisis of 1932 programmes became more 'nationally' orientated, and after July the government was allotted a daily time period in order to address the population. Irrespective of the political future, German broadcasting was being centralised by the government and the whole concept of regionalism had been abandoned.

Within a matter of ten years, in three of the world's major industrial societies, radio had developed from being a form of two-way communication into one of the most important channels of cultural, economic and political values in society. The existence of broadcasting had posed problems for governments, faced with new technical and administrative practices. There was no guide, and paths followed in any state reflected the general principles of political and economic life. It was, however, inherent in the nature of the medium, with high capital outlay and large running costs, that similar institutional frameworks would be constructed. One common aspect was that the organisations took little account of the audience, except as a public to be entertained, informed, or more particularly in the case of the United States, sold to.

However, in the competitive atmosphere of US broadcasting the relationship with the audience began to change. What newspaper owners had discovered in the previous century became obvious to the organisers of a medium in more immediate contact with consumers. Audiences had to be recognised and cultivated. Broadcasting and the press had complementary features: in some cases they were channels of advertising, but in all cases they were purveyors of information. It is easy to understand the suspicion with which newspaper proprietors viewed the development of broadcasting, and their unwillingness to offer, and often attempt to restrict, news services to broadcasting organisations. The newspaper industries had enough problems without the added complication of an alternative and immediate news service and advertising channel.

The general characteristic of the press in the inter-war period was a movement towards a greater concentration of ownership and control – newspapers were merged, chains consolidated and individual proprietors became national figures, motivated, it appeared, as much by political ambition as by economic gain. A commercialised press was always susceptible to changes in the economic climate, and the disruption caused by the First World War had created opportunities for entrepreneurs to acquire newspaper titles, or influence in publishing. Of our three cases, Germany, with its decentralised press structure and chronic economic condition in the post-war period offered the greatest opportunity for this development. It was not alone. In Britain, the consolidation of ownership of regional newspapers in chains was paralleled by the expansion and the greater penetration of a national press emanating from London. The United States witnessed a more widespread amalgamation of titles, the further development of chains, and the emergence of a news magazine. The political ambitions of some press owners in Britain were well known, but rarely successful; in Germany, however, political influence in the press was less direct but eventually of more lasting importance.

The decentralised character of the German press meant that there was a large number of papers with small circulations; in 1919–20 there were 3689 newspapers in the Weimar Republic, of which 2470 had printings of 5000 or less. No paper had a circulation approaching a million. With the post-war inflation, the alternatives for many were closure, or support from outside agencies. A major source of finance for provincial newspapers came from a financial trust organised by Alfred Hugenberg. As explained above, the origin of the trust lay in an attempt by the heavy industrialists of the Rhineland to influence public opinion through the press in the period immediately before 1914. During the war the aims of the organisation had been linked to those of the Pan-German League, and complicated financial links had masked the central control which lay with conservative businessmen in the Rhineland. In seeking to organise opinion at home and abroad in its own favour through judicious investment the trust had acquired extensive interests in publishing and news agency business by 1918. One important endeavour during and after the war was the subvention of small nationalist newspapers, with the trust rarely taking direct control, but using its economic influence to support editorial policy.

This economic power was exercised through two investment loan organisations formed in 1922, *Alterum Kredit AG* and *Mutuum Darlehens AG*, which both provided capital for small provincial newspapers. At the same time Hugenberg used his funds to set up the *Wirtschaftstelle für die Provinzpresse*, providing syndicated stories for subscribers, as well as manufacturing printing plates of pages to be inserted in local papers. This firm was connected to the *Telegraphen-Union (TU)*, a news agency which offered a competitive service to that of the government sponsored *Wolff Telegraphen Buero*. The trust had invested heavily in *TU* during the war, and the agency produced stories slanted to the right-wing nationalist position. Any newspaper which accepted help from one of the financial organisations linked to the trust was obliged to subscribe to the *TU* news service. This complex system of support enabled small papers to survive, and continue in private ownership, since problems of newsgathering, auditing, and selling advertising space were taken over by Hugenberg's organisations.

It was a common belief among politicians of all parties that newspapers were a key factor in the political education of the population. A large number of papers were subsidised directly by political parties of the right and left, and the burgeoning National Socialist movement found it necessary to have its own press in the late 1920s. In the politically fragmented republic such newspapers were important channels of information to the party faithful, rather than a means to capture new voters. For instance, there was no correlation between the circulation of the National Socialist press and the size of their vote: people might still read the liberal press because it was more interesting and informed, but in elections vote for the radical right. On the other hand, the effectiveness of the liberal press in organising opinion behind the Republic was restricted by the belief that such an overt manipulation of news was detrimental to the ideals of democracy. In the late 1920s there was little room for such idealism, which, in practice, depended on a population having access to accurate news reporting and a free range of opinions.

Since the bulk of newspapers had a local circulation they depended on the services of news agencies and other concerns for their national and international news. The control which Hugenberg and his associates were able to exercise over the content and outlook of many of the German local newspapers had important consequences for the future. While apparently apolitical there was a clear 'national' bias in their news reporting. They appeared to stand above parties, presenting a Germany which needed to revert to old values to withstand the present troubles. It was the outlook of the German Nationalist Party (DNVP), of which Hugenberg became the leader in 1928.

With his publishing connections, he had a basis of influence unchallenged by other nationalist leaders, and took the lead in forming a 'national opposition' against the government in 1929. Hugenberg was no orator, and had little physical presence, unlike the leader of the NSDAP, Adolf Hitler, who was organising his movement to challenge the predominant position of the Nationalist Party on the right wing of the political spectrum. However, Hugenberg was able to restrict the national coverage of NSDAP activities in much of the press and emphasise his own position.

As German politics polarised, and the economic crisis deepened Hugenberg found it necessary to bring the NSDAP into his coalition of right-wing interests, although Hitler was already lukewarm about his support for the so-called Harzburg Front which was formed in 1931. The inclusion of the NSDAP had two effects: it weakened the overall position of Hugenberg, and gave valuable national publicity to Hitler through the channels of the regional press orientated to the nationalist position. A wider public were presented with the

NSDAP Führer as a potential candidate for the leadership of the right wing in Germany. The access to a medium of mass communication became available to Hitler as the finances of many newspapers became more straitened and they depended even more for their existence on the news services which had been provided throughout the 1920s. It would be impossible to calculate the importance of this press exposure to Hitler's electoral successes since voting attitudes of many German voters were swayed more by their physical circumstances than by their newspaper reading. It was the general presentation of politics, national and international, which provided an understandable framework for the arguments of Hitler as they were developed in the late 1920s. The complexity of the situation in Germany was reduced to a number of statements, reiterated uniformly through large sections of the German press. The population were not encouraged to think about the problems, but to indulge in prejudices which were reinforced as the crisis of German democracy deepened.

Many of the newspapers in Germany had been able to continue under private ownership in the worst of the crisis, even though real forms of control were exercised through the organisations of financial subvention. In the United States consolidation of control took a different form in the 1920s, following the pattern of the pre-war years.

The extension of the telegraph, and the organisation of news agencies had encouraged the growth of ownership chains across particular areas of the United States. In the post-war period the practice of amalgamating titles in specific cities and towns was undertaken with the intention of maximising the available readership which would attract advertising. The challenge of broadcasting in this area in the late 1920s accelerated a trend which had originally been a response to the problems of running uneconomic papers.

Chain ownership rarely affected the content of individual newspapers. The Scripps–Macrae, later Scripps–Howard, 'League', which had twenty-three titles in 1914 had added a further twenty-one by the middle 1930s, but its emphasis lay in local commitment. The publishing group took up to 40 per cent of stock in a paper, leaving the rest in local hands. If the paper was successful the group continued to support it; if not, they withdrew. The editors had complete freedom in reporting local affairs, and on national issues they had a consultative function in the group.

In contrast to Germany, newspaper publishing in the United States was a source of profit to those with financial resources, and courage. The period up to 1929 witnessed an expansion of circulation and advertising revenue, but also increasing costs. Circulation continued high through the Depression, but advertising slumped dramatically; in 1933 it was 45 per cent below the figure for 1929. By then the bulk of mergers had already taken place and, although some newspapers had perished, the consolidation of the 1920s enabled the majority to weather the storm.

Yet they still had to face the advent of broadcasting, which offered a twofold challenge to the press. Scarce advertising revenue would be creamed off into a medium which had an audience capable of being reached at a national level. Simultaneously, radio could transmit news directly into people's homes. As we have noted, one answer was for newspapers to own stations and undermine the challenge. Associated Press and other news agencies did not allow their reports to be used by stations until 1939, but by then three radio-news agencies had been established to fill the void. However, news was a small part of the content of the new medium, and radio had little real effect on the organisation of newspapers before 1933.

The consolidation of chains often took on a national complexion, and agencies offered a news service to papers across the United States, but even the most prestigious east and west coast newspapers had a local and regional circulation. There were a number of weekly reviews with a national circulation which commented, in depth, on current affairs, but often two to three weeks after the event. There was no journal which attempted to give comprehensive factual coverage of national and international news every week, until Henry Luce and Briton Hadden founded *Time* in 1923. The weekly news magazine was aimed at a new readership which sought background information on as many subjects as could be culled from the press of the world. It did not get into profit until 1927 but from then on profits soared, as circulation, based upon subscriptions, grew.

Hadden was responsible for the characteristics which set *Time* apart in modern journalism; the style of writing, and the outrageous use of captions. News was a marketable commodity, packaged attractively, and delivered to the door across the United States. It caught the attention of the busy reader, and offered no deep analysis of issues, but simplified and personalised complex problems. As a weekly digest of world events *Time* was important in offering to professional groups across the continent a unified outlook about the United States and its place in the international environment. It also produced, in Henry Luce, a nationally known figure who, by his selection and presentation of items, had an increasingly important political function in the United States, while staying out of the political limelight.

The old-style magnate, William Randolph Hearst, found himself out of touch in this new environment. By 1922 he owned twenty daily and eleven Sunday newspapers, two wire services, and a number of magazines, and yet the personal publicity he gained through his press holdings had never furthered his political ambitions. He was still an outsider, who saw his empire disintegrate as he milked its resources to build grandiose properties and further the film career of his protégée Marion Davies.

Hearst became the eponymous hero of Orson Welles's film *Citizen Kane* and the epitome of a megalomaniac newspaper magnate, just as Evelyn Waugh's Lord Copper apparently encapsulated in *Scoop* the British press lord of the same period. It is difficult, at times, to disentangle fact from fiction.

The frustration of British politicians with the owners of the press was articulated by Stanley Baldwin, a Conservative leader, in 1931, when he compared their position to a harlot, exercising 'power without responsibility'. There is no doubt that some owners, such as Lord Beaverbrook and Lord Rothermere, did wish to use their respective *Daily Express* and *Daily Mail* as vehicles for their own political views, but it is unlikely that they had very much effect. Their papers were successful, not because of their political message, but because of the style and content of their news and feature pages. What also concerned Baldwin was the concentration of ownership in few hands, although the bulk of the papers were essentially conservative in tone.

The distinctive feature of the British newspaper industry was a national press, distributed from London, and penetrating most areas of the mainland. This had developed in the two decades before the First World War, and was to increase in size and importance in the inter-war period to the detriment of the provincial press. Both provincial and national press during these years were subject to a concentration of ownership.

The 1920s witnessed a period of increased circulation for the national dailies. In 1918, the total circulation stood at 3.1 million, and within a decade it was close to 5 million, doubling again in the next ten years. This was caused mainly by the aggressive marketing of the papers who sought out readership by promotional gimmicks and then tried to hang on to them. The relaunching of a left-wing paper, the *Daily Herald* in 1929, accelerated this 'circulation war' with offers ranging from free insurance to sets of encyclopaedias available to new subscribers. Circulations had then to stay high in order to keep the cover price low, and encourage advertisers; but the concomitant effect was to undermine the weaker provincial newspapers which could not afford to offer incentives to readers, or to produce a comparable range of news and features.

As in the United States there were a number of amalgamations and closures. These increased the market dominance of the surviving groups which began to consolidate their position in the provinces, and this, in turn, reinforced their national position. The two largest groups were owned by members of the Harmsworth and Berry families. By the 1930s they held between them ten morning, nineteen evening, eight Sunday and twelve weekly newspapers in Britain, although it was only in London where they were in competition. On the death of Lord Northcliffe in 1922, most of his holdings went to his brother, Lord Rothermere, who by a series of financial manoeuvres kept an interest in the papers through a holding company, the Associated Press, without, it appeared, having total control. Similarly, the Berry brothers, who were translated into the Lords Camrose, Kemsley and Iliffe, took over the Amalgamated Press in 1926 with its large periodical holdings, and developed a structure which was vertically integrated, ranging from ownership of paper mills to newspaper distributors.

The Westminster Press was the other main provincial holding company, and with the other two national groups, Beaverbrook and Cadbury, much of the daily and weekly press in Great Britain was controlled by five main companies. Concentration of ownership provided a strong economic base, and appeared to give the proprietors a disproportionate influence on affairs of state.

From 1916 to 1922, when Lloyd George was Prime Minister, the three press lords, Rothermere, Beaverbrook, and, until his death, Northcliffe, became frequent visitors to Downing Street, and as we have seen, members of his government during the war. The personal position of Lloyd George appeared to depend on the publicity which could be garnered from the relationship, but on his fall in 1922 the press lords found themselves at odds with the political establishment, and particularly the Conservative Party leadership.

During the late 1920s, policies promoted by the proprietors through their newspapers, whether Empire Free Trade in the *Express* by Beaverbrook, or opposition to the government's Indian policy in the *Mail* by Rothermere, seemed to have no effect on public opinion at large. The popular national dailies did, however, succeed in creating a climate of opposition to the Labour Party in its periods of office. Baldwin's exasperated cry showed how far the political establishment in Britain had failed to recognise the essentially integrative character of the national press, and the misunderstanding about the organisation of public opinion, encouraged by the press lords themselves.

The political power of the newspaper proprietors was much exaggerated, and a glance at the bulk of national daily newspapers in the 1920s and early 1930s would show an emphasis on the trivial and sensational. The key to survival lay in attracting readers, and particularly advertising. Overt political messages did not sell to either group, but the importance lay in the implicit statements about Britain and the world which were produced every day.

The penetration of the national dailies and the relative decline of provincial newspapers symbolised the predominant position of London in national life and the importance of metropolitan opinion. The size of the country, the transport network, and unified character of political life made such a development not only possible, but generally acceptable. It was not a state of affairs paralleled in Germany and the United States where particularism was not only much stronger, but considered a virtue in the organisation of political society. However, because of the consolidation of ownership, use of news agencies, and the importance of a large market to attract advertising newspapers had more uniformity of content and outlook.

The mechanistic view that the mass media had an immediate influence on individuals was more generally accepted by many observers, who were less concerned by the press, which appeared to offer a range of opinions and outlooks, and required a certain level of literacy for comprehension. There was greater worry about the growing influence of the cinema.

Films had been used for propaganda purposes during the war by all the main belligerents. There had been no clear understanding of their effect, but an awareness of the potential that lay in a medium

rtTt99nt

which was open to manipulation through the positioning of the camera and editing of the film. While being used for the national effort such manipulation was praiseworthy. In a post-war world where absolute values appeared to have vanished the cinema could be used as a scapegoat identified as a major factor in the decline of society. The development of the cinema in the inter-war period certainly did have an effect on international society, but hardly in the ways which some observers feared in the 1920s.

The First World War had witnessed the virtual demise of European film production, and the American industry was poised to take advantage of the situation. By 1918 it held an 80 per cent share of the world market in films, a position which it was able to maintain over the next two decades. With a large domestic market to provide a return on capital, the exporting of films became the source of continuous profit for an industry which had always been geared to the needs and expectations of the market. In order to satisfy the increased demand, studios became the equivalent of factory systems with integrated production schedules, marketing organisations, amalgamations for economies of scale, and control of that essential human constituent, the star. The product was a cultural package, aimed in the first instance at the cosmopolitan American audience, but able to enter other cultural enclaves through its universal appeal and superior production values.

The horizontal integration of the industry had begun before the First World War and was to continue in phases through the inter-war period, with production companies becoming absorbed into larger groupings, and all facets of film-making being organised on a few sites. The companies also participated increasingly in the vertical integration of the industry, by involvement in the distribution network, and the ownership of cinemas. Independent film-makers suffered accordingly, the more so as a consequence of the practice of block booking by which studios secured consistent outlets for their products. It was this control of the domestic market which gave the US film industry its springboard for world supremacy, and which also produced a specific kind of product which appeared to reflect American popular taste, and presented it to the world as something essentially American.

European film industries never had the level of capital investment required to compete effectively with Hollywood. The domestic markets were smaller, and the opportunities for exporting abroad, particularly to the United States, were severely restricted. One exception was Germany in the immediate post-war period, when with the economy severely hit by inflation, many investors saw immediate profits in popular films and formed production companies, particularly to export to the US. The stabilisation of the Mark in 1924 effectively pricked the bubble of speculation and the cheapness of German films abroad. The German domestic market was once more open to American films.

The industry in Britain found it even more difficult to recover from the war and by 1927 it held only 5 per cent of the British market. The financial viability of national film production in both countries was in doubt, and raised wider questions of political and cultural influence. The war had demonstrated the importance of film as a channel of public information, and the problem for democratic governments lay in producing the necessary response to safeguard a national industry.

The German government had been involved in the organisation of *Universum Film Aktiengesellschaft (Ufa)* during the war, but the Weimar regime subsequently relinquished its financial interest. Its role in the post-inflation period was to pass legislation requiring the production of one German film for every foreign film released in Germany, the so-called 'quota-system'. The aim was to promote the survival of the indigenous film industry, and it was a measure paralleled in Britain in 1927 when an Act was passed requiring exhibitors and renters to allot an increasing share of screen time to British films, rising from between 5 and 7 per cent in 1929 to 20 per cent in 1936–9. The British Act also defined the character of a British film in terms of the production and directorial staff involved. The result of these legislative activities was, as hoped, a general increase in national productions, but less fortunately, the emergence of the 'quota quickies', or *Kontingentfilm* in Germany, which would satisfy the demands of the law, but had no intrinsic merit. Very often they were not intended for public exhibition. In many cases they were made by American production units, or companies financed from the United States, with the express intention of obtaining the necessary quota certificates to ensure access for their main productions.

Economic penetration took another form with direct American financial intervention in Germany when Paramount and Metro-Goldwyn collaborated with a $4 million loan to prevent *Ufa* from collapsing in 1925. When, in 1927, this was found to be insufficient to satisfy older debts, a coalition of German financial interests bought out the American companies. The leading figure in this consortium was Alfred Hugenberg, extending his wide publishing interests into another medium. Not only did he acquire the main production company in Germany, but through this, and other purchases, substantial distribution facilities. Hugenberg and his group had acted for two reasons: to obtain a potential source of profit, and to secure an important outlet for the presentation of the nationalist political position. The acquisition could be seen as both a symbolic and an actual rejection of American cultural and economic imperialism.

Although *Ufa* had been saved as a major production company, there were many more smaller companies at risk, particularly after 1929. Their survival depended on the distribution outlets which were the central element in the vertical integration of the industry. Many of these were now under the control of Hugenberg and his associates.

Distribution was also the key area of integration in Britain when, after 1927, two main circuits became linked to specific studio operations. The Gaumont–British Picture Corporation linked up with Gainsborough Productions in 1928, and Associated British Cinemas developed its relationship with British International Pictures. Although both circuits owned about 400 cinemas in 1930, this comprised only a small proportion of the total number in Britain; nevertheless, they dominated the distribution system by occupying the best sites and being able to construct the most attractive programmes, setting a pattern of releases for independent exhibitors. While American films still dominated the market, the financial control of British production and distribution fell into fewer hands.

The introduction of sound films after 1927 put greater pressure, world-wide, on industries already concentrating their resources on finding new ways to control the market. Patent battles were fought over the sound systems to be used, between electrical companies heavily involved in broadcasting. Studios had to re-equip, and cinemas instal new projectors and loudspeakers. Hollywood studios had invariably looked to the east coast for their finance, but they now became totally dependent on the merchant banking houses of Wall Street for the huge amounts of capital needed. Furthermore, control of the market was even more necessary to assure the studios, and the banks, of a definite return on investment.

One effect of sound was to restrict the apparent universality of the cinema. Dubbing, subtitling, or even duplicate copies were alternatives, but every solution was a costly addition to the budget, and it seemed that Britain was at an advantage in sharing a common language with the Americans, although some people suggested it was more a cause of division. Sound did revitalise audience figures, which had begun to decline after 1926.

The stylisation of the 'silent' cinema would give way to a new, more fluid narrative treatment, as film-makers explored the problems and possibilities of integrating natural sound into the picture. The conventions of editing and montage would still be important in film language, but sound offered an opportunity for the real world to be explored in a way hitherto impossible.

The 'silent' cinema had always concerned itself with recording actuality in newsreels, which had been developed into part of the entertainment package available in cinemas. In the 1920s there was also the development of factual film production which was given the generic title of 'documentary' under the guiding hand of John Grierson in Britain. He had come under a number of influences; the quasi-anthropological films of Robert Flaherty, such as *Nanook of the North*, the revolutionary films of Soviet Russia, and the ideas of Lippmann. From these he formulated a concept of the role of film as an educational force in democracy. He would argue later that, through the 'creative treatment of actuality' in film, a government would make clearer to the citizen both the role of the individual in the state, and the way in which the state acted for the individual. Working outside the British film industry, and with no encouragement from the British government, Grierson was to propagandise his own 'realist' viewpoint, and to collect around him a band of followers, who were to bring his ideas to fruition in the Second World War.

For most film-goers in the 1920s the newsreels continued to be the main source of visual information about the world. They were weekly reviews bringing together a number of disparate stories, and designed to entertain rather than inform. While at their best in covering planned or expected events, whether sporting, ceremonial or political, the newsreels could only provide, at best, a partial background to the issues of the day. Their content was also affected by the competition between companies to be the most entertaining, or most topical newsreel, and the attitude of exhibitors, who often saw them, at best, as fillers in the programme, or at worst, as a way of clearing the cinema between shows.

Sound was to have two main effects. It was now possible to place a commentary over the film, providing continuity and an explanatory framework for the pictures. Sound effects could also be dubbed on. It also meant that newsreel companies faced increased costs as they re-equipped, or lost their place in the market if they were slow to take up the new technology. The result was the sharing of the domestic market between a number of companies, four in the United States and five in Britain, which had arrangements with the major producing and distributing organisations in the industry. The American company Fox Movietone produced the first sound newsreel in Britain in 1929, and with the Harmsworth press as one of the investors formed British Movietone News. While Gaumont British News and Pathé were associated with major British production companies, Paramount and Universal, the other major producers were linked to their parent companies in the United States. The major Hollywood studios had recognised, after 1927, that they could offer a complete package to exhibitors, thus encouraging block bookings, if they had control of the newsreel companies.

Although there was still competition to get the best stories, market shares had stabilised by 1933. There was a clearly defined product which was acceptable to producers, exhibitors and audiences. There was no scope for, or intention of, investigating the nature of society: the 'real' world was packaged and delivered in newsreels which differed very little from their competitors.

Party politics in the democracies had a lot to gain from the development of the newsreels. For the first time leaders could be heard as well as seen, and a more rounded personality presented, particularly on those occasions when the politician was able to speak directly to the cinema audience. It would not be long before stories would be made by political organisations for inclusion in a newsreel, thus saving the company both time and money.

The alternative was to own a newsreel and control the political content. Alfred Hugenberg was in this fortunate position, since *Ufa* was the main newsreel-producing company in Germany. Before 1931 the German Nationalist Party position had been exploited, to the detriment of Hitler and his associates, but it became more difficult to ignore the NSDAP as the movement challenged the government in association with the Nationalist Party. Many Germans had their first glimpse of Hitler on film in their local cinemas.

It is unlikely that the newsreels had an immediate political effect in any country, but in personalising issues and placing stories within a particular framework, invariably the same framework, irrespective of the newsreel company, they were able to provide the cinema audience with a simplified picture of the issues affecting the national and international environment. It complemented and reinforced the information they received from other areas of the mass media.

The presentation of factual material on film had been a mainstay of the cinema since its earliest days even when it was necessary to reconstruct news stories for the sake of the camera. The question of the possible manipulation of the contents of film, and its manipulative effect on the audience was sharply focused during the First World War and during the 1920s there was concern in some quarters, not only among politicians, about the presentation of social and political issues in the newsreels, particularly violence. It raised the whole question of censorship in the cinema.

The British Board of Film Censors (BBFC) had been established by the industry in 1912 as a regulatory body to obviate the danger of central or local government interference in its products. While not obligatory, companies could place their films before the Board for certification giving them some security when faced with some licensing authorities. The particular concern had been the protection of children, but as the BBFC developed its procedures it extended its competence, and created general guidelines for British producers, and set of criteria for imported films. However, the Board had never taken responsibility for newsreels, mainly because it did not have the organisation to certificate each edition at the speed required, and was essentially concerned with fictional films.

Since they were susceptible to local censorship newsreel companies exercised appropriate caution in the content and style of their product. Exhibitors, concerned that nothing controversial should put their own position at risk, put further pressure on the companies. Therefore, without overt political pressure, or direct censorship, the presentation of society, at home and abroad, was essentially bland.

The BBFC were mainly concerned with the moral content of feature films although this was a very wide brief, and allowed proscription of scenes which were felt to bring into question accepted beliefs and standards of behaviour in public life. This might range from refusing a certificate to a film from Soviet Russia, to expressing disquiet about the presentation of royalty on the screen. Official bodies and the film industry itself recognised the Board as a satisfactory solution to the problem of control of a medium which appeared to have such an important influence upon the life-styles of so many people.

The guardians of public morality were mainly concerned with the possibility that audiences would imitate the behaviour witnessed on the cinema screens. Relationships between the sexes was a particular problem, and compounded by the fact that films were often sold to an audience on the basis of their titillating content, and the reputation of the actors, male and female. The stars were presented, through carefully written magazine and newspaper articles, as specific kinds of people, with interests not unlike the audience, but through the 'magic of the movies' able to indulge themselves in luxuries normally unattainable to the general public. Woman stars, while sexually attractive, posed no threat to the establishment of marriage, which they affirmed they believed in, although love occasionally intervened.

This carefully constructed picture of Hollywood was undermined in the early 1920s when a series of scandals, mainly of a sexual character, reflected on the moral probity of those who were involved in the production of films. In order to divert criticism, particularly from those sections of society which were always suspicious of the intentions of the studios, Will Hays, a noted Republican politician, was appointed chief executive of the Motion Picture Producers and Distributors of America Inc. in 1922. In essence, he was the intermediary between the studios and the pressure groups representing public opinion. Producers were able to seek advice from his staff, and films with the Hays Office imprimatur were accepted by exhibitors with no fear of content or outlook. By the 1930s the Office had laid down a rigid production code which set the pattern for Hollywood films, and effectively acted as an internal censor for the studios.

While the reason for interference in film content, in Britain and the US, was ostensibly the possible effects on public morality, there was more overt political action in Germany in the 1920s, conducted through government agencies. After May 1920 the Ministry of the Interior became particularly concerned with internal security, and began to censor films which appeared to threaten the state, or endanger German prestige abroad. Two bodies, in Berlin and Munich, were established to examine all films to be exhibited in Germany, above them being a court of appeal. Unlike Britain or the US, there were no guidelines established for production companies, or prior consultation. Film-makers had to test the limits of discretion, which tended to vary with the political stability in the period. Until 1931 the opportunities for political intervention were rarely exercised, but after that date the category 'being liable to endanger important state interests' was introduced into the list of criteria. The ground had been prepared for the regulatory structure which was developed under the National Socialists after 1933.

Questions of censorship brought out more clearly the relationship between politics and culture in society. Lenin, in Soviet Russia, had stated clearly the importance of artists in the political development of the state. Film in Bolshevik Russia was considered to have a role as an art form which not only reflected the nature of society and the ideologies which underpinned it, but actively promoted their acceptance in that society. Censorship by the state was recognised as an essential characteristic of political and cultural life.

The emergency of the First World War had promoted similar attitudes in democratic countries. However, the apparatuses of control were quickly dismantled, and the interests of the state were seen to lie in the promotion of debate and the exchange of opinion. It was in Germany after 1919 that one can discern the crisis, in peacetime, of a democratic government faced with internal and external challenges to its existence, aware of the need to promote discussion, but fearful of the effect. Freedom of the press was safeguarded under Article 118 of the Weimar Constitution, but could be retracted under the emergency provisions of Article 48. This power was used in times of political crisis, particularly after 1930, but it was not used in a continuous way throughout the 1920s to determine the content of newspapers. Similarly, the government was rarely bothered with the content of broadcasting in the 1920s, but was concerned with the institutional framework of the medium. In the case of cinema a state-controlled framework was established to adjudicate on content.

The different approaches to the problem of control reflect the general attitudes in the state to government intervention, the responses of the authorities to new forms of communication, and the aspects of the media which were capable of control in a democratic society. The responses in Britain and the United States reflected the same conditions. The stability of the political systems allowed greater freedom of the press, a wider use of indirect control of institutions and little direct intervention in content.

Most of this chapter has considered the organisation of the mass media, and their relationship to government agencies. In the development of political society in the inter-war period it was of increasing importance, but was only one influence upon the development of the mass media. A continuing theme throughout the chapter has been the financial framework through which a medium was financed. Advertising was already a major factor in the development of the press before the First World War, and would continue to be a factor in the debate about broadcasting finance, either in Britain or the United States. Both media were seen as ideal channels for the form of consumer advertising which reflected the economic development in industrialised countries.

Modern advertising began towards the end of the nineteenth century with the growth of agencies specialising in the promotion of firms and products in specific newspapers. The result was a growing expertise in the design and lay-out of advertising in order to achieve the desired effect. The experience of wartime had focused the attention of governments on the problem of direct communication with the mass of the people, particularly in the promotion of national outlooks and values. This in turn provoked the specialised debate with which this chapter opened.

The developments in the organisation of the mass media have to be placed within the context of the growth of advertising. The development of an enlarged consumer sector had already had an important effect on the character of newspapers, particularly in Britain and the United States. Broadcasting offered further channels of information for the commercial entrepreneur to engage with the public. Even when these were refused, as in Britain and Germany, the experience of the United States was never far from the minds of administrators, necessitating the search for other forms of finance, and the presentation of 'public service' as something more worth-while than the demands of the advertiser.

There was little direct advertising of products in the cinema, but the film industries of all countries depended upon the other channels of communication to sell their products in the market place. While studios attempted to control the market as much as possible, they also required constant exposure in the press for their stars, and new films. Popular newspapers found in the cinema a subject which would appeal to the readers who often saw two or three films a week. By the 1930s in Britain and the US radio personalities were performing the same function, opening the whole question of broadcasting to a wider audience, particularly in Britain.

Simultaneously there was the growth of a more 'scientific' outlook in the organisation of advertising. 'Market Research' investigated the consumer, finding evidence of tastes and preferences for the producer and advertiser alike. The refinement of polling techniques and the systematic analysis of results became the preserve of experts working independently, or for advertising agencies. Products could be shaped for a known market and adverts placed in newspapers selling to a known audience. Market research was of particular importance to manufacturers as well as the broadcasting networks in the United States who were able to obtain a reasonably accurate picture of a national audience, its interests and its prejudices.

Complementing market research was the activity of 'public relations'. It too was in a formative stage after the war, but in the corporate world of US industry was beginning to be established as an important form of general advertising. The practitioners used all forms of communication to present to the general public an aspect of an industry or a firm. The aim was not to advertise a specific product, but to demonstrate how a particular organisation provided a service for the community as a whole. The emphasis was placed upon the creation of an image, a pseudo-reality, and the means were now available to reach the widest number of people through a variety of channels, as long as access could be guaranteed.

Mass communication organisations were the key elements in the growth of such activity. They were never merely neutral channels, but continually defining their own relationship with the public and the state. The processes of change in the press, broadcasting and film industries had to be understood within society at large, and it was largely left to individuals within the organisations to promote particular outlooks. Whether it be the role of the press as the 'Fourth Estate' acting as an element in the political process representing the people, or a broadcasting system acting in the 'public interest', the presentation of the role was in itself a form of 'public relations'.

Whereas Lippmann had been concerned with the role of the press as the organiser of opinion, there were, by the 1930s, two other channels of equal, and some thought, more importance, in the presentation of society to itself. The immediate post-war years had witnessed substantial changes in all areas of social and economic life, and the mass communication institutions had reflected these developments, not only in their products, but in their organisation.

This mainly took the form of consolidation of resources for economic reasons. Only in Germany had there been overt control of media resources in the interests of state security, and this for a short time. However, every development in the institutions had political ramifications. Access to the media lay with those who took financial and administrative decisions inside the organisations. They were essentially conservative, and concerned mainly with the success of their own enterprise. At one level this meant developing a relationship with an audience, at another, not coming into conflict with the increasing power of the state.

A combination of both factors produced channels of communication in the 1920s, which rarely reflected the true state of European and American society, but a view which was acceptable to those with immediate control over content. Their motives were primarily commercial, but while apparently apolitical they were not the guardians of the civic conscience envisaged by Lippmann. However, media use was taking the form he had suggested in 1922, and it would not be long before politicians, including those who claimed to be democratic, recognised the importance of the mass media as a key element in good government, and a possible instrument of social control. The framework within which they would develop their concern had been constructed in the immediate post-war period.

6. The Media and the State in the 1930s

THE economic crisis which enveloped the United States and much of Europe after 1929 undermined still further the fragile stability which had been created, both nationally and internationally, in the post-war period. It became a crisis of confidence in man's ability to organise himself politically and socially for the benefit of all. The principles upon which the post-war world had been built, democracy and self-determination allied to international cooperation, had already been challenged by the success of Bolshevism in Russia and the advent to power of the Fascist movement in Italy. The former proselytised for an international society based upon communist principles, the latter for a nationally orientated political and social integration. The economic crisis of the early 1930s exacerbated this ideological struggle with many states attempting to solve their problems without recourse to either alternative.

Liberal democracy was apparently ineffective in solving the problems of economic inequality and ethnic rivalry because the ideals of compromise and freedom of the individual were impossible to maintain in a world in which economic and military power were the main determinants of control. The underlying power structures had not been changed in the post-war settlement and to many people the only way forward was a wholesale reconstruction of European and world society. The changes which were contemplated had moral as well as political connotations. The crisis concerned the role of liberalism as a moral creed. To many people freedom had been equivalent to licence and natural authority had been undermined. In the 1930s there was a new search for a moral certainty upon which political and social life might be based. The mass media were to play an important part in the construction of a new moral base situated in the nation. It was not a new concept, but the novelty lay in the way the new forms of mass communication were used to create and sustain the idea for millions of people, and to produce a legitimate reason for the possession of power by political leaders. The effect of the economic crisis was to make government by consent more difficult. In the face of political polarisation to left and right the Brüning government in Germany, after 1930, relied more and more on presidential decrees since it was impossible to obtain a majority in the Reichstag. After 1931, in Britain, the main parties formed a coalition, called the National Government, to carry out the necessary measures. The executive in the United States tried to increase Federal control after 1933 in order to restructure the inefficient areas of economic life. The institutions of democratic government were well established in Britain and the United States and capable of adapting to the changes required to overcome the crisis. In Germany the Weimar Constitution had been rejected by many of the population as an alien imposition, and little valued and trusted as a political system by many of the leaders. Hitler's declared aim was to destroy the whole edifice, and to recreate a more Germanic form of government. Whether impelled by motives of preservation or destruction, all politicians required the support, either active or passive, of their populations: one way of achieving this was through the mass media.

In the main, statesmen who sought consolidation of their societies had the support of owners and managers of mass communication organisations. Where privately owned and commercially orientated they sought political and economic stability for their continued existence. Where governments were concerned with licensing and the regulation of activities, particularly in film and broadcasting, there were opportunities for more influence since there was a greater dependence on the survival of the system by the institutions of the medium.

The most problematical issue is how far films, broadcasts and the press actually influenced populations. Assumptions were made that the mass media were both a symptom and a cause of moral decline, but there was no coherent body of evidence to support either claim. What was being recognised was that populations were getting the bulk of their entertainment, and information about their national political environment, from such sources.

Irrespective of the continuing influence of other socialising factors, the immediacy and overwhelming character of the mass media suggested power. Although we may be more sanguine today, we can only guess at the possible effects of the products of the mass communications industries.

The power of the mass media lay in offering a single outlook on particular issues to large numbers of people. The more coherent the outlook and insistent the presentation the more likely it was to influence the attitude of individuals to the world about them, and their own role in it.

The societies which we are considering were complicated, industrial organisms which were put under enormous strain by economic dislocation. All sectors of the community were affected, including the institutions which were concerned with presenting information, or producing entertainment for large numbers of people. As channels of communication they were of importance to governments, but they had also to survive as economic units in their own right. The influences upon them are not easy to unravel, but no government, either democratic or totalitarian in outlook, had direct control over all aspects of the mass media in the years before the Second World War. What they had in common was a requirement to construct an ideal community which could survive in a hostile world. The very nature of individual societies and the character of mass media systems made this community a national entity, and encouraged the conception of a divided world which led to war in 1939. The main responsibility for that war must still lie with politicians, particularly Adolf Hitler.

The emergence of Hitler as German Chancellor in January 1933 was made possible, in part, by the use he had made of the mass media which lay outside his immediate control. Although the final accession to power was by 'backstairs intrigue' he was still able to claim that it was his natural right, not only as leader of the largest party in the Reichstag, but also as the only leader capable of uniting the country. This reputation had been created by the mass media.

He had been helped by the disarray in traditional nationalist circles who tried to construct a unified front, including the NSDAP, under the leadership of Hugenberg, the Nationalist Party leader. The 'Harzburg Front' of October 1931 only succeeded in providing Hitler with more publicity through the newsreels and press organisations in which Hugenberg had a controlling interest. As we have seen, the German provincial press was overwhelmingly nationalist in outlook and willingly gave space to a young leader on the radical right.

Furthermore, the mass rallies of the NSDAP, the challenges to and by the Communists, and the presidential elections of 1932 kept the leader in the news. He encouraged further interest in his activities by publicity coups such as the use of aircraft to fly from city to city in the presidential campaign. Symbolically, if ambiguously, it was called 'Hitler over Germany'.

While much of the press might have been sympathetic to Hitler, he owed much to the work of Josef Goebbels. This one-time seminarist had considerable gifts as an administrator and orator, which he had demonstrated while party leader in Berlin in the late 1920s. He was the party's leading propagandist in 1932, and not only supported Hitler's views, but appeared at times to outdo the Führer in his vehemence.

Goebbels took the 'leadership principle' which was the basis of authority in the NSDAP and constructed an image of Hitler, not only as party leader, but as the future head of a regenerated society. The focus of attention was constantly placed on the Führer, and the channels of mass communication were perfectly suited to magnify and support such a construction. Hitler's speeches were full of quotable remarks; he rarely deviated from castigating the supposed originators of the crisis, never explaining, merely asserting. Complex problems were blamed on the Versailles Settlement or the upholders of the Weimar Constitution. The individual alien presence was personified in the Jew. He was not alone in his views, but the constant reiteration, and the way in which he dominated the argument seemed to give him the leadership of many who held, or were willing to hold such opinions. Radio broadcasts caught the atmosphere of the mass rallies, and films were dominated by his presence. He appeared to personify dynamic youth, moving forward: no audience was ever able to question him, the communication was all one way.

To have achieved power in 1933 was not enough. The maintenance of power was now the primary task of the NSDAP. In the first days of the new government there were only three National Socialist ministers. It was not until 12 March 1933, that a new ministry was proclaimed by presidential decree, that of

Public Enlightenment and Propaganda (RMVP), under the leadership of Goebbels. The delay in forming a ministry may have been through Hitler's caution until his position was strengthened by the elections of 5 March. However, with the Reichstag Fire, and the declaration of the State of Emergency, the creation of a new organisation was not only possible but, it could be argued, necessary. It had certainly been part of National Socialist thinking since the previous year.

Under the new regime there was to be no free exchange of information. The Propaganda Ministry had the responsibility for the presentation of Germany to itself and to the outside world. The loyalty of the state was to be directed at Hitler and the NSDAP: the aim of the ministry was to construct a view of Germany united on the basis of National Socialism, and particularly, the leadership principle.

The new ministry cut across old state and party responsibilities: broadcasting policy came from the Post Office, film censorship from the Ministry of the Interior. The biggest opposition came from Otto Dietrich, who was Press Chief of the party, and Max Amann, who was in control of the party's publishing operations. Financial control was as important to them as political and cultural unanimity. The RMVP was never able to secure complete control of the press in the Reich because of the relationship which each of the men had with Hitler. It is one illustration of how the apparent monopoly of power in the state was diffused through a number of individuals and organisations.

The ministry was organised into a number of divisions which were concerned with the general direction of policy, but left day-to-day regulation to subsidiary organisations (Chambers) to which all accredited workers in the separate areas of culture and information services had to belong. Within the Reich Chamber of Culture, the umbrella organisation, were sections for the Press, Film, Broadcasting, Theatre, Music, the Graphic Arts, and Writing. Each Chamber had a President and administrative personnel linked to the RMVP. In some cases the Chambers were allowed a measure of control over individual enterprises. One example occurred in April 1935, when the Reich Press Chamber, whose President was Amann, issued ordinances allowing it to close down newspapers which were accused of sensationalism or sectarianism, or were in too great competition with others. The result was an opportunity for a further extension of control by the party press in all areas of Germany.

The Ministry was involved in the amalgamation of Wolff's *Telegraphisches Büro* and the *Telegraphen-Union* in December 1933, leading to the formation of the *Deutsches Nachrichten Büro* (*DNB*). This was the government agency which produced internal and external news for over half the papers in Germany in the first instance, and acted as the mouthpiece of Germany to overseas newspapers.

One form of influence which was developed by the ministry was the briefings for journalists and editors, explaining government policy, and giving guidelines for treatment. Attendance at such briefings was necessary, and they were one way in which conformity of outlook might be achieved.

There was no attempt in the early days to shut down the non-National Socialist press, apart from Socialist and Communist papers; however, the accreditation system through the Chamber, the threat of closure, and the unwillingness to alienate a readership which was often supporting National Socialism led to newspapers taking a passive line. The further measures after 1935 decimated what was left of the liberal press.

By a system of intimidation the press became an instrument of the party and the state. However, the actual organisation of press policy was often confused because of the rivalry between competing groups in and out of government. Broadcasting, however, was most easily assimilated into the new structure. Its organisation had become more centralised under Brüning and von Papen, but not until the individual Länder became assimilated into the Reich in July 1933 was it possible for reorganisation to be fully achieved. The Broadcasting Division of the RMVP took control of the *Reichs Rundfunk Gesellschaft* (RRG), and appointed managers in the nine regions. Output was centralised in Berlin, with programmes consisting mainly of music and news.

The importance of broadcasting to the new regime lay in the immediate contact with the listener. However, while it offered a one-way medium of communication Hitler still needed the responsiveness of a live audience to be an effective speaker. After March 1933 he never broadcast from a studio, but his speeches were relayed from mass rallies so that the radio audience could catch the excitement of the occasion. The listener's imagination was engaged, and the apparent spontaneity of the meeting encouraged a feeling of dynamism.

Broadcasting also allowed the National Socialist viewpoint to cross national boundaries. It was an expansionist ideology which claimed to speak for Germans inside and outside the frontiers of the Reich. It was now possible to speak to them. Wireless campaigns against the Austrian government were organised in 1934, and in support of a 'Yes' vote in the Saar plebiscite in 1935. Short-wave transmitters allowed the German government and party officials to link up with their fellow nationals in other parts of the world. By 1936 a network of transmitters was providing foreign language broadcasts which were important in putting Germany's case as the international political crisis deepened.

The regime was concerned that the German people should not only have programmes of a suitable national and political outlook, but that as many as possible should have the means to receive them. Cheap receivers were sold to encourage more people to listen in their own homes, and public buildings and factories were wired for sound – no one was to be out of range of the voice of the government.

Yet the cinema, combining sound and pictures, seemed to offer even more scope for the organisation of opinion. Both Hitler and Goebbels had an interest in film, and for the first time it was possible for a political leader literally to tower above his people on a screen.

There were, however, fundamental problems in the German film industry to be solved. Producers had been hit by increased costs while exhibitors had been undermined by falling audiences and the need to re-equip cinemas for sound. While unwilling to centralise funding Goebbels was concerned that the industry should work for the benefit of the regime. He oversaw the creation of a Film Credit Bank in June 1933 in order to finance smaller producers, and the Reich Film Chamber organised the workers in the industry. Both organisations were linked to the Film Division of the Propaganda Ministry which had responsibility for the censorship of films. A new cinema law of 1934 widened the scope of activity of this section, allowing films to be banned because of their treatment of politics or race, and giving tax concessions on those films which were particularly acceptable to the regime.

The aim had been to create a financially viable, nationally

orientated film industry – the problem was how the two aspects might be combined successfully. Films were difficult to export since some states rejected them on political grounds, or merely to protect their own industries; something which Germany itself was trying to achieve. The constraints in the domestic market were mainly financial, but with clear political overtones. The emigration of actors and producers after 1933 had raised the salaries of those who remained: pre-production censorship by a ministry official led to confusion and a lack of confidence. Production costs rose still further, and there were fewer films for exhibitors to show as American productions began to be banned. Eventually, by a complicated financial manoeuvre in 1937, the Reich Finance Ministry took responsibility for placing the necessary capital in film companies, thus placing them under government control, but keeping their separate identities. Goebbels became the arbiter of subjects and producers.

The subjects tackled by the film industry were in the main the same as in any other country. Political topics were soon found to have little box-office value, and Goebbels recognised that entertainment was the first priority. However, through the system of censorship, the values upon which National Socialist society was to be based were continually reaffirmed. Through the use of newsreels too he was able to construct a picture of the world which conformed to that produced by other sources available to the general public. It is worth noting, though, that the film by which many people outside Germany saw the manifestation of National Socialism for the first time was made outside the auspices of the Propaganda Ministry. *Triumph of the Will* was made by a woman, Leni Riefenstahl, on the direct invitation of Hitler to record the National Socialist Rally at Nuremberg in 1934. For many people today its images are those which best encapsulate the nature of National Socialism, but whereas the pictures of men and soldiers marching has a particular meaning after the events of the Second World War, in the context of their own time they demonstrated a nation on the move and the unification of party and State. The more humdrum nature of the Propaganda Ministry work was concerned with the same objective over a wide field, and slowly established a conformity in the presentation and organisation of information.

In the main Goebbels did not take over an organisation if it was not necessary; he allowed the Chamber structure to exert local control, while the institutions of the mass media outside broadcasting stayed in private hands. This reflected the general character of the National Socialist economy before the war, and as in the case of that economy after 1939, the general trend of propaganda activities in Germany took a new turn in the light of a fresh situation.

The cohesion with which Germany went to war in 1939 reflected, to some extent, the success of the Propaganda Ministry in constructing the idea of a national community, National Socialist in outlook, and based upon the 'leadership principle'. The British people had also been presented with a picture of themselves as a nation through the mass media, but without the direct organisation of opinion through a government ministry. There was pressure upon mass communications organisations in different ways, and at different levels, but much of the impetus for the construction of the national image in the 1930s arose from the immediate needs of the organisations themselves to survive in an economically and politically hostile environment.

In 1932 the BBC moved into a custom-built edifice in Portland Place, London, which to many people had the appearance of a ship. The hierarchic levels of control were embodied in the internal organisation of the building, with Sir John Reith, the Director-General, as a captain whose main aim was to preserve the craft from the outside storms of government interference, and the threat of insubordination in the lower ranks. By centralising control in London and taking away regional responsibilities for planning at all levels he had been able to create a uniformity in financing and production. A metropolitan outlook dominated the medium, and the 'public service' ethos was translated into an attempt to raise the cultural level of the nation as a whole. Such cultural 'gatekeeping' was effected by administrators who often frustrated the attempts of programme-makers to influence the pattern and content of broadcasting. The established format, with a variegated mixture of music, talks and plays but no distinct pattern, was intended to encourage the audience to be alert and not to use the radio as background to other activities. There was certainly a diversity of programmes, but no attempt to specialise and capture specific audiences at particular times. Cultural uniformity was one result of the centralising process, and although regional dialects still persisted, BBC English became the standard for pronunciation throughout the country. Reith acted in the best interests of broadasting as he perceived them since the BBC had been charged with creating a national service as a monopoly position. It was a role fraught with difficulties, and his solution was paternalistic, constructing an image of the nation he should serve, rather than responding to the needs of the nation.

The BBC had more than an internal role. Wireless was a medium which could cross frontiers, as we have noted in the case of Germany. Britain was the centre of an empire and Commonwealth which was coming under increasing pressure, from within and without, in the 1930s. With the development of short-wave transmitters, and the recognition of their use in other European countries, the BBC took on the role of Britain's voice in the world, particularly to those areas politically and emotionally linked to the United Kingdom. The far-flung parts of the empire could be tied to the mother country physically by means of wireless, but the symbolic aspect was no less important.

The Empire Service was inaugurated in December 1932, and on Christmas Day of the same year King George V broadcast for the first time, not only to his subjects in Britain but throughout the world. At a time when the role of Britain as an imperial power was coming into question, the appearance of world power was reinforced, not least to the population at home. It was, in the long run, more symbolic than real.

The impetus was created for the further extension of BBC broadcasts to Europe and the rest of the world. It was recognised both in government circles and within the BBC that foreign opinion was of crucial importance in the international environment of the 1930s. Views were divided as to the best method of influencing such opinion, whether through more traditional channels, such as the Foreign Service, which dealt with opinion-makers, or by addressing the mass of the people in other countries. The BBC began to offer the second option, and it was to be of national and international importance in the Second World War.

Film too had a national and international significance in Britain in the 1930s. 'A film has a national conception and an international life', declared a report which recommended the inauguration of a British Film Institute in 1932. It was one of a number of statements published at the time which argued that film should be used as a tool for cultural and educational advancement. One concern of the report, echoing a continuing complaint from the 1920s, and reiterated in many other countries, was the ubiquitous nature of the American cinema and its possible effect on the moral outlook of young people. A British Film Institute would have a number of functions, but it should primarily educate audiences in film appreciation, thus echoing the BBC view that it should be serving a discriminating public. It was also to encourage the production of British films which would be competitive in the world market, while portraying all that was best in British life. The aim was a cultural nationalism which would oust the alien influence of the American cinema.

As in the 1920s, the British commercial cinema tried to emulate Hollywood studio productions without the financial resources or, some thought, the talent. Only Alexander Korda, an expatriate Hungarian, managed to secure some success in the United States in 1935 with *The Private Life of Henry VIII* which opened up a co-production agreement with United Artists. However, this assault on the main overseas market could not be sustained and by 1938 Korda had even lost control of his studios. His view of British history which appealed to the Americans was only one example of the way in which an examination of the past presented an idealised picture of the community for the present. Kingship was personalised, almost democratised, and yet clearly distanced from the people. The British cinema industry was constructing a mythical past, and at the same time a mythical present.

With costs increasing because of the re-equipment required for sound producers sought safe markets for their films. This required some arrangement with the distribution circuits which were more in tune with public taste, but there were also other influences. The British Board of Film Censors acted as the watchdog for the industry and producers took care generally to keep within the guidelines of good taste and appropriate attitudes which were suggested by the Board. The results of these constraints, both financial and moral, were films which were politically anodyne, personalising social problems and showing resolution of conflict within the community by the upholding of traditional values. Diversity within the wider community was shown, but not as a challenge to the stability of life. When not being influenced by the American films which made up 80 per cent of those released in

Britain, the public saw a reflection of British society which had little connection with real life around them but constructed an ideal sense of the British national community.

There was a small group of film-makers who wanted to show the real character of British life to an audience. Reference has already been made to John Grierson who, under the auspices of various quasi-governmental and commercial bodies, brought together the 'documentary movement'. Their work must be seen in terms of the development of public relations in Britain, and for all their fine intentions they were inevitably restricted by their sources of finance. Sponsoring bodies required films which were optimistic: even when investigating and illustrating social problems the tenor of the films suggested that in a more efficient and organised society they were soluble.

The result was a construction of values which appeared to be characteristic of British society. They emphasised individuality responsibly organised within the wider community: diversity subsumed. into a general uniformity for the public good. *Night Mail* (1936) provides a good example of this. Made by the General Post Office Film Unit it portrayed the efficient running of the train service from London to Glasgow every night, collecting and distributing mail on the way. Both the railway and the Post Office were concerned with service to the individual consumer, and at the same time employing hundreds of individuals whose role was explored in the film. At one level it was an educational film explaining a complex operation, at another it constructed a sense of national unity through the network of railways, ideals of service through the Post Office, and more importantly, placed the individual worker and consumer within a large industrial organisation.

The mirrors which the documentary film-makers held up to society were seen by very few of the population, since the films were rarely distributed in cinemas. However, their work was of importance because the skills they acquired in constructing images of unity in peacetime were to be fully utilised when they formed the core of the Crown Film Unit after 1940, portraying Britain at war as a nation diverse but unified in the face of the enemy.

The closest the British cinema audiences came to 'factual' reporting on film in the 1930s was in the newsreels which accompanied the main features in most cinemas. As was the case in other countries, they were a collection of filmed topical events, serious and amusing, with a commentator who linked them together. While concerned with topicality, their main aim was to entertain, and to keep before the audience the names of the major film corporations to which the newsreel companies were affiliated. Such a mixture of news presentation and public relations was susceptible to pressure from the censors and government. Reporting of domestic and foreign events was suitably structured to divert any criticism from public bodies or government agencies. The prevailing picture in the newsreels was of a country united in purpose and capable of absorbing or thwarting any elements, both internal and external, which threatened its existence.

Concern for commercial viability was a major factor in the presentation of British society in films. Success was measured in box-office returns and, while there were some independent surveys of the cinema audience, producers had a preferred image of their audience which was of an undifferentiated mass who were easily satisfied by non-controversial fare. It was an outlook not unlike that of BBC administrators in the same period.

The middle of the decade saw the most prosperous years for the film industry, but pressure grew on the BBC from two quarters. The Ullswater Committee sat in 1935 to enquire into British broadcasting, and questions about the performance of the BBC as a national organisation were raised in the press. Furthermore, producers expressed annoyance that they had little real idea of the effect their programmes were having on the general public. Clearly the BBC had to look to its relationship with the public as a whole, as well as that with opinion-formers and decision-makers in the establishment.

The result was the creation of a Public Relations Department in 1935, which had a listener research organisation attached to it in the following year. In effect, the BBC began to engage in listener research. The management of the organisation had little enthusiasm for the exercise since it smacked too much of commercialism. Advertisers on the broadcasting networks in America had already investigated their audiences for nearly a decade, and techniques of sampling were already being used by the agencies in Britain. Their aim was to identify the market for a product so that advertising might be targeted to maximise sales. In such an operation the risk to the manufacturer was minimised, while the apparent needs of the consumer were gratified. It appeared to be a scientific form of manipulation, and had obvious ramifications in the field of political persuasion.

Commercial needs dictated some forms of social research, but there was a more academic interest which found expression among some businessmen and bureaucrats who believed that a scientific examination of society would enable a more efficient system to be developed. It was an idea which motivated some of the 'documentary movement'.

Political and Economic Planning (PEP) was founded by a non-political grouping in 1933 to carry out investigations into the main institutional structures in Britain. Mass Observation, formed in 1937, looked more specifically at the habits and attitudes of individuals in society. Both organisations were constructing techniques of enquiry which were to be of enormous importance to the British government in the Second World War.

In the 1930s it was the British press which most utilised market research. The relaunch of the *Daily Mirror* in 1934 as a downmarket, leftist tabloid was master-minded by J. Walter Thompson, the advertising agency. It conducted readership surveys, developed strategies of marketing, considered the editorial position, and encouraged potential advertisers. With an increase in national newspaper circulations from 3.1 million in 1918 to 10.6 million in 1937 there was a market to be captured by the newspaper proprietor and the advertiser in tandem. The spiralling costs of production, and the need to keep cover prices as low as possible, made advertising revenue, which was over half the income of most newspapers, the key to financial stability. Large circulations led to increased revenue, and the knowledge that a buying public existed in the lower-income households encouraged advertisers to use those popular national dailies which could penetrate that market. This connection, leading to mutual advantage, had an effect upon the content of the national dailies which aimed to cater for as many groups as possible. The most obvious result was a further deterioration in the amount and quality of political reporting, and an increase in features of general interest and sports coverage.

While rarely tied to one political party the bulk of the national press was conservative in outlook, and by the selection and framing of news the papers aimed to appeal to the widest possible audience. There was an emphasis on collective values; those elements, mainly of the left, which challenged and appeared to threaten the stability of society, were shown as troublemakers who had little in common with the bulk of British society. The unifying aspect in most papers was the presentation of Britain as the centre of an empire. Foreign news was presented from a British viewpoint, and Chamberlain spoke for the majority of the people when he displayed his attitude towards Czechoslovakia as a 'far-away country' in 1938.

There were few effective voices in the national press which challenged this construction of consensus. Even the regional accents became as muted as they were in the BBC as the provincial morning and evening newspapers became amalgamated in chains, and declined in number over the twenty-year period. The concentration of ownership which was noted in the previous chapter was impelled by financial motives, but had political and cultural ramifications. The main source of domestic news was London, and the penetration of the national dailies strengthened the metropolitan bias still further. It was the growing movement towards a centralisation of news sources through the Press Association, and the location of correspondents in and around government sources which offered an opportunity for the management of news stories by the growing number of public relations departments attached to large firms and government departments.

Such organisations were concerned with selling an image rather than a product. By the use of all means of communication they tried to create a frame of reference in which the activities of the organisation might be viewed. There was no compulsion on newspapers to use press releases, but they were often conveniently timed, filled space, and were well written, in order to appeal to the readership of a particular newspaper. Such activities would also be of importance in wartime.

In 1936 the British government, faced with the possibility of a European war in the future, began to discuss the creation of a Ministry of Information. It had the experience of the First World War, and the knowledge of developments in Germany to work on. It also had some expertise in the fields of advertising and public relations to call upon. The issue was debated in government circles until 1939, when a ministry was set up, but it was not until

1942 that the organisation and principles upon which it might be based were successfully established.

Before 1939 the argument revolved around two issues. What form should the organisation take and who should head it? There were proponents of a single ministry, similar to that in Germany, which would pull together all aspects of censorship and the preparation of information. Others sought the coordination of activities already being conducted by various organisations, for example the BBC or the Foreign Office, without any real central direction. The result was that by 1939 there was a ministry formed with no real idea of its function, and a great number of vested interests to overcome.

The question of who should head it clearly depended on the form it might take, but there was suspicion in British parliamentary circles that any politician who took on such a task would be able to manipulate opinion on his own behalf. They need only have looked to Neville Chamberlain, the Prime Minister after 1937, for evidence of the use of the mass media in order to create an image as a statesman. As a leader of the Conservative Party he had encouraged it to make films, and as a Cabinet minister he had used the newsreels to address the public directly. He had developed a personal style, and was the first British politician to understand the specific qualities of each medium and use them to advantage.

By 1938 Chamberlain had constructed an image of an international statesman, by the use of newsreels, the press and broadcasting. He embodied the ideals of British society, and the Munich Settlement appeared to represent the results of negotiation and fair-dealing. Chamberlain had apparently sought peace for its own sake. He represented the concept of freedom against the might of National Socialist Germany, and appeared to have shown its efficacy in the international arena.

Chamberlain himself knew the truth, as did the British people within six months. Rather than following British opinion before 1938 he had helped to make it. The government had been in constant contact with the owners of newspapers, newsreel owners, and the BBC, in order to make sure that the presentation of its policies was correct. The influence was indirect, but all the owners and managers of opinion-forming institutions were susceptible to government pressure.

Whereas in National Socialist Germany there was overt control, in Britain there were two forms of indirect influence on the mass media. One was financial, the other governmental, but they were never totally separate. A government used to working through 'middle-men' to secure the right kind of publicity was removed from the people – it was this deficiency which undermined the early attempts to organise opinion directly through a government agency. Not until the expertise of those men who had constructed and examined the nation before the war was brought into play could the Ministry of Information function effectively, and it also helped that by then Britain was winning the war.

The continuous challenge to international stability which affected European countries after 1936 hardly appeared to involve the United States of America. The effects of the Depression in the early 1930s had thrown the USA back on itself as the country attempted to solve its enormous economic and social problems. This introspective attitude was encouraged by the mass media which were also struggling to survive in a sorely dislocated economy. Film audiences were in decline by 1933, newspaper revenues and circulations were down, and a mood of pessimism and self-doubt appeared to pervade the country. There was an ambivalence towards accepted ideals in American society which found expression in the treatment of vice and violence in Hollywood films of the period. Gangsters were portrayed as rebels against an uncaring society which had failed to support those who had fought for those ideals in the First World War. Individual survival seemed of more importance than the subscription to false values.

The challenge to such a pessimistic outlook came with the inauguration of Franklin Delano Roosevelt (FDR) as President in March 1933. He pinpointed the problem in a telling phrase: the American nation, he said, 'had nothing to fear but fear itself'. It was a question of engendering a feeling of confidence, irrespective of the attempts to restructure American economic life. There had to be an impression of dynamism, of caring leadership, and an emphasis on goals which would bind the nation together. The reconstruction of the economy could only take place if people believed it was possible. The channels of communication between the government and the public were to be of crucial importance, and he started by mending fences with the press.

FDR's immediate predecessors had often been openly hostile to journalists, and sporadic news conferences had been tightly structured with prepared questions and answers. Roosevelt kept the old categories of attribution which were allowed from presidential replies. This meant that information was divided into that available for direct quotation, that for background only, and that which was strictly 'off the record'. The difference now was that he took questions from the floor in regular conferences, knew the journalists individually, and allowed them to ascribe a statement to him indirectly without quotation. This allowed the pressmen more freedom, and Roosevelt was aware that they wanted good copy which would meet deadlines. He was also adept at coining phrases which could encapsulate an idea. The 'Hundred Days' focused attention on the series of measures put forward by the administration at the beginning of its term – it encapsulated the urgency with which regeneration should proceed.

Roosevelt, himself, was a symbol of that regeneration. Although physically disabled through poliomyelitis, his strength of purpose and character as a national leader had to be displayed to the national audience. Broadcasting, which by 1933 had become an integral element in the lives of the majority of the American public, offered the most effective channel for the construction of such an image. Between March and October 1933, FDR addressed the radio audience four times in what became known as 'fireside chats'. His style was intimate and friendly, not hectoring. He set out the problems, and the way in which the nation, government and people, would have to work together to solve them. He came across as a rational democratic leader speaking directly to individual citizens in their own homes. The patrician became a populist, speaking over the heads of the legislature, which might be less inclined to carry through his measures. It was a 'milestone in politics and broadcasting' for, whereas Hitler's use of the radio was an adjunct to the mass rallies and confirmed his position above the people, Roosevelt used the medium to construct his role as the leader of the nation which responded not as an undifferentiated mass but as individuals and families. Throughout his terms of office Roosevelt used the 'chats' to inform and cajole the American people – by the use of radio, democracy was strengthened, and the concept of responsible leadership reinforced.

Yet the programme which Roosevelt put forward to Congress and publicised so effectively had implications for the future development of the mass media in the USA and created some antagonism towards the new government among owners and producers. Federal intervention, which was meant to iron out inequalities and promote greater efficiency in commercial life, could have meant an investigation into the internal affairs of the organisations which ran the networks, the studios and publishing. It was likely that the 'honeymoon' period which Roosevelt exploited so successfully would soon come to an end.

In order to rationalise the internal communications system the Federal government proposed to widen the scope of the FRC (Federal Radio Commission) to include supervision of the telephone network which was controlled by AT&T. The Communications Act of 1934 created a Federal Communications Commission (FCC) with the same powers as the FRC to license individual radio stations and to monitor their performance. Since the telephone lines were an integral element in network broadcasting the further supervision had implications for the future. Of greater immediate danger to the networks was the debate on the content and general standard of broadcasting which accompanied the passage of the bill through Congress.

By 1933 advertising agencies were key elements in the programming of the networks. They were not only concerned with buying and selling time but also made programmes for sponsors and placed them within the schedules. Many educationalists saw this as detrimental to cultural standards since there was little room on the air for anything which was not demonstrably 'popular', unless it was broadcast outside the hours of peak listening. The aim of the agencies was to deliver the largest number of consumers to the sponsors in the cheapest and most acceptable way possible. The aim of the critics was to encourage the new Commission to look more carefully at the 'public service' role of the radio stations. They argued that more time should be allocated to educational and 'cultural' programmes which would attract smaller but interested groups in the community.

The amendment to the Bill was lost, and the FCC had no right to interfere in the day-to-day running of stations. The ultimate sanction of closure was too draconian to contemplate except in the most extreme cases, and in any case the Commission had no right to interfere in the real organisation of broadcasting in the US, network control. The government had no intention of interfering in sound business practice, and the agencies argued that they were indispensable to the creation of wealth for everyone in society.

By appealing to a national audience, and emphasising social and economic values which would pull the country together, the radio networks were able to construct an outlook of community feeling. The government was not averse to this, or in the end how, and why, it was achieved. The complex character of American society was rarely examined in the need to maximise audiences.

If broadcasting had been castigated in some quarters for contributing to the national decline in the early 1930s, the major culprit was identified by many more as the cinema. A simple solution was sought to the apparent decline in morals, particularly of young people, and it was found in the effects of a combination of sound and pictures upon impressionable minds. This monocausal approach to the effect of the cinema in society stimulated a number of studies which were published in 1932 and 1933, producing evidence for the view that films had been responsible for cases of deviant behaviour, and generally adding to the moral degradation of American life. Although lacking academic rigour the surveys seemed to provide 'scientific' support for the concern many citizens had about the picture of American society that was emanating from Hollywood studios.

In 1930 the Hays Code, which suggested guidelines to producers on what was morally and socially acceptable in their films, had been reframed in order to take account of the advent of sound. These recommendations had been studiously ignored by producers and directors who, concerned by dwindling audiences as the Depression deepened, offered as much titillation as possible. The framers of the 1930 code, with the support of the Roman Catholic hierarchy, Protestant leaders, and the National Legion of Decency, began to mobilise public support in order to put pressure on the Hollywood establishment. Fearful of a further deterioration in box-office receipts Will Hays, as the industry's censor, appointed Joseph Breen to act as the Production Code Administrator in 1934. Such a move precluded any government legislation, and Breen's office was one factor in the change of content and style of Hollywood pictures.

Another lay in the resurgence of the industry itself. In a more confident atmosphere audiences began to return. The studios became more cost-effective as the main financial institutions which provided the risk capital put in managers to safeguard their investments, and oversee production costs. New producers, working within a factory-style environment, made products which would sell in a more buoyant and receptive market.

Censorship pressures and the reorganisation of the industry produced films which offered a more positive statement about American society, and man's general predicament. Hollywood movies became more affirmative, surer of the market, and based upon properties which had already been proved successes as novels or plays. Musicals were lavish, offering style, which might be emulated in society at large. They were more than escapist entertainment since they reflected a new opulence which was attainable to the ordinary man by sticking to the values which were celebrated in the films themselves: individual competence, respect for principled authority, awareness of the wider community and its heritage of freedom. The films of Frank Capra which explored these concepts were box-office successes; many other productions reiterated the same outlooks. Out of a period of self-doubt Hollywood constructed and celebrated a new self-belief. Selling in the largest domestic market in the world the films offered a view of American society which was progressive, unified, and free from the traumas which were affecting other areas of the world. They were an element in the reinforcement of isolationism which permeated American society in the inter-war period.

By its size, wealth and domination of the world market in films the American industry also acted as a magnet for talent from other countries. Political refugees were taken in, other writers and actors were bought in. They were all integrated into the conveyor-belt system of production, their influence only beginning to show in the 1940s. To survive in the 1930s they adapted to American needs, but the problem they had to face in a time of increased nationalism was how to demonstrate their new allegiance. It was to be a particular problem as war approached.

The nationalist outlook in Europe also affected the Hollywood industry since, as we have seen, governments became concerned about the effects of products from America upon their own culture. The only way to withstand the flood of well-made films was by outright banning. Some were censored or prohibited on grounds of immorality, even though they were made within the guidelines of the Production Code. More often in the late 1930s they were considered politically suspect, particularly in Germany. The counter-response to the dominance of Hollywood was further cultural and political alienation in Europe which encouraged a division between the old world and the new.

It was American broadcasting which began to bridge the gap, and it was the result of a developing interest in news among network heads, particularly William Paley, the founder of the Columbia Broadcasting System. Throughout the early 1930s Paley had to fight against the two networks owned by NBC, securing affiliate stations as best he could. He tried new forms of advertising, and promoted his network as more go-ahead than the others.

However, in 1933 the whole news-reporting role of broadcasting was brought into question when the press which provided the stations and networks with information called a halt, conscious that many of their own problems sprang from the amount of advertising which had been taken from them by the newer medium. The networks could either cease to be news media or they could create their own service for the collection and dissemination of material. The result had been a compromise whereby the major news agencies would supply bulletins to the stations, making two five-minute news broadcasts daily. None of this 'news' was to be less than twelve hours old, and the broadcasts were not to be sponsored.

Circumstances quickly destroyed any such form of control by the news agencies. Advertisers came forward to sponsor broadcasts, and there was enough incentive for the networks themselves to build up news-gathering teams. The future reputation of CBS lay in the personnel who not only reported events in America, but relayed the events in Europe to the USA.

H. V. Kalternborn was the archetypal news analyst who not only described a scene but commented on its significance. Whereas Reith had never allowed the identity of his newsreaders to be revealed in case their personalities interfered with the important facts they were presenting, newsmen in the United States sold the news to the listening audience. They created the framework in which Americans should see the war in Spain, or the rise of National Socialism in Europe. In 1937 Kaltenborn was joined by William Shirer, and as European director of CBS operations, Edward R. Murrow. This was the basis of the team which brought to American the unfolding drama of Munich, 'the greatest show yet heard on American radio'. The United States was being informed of the events into which it would be drawn inexorably within three years, and reminded of its role as a world power.

In the early 1930s most men had been too concerned about their everyday existence to worry about the international ramifications of the economic crisis and the subsequent political changes. The cinema, the radio and newspapers had provided a steady diet of entertainment and news which satisfied the majority of a population. The developing nationalism was reflected in the media, but it was also constructed: the unified nation became the central element in many peoples' lives. During the 1930s governments had developed strong ties with the owners and leaders of mass communication organisations. Some were direct, some indirect, depending on the ethos of the society involved, but the result had been a community of interests which would be tested in wartime. The initiatives which had originated in the inter-war period in the understanding and organisation of a population would also be used in the social laboratory of an international conflict.

7. Propaganda in War and Peace

As we have seen, the nature of the modern world had been brought
into sharper focus as a result of the First World War and its influence
over developments in the next two decades. Old patterns of political,
social and economic domination had been undermined; beliefs, both
religious and secular, had been thrown into disarray and new
channels of thought and expression had been developed. The USSR,
under Bolshevik and Stalinist control, had emerged as a major
industrial and ideological power in the east of Europe. National
Socialism in Germany, Fascism in Italy, and similar right-wing
radical movements throughout Europe turned not only against
socialism, with its international outlook, but also the liberal democratic regimes which represented in concrete terms the ideals
embodied in the post-war settlement. Germany, after 1933, posed a
continuous challenge to the territorial provisions of the Versailles
Treaty. Meanwhile in Asia, Japan, an Allied Power in the First
World War, began to establish a power basis on the continental
mainland, in Manchuria and China, posing a potential threat to the
west European imperial powers, and the position of the United
States in the Pacific.

After 1919 the USA had retreated on itself politically yet it
continued to dominate the world economy as a major creditor state,
and as a leading industrialised society. The economic and social
problems of the late 1920s and 1930s had increased its political
introversion and the international responsibility of the United States
had yet to be recognised and accepted by the majority of the
population by the late 1930s. They were ill-prepared to assume such
a role, given their lack of knowledge of the outside world; a world
only slightly better informed about the USA because of the images
manufactured in Hollywood and distributed throughout the world.

Although there were developments in communications technology, they served the growing political nationalism of individual states. Together with the forms of cultural nationalism, which had been promoted by elite groups in Europe to counter the popular cultural predominance of the United States, they produced a form of political introversion which further undermined international stability.

By the late 1930s there were few statesmen in Europe who did not accept the need for territorial changes in the east of the continent; there was only one, Hitler, who accepted the necessity of war as a means to achieve his foreign political ends. However, given the possibility of conflict, democratic states sought to prepare for a future war while not precipitating it. The organisation of propaganda, both domestic and foreign, became one element in that preparation, but as we have noted, in Britain competing agencies undermined its development. Since a Ministry of Information would not come into existence until the declaration of war there was little opportunity, or willingness, to construct procedures for news censorship, for administrative relationships with other ministries, and to finalise the role of newspapers and the BBC.

Goebbels had found his own position difficult enough in National Socialist Germany after 1933. Nevertheless, on 1 September 1939, when the European war began, he had an organisation which was immediately capable of exploiting the initial successes of the German army, although Goebbels himself was not a fervent supporter of the conflict, mainly for reasons of personal ambition. He recognised that his control over the aims, objectives and content of propaganda at home and abroad would be circumscribed by foreign policy requirements and military needs, leading to a decline of his own influence over Hitler.

Goebbel's own reluctance about the war with Poland in 1939 was shared by large numbers of his fellow citizens according to reports on public opinion which were returned from *Gau* (regional) propaganda offices to Berlin. The identification of public attitudes towards government policy and the party leadership had been well established in peacetime, particularly by the Security Service. Feedback, by whatever form, was a key aspect in presentation and content of propaganda in Germany throughout the war, but the content and circulation of the reports became part of the Byzantine power struggle amongst the leadership of the Third Reich.

Lord Macmillan, who had been appointed as Minister of Information in Britain at the outbreak of war, restricted the development of enquiries into public opinion because of the use that might be made of them by competing elements in the ministry. Such short-term thinking displayed his own lack of understanding of propaganda, and lack of leadership. The development of reporting on public opinion was rather haphazard, calling upon the resources of Mass Observation, the British Institute of Public Opinion and other social surveys. A weekly report on Home Intelligence was made available by the ministry only after September 1940, and then with some trepidation since they were far from 'scientific' and objective. The reports continually reflected public apprehension and concern, not only about the conduct of the war but also about the performance of the ministry itself.

It took two years, and three ministers, before there was a clear idea of its relationship to other areas of government, and the institutions of the mass media. Macmillan, as a member of the House of Lords, was divorced from day-to-day politics in the Commons, and gave way to Sir John Reith, who was found a seat in the Commons, in January 1940. His tenure lasted until the fall of the Chamberlain government in May, when the new Prime Minister, Winston Churchill, appointed Duff Cooper, who had resigned from the Chamberlain government in 1938 over the Munich Agreement, and expected a more senior government position. While Reith had wide experience with the BBC, he did not have the breadth of outlook or political weight to develop a clear strategy, and Duff Cooper had little real interest in propaganda. Although, personally, they lacked the ability to deal with the main problems affecting the ministry, they also had the disadvantage of attempting these tasks during one of the worst phases of the war for Britain.

There were three distinct, but inter-related, problems: firstly, how to devise a system of censorship which satisfied the needs of newspapers, public and government alike; secondly, how best to create a positive propaganda outlook both at home and abroad, and how to define the role of the BBC; thirdly, how to coordinate through the ministry the information services of the numerous government departments, particularly the military, which sought to preserve their own independence. In July 1941 Duff Cooper eventually gave up trying to solve these problems, and Churchill, after consultations with Beaverbrook, asked Brendan Bracken to take over the ministry; he stayed for the duration of the war.

Bracken's career in British politics was similar to that of his mentor, Beaverbrook. He was essentially an outsider, the rumour had circulated that he was Churchill's illegitimate son; however, the truth was more mundane. He came from Ireland, and by use of a forceful personality had integrated himself into the higher reaches of political life. As Minister of Information he had the support of the majority of the British press, led by Beaverbrook; an awareness of the political atmosphere in which he worked, and the advantage of the confidence of Churchill, through whom he was able to establish a better relationship with the service departments. Bracken had a genuine interest in propaganda, not least because of the way he had projected himself in society, and recognised that the ministry's function was not to exhort the domestic population, but to inform as accurately as possible. This required access to sources of military information, which he achieved with the help of the Prime Minister, and the cooperation of newspapers to use it in a responsible way. The system of press censorship was purely voluntary, although editors were alerted through the D-Notice system of what should not be published for security reasons. They had freedom to criticise the government, and individual departments, although the *Daily Mirror*, a left-of-centre paper, incurred the wrath of Churchill for impugning the administrative capability of the army in 1942.

While the ministry guided the press, it also acted as adviser for other ministries who had to communicate with the general public. It was able to coordinate requirements of departments competing for advertising space in newspapers, and take on an innovatory role, suggesting how best the message might be presented. It was a task which required discretion mixed with political authority, virtues which were also needed in clarifying the role of the BBC in wartime.

There was no doubt that broadcasting would be a key factor in the provision of information, both at home and abroad. However, since 1922 the BBC had developed as an institution free of government interference, under the guiding hand of John Reith. He was succeeded as Director-General in 1938 by J. W. Ogilvie, an academic totally unsuited for the task of organising the BBC in wartime, or for establishing a working relationship with the government.

Personnel in the BBC, jealous of the independence of the organisation, suspected any attempt by the Ministry of Information to interfere in its services. However, broadcasting was ultimately the responsibility of the government, which toyed with the idea of taking over the Corporation completely. Wiser counsels prevailed, and a clearer line of responsibility, started under Cooper and developed by Bracken, began to restore confidence inside the Corporation. A. P. Ryan and Ivone Kirkpatrick, the former a BBC employee, the latter a diplomat, were appointed by the government as 'advisers' to the Corporation in home and foreign broadcasting. Within a few months they had become the key personnel in linking the needs of the government to the capabilities of the BBC. The Corporation remained constitutionally independent, but the government position was clearly represented in policy decisions on content and interpret- ation of news in two vital areas. The combined talents of Bracken, Ryan, Kirkpatrick and Robert Foot, who succeeded Ogilvie in 1942, allowed the system to work reasonably well. The BBC was able to present itself as the voice of Britain, broadcasting accurate news, without appearing to be the mouthpiece of the British government.

The Corporation had also to take account of the interests and needs of its domestic audience. The war brought the BBC closer to the mass of the people, and it sought more clearly to reflect the regional diversity and differing attitudes towards entertainment and culture which were apparent from the results of listener research. The development of a Forces programme in 1941 began to satisfy a demand, both civilian and military, for more 'popular' entertain- ment; something which was also needed to satisfy the American troops who began to arrive in 1942 and who had experience of commercial broadcasting in the United States. Changes in content had been envisaged before 1939, but the war accelerated the movement, and left the BBC stronger to challenge the argument against its monopoly in the post-war period.

During the war the British public, faced with smaller newspapers because of newsprint shortages, looked to the BBC for accurate and responsible reporting of events. It truly became a 'national institution' in which the people put their trust. At the same time populations in Europe and farther afield looked to the BBC news broadcasts for a reliable statement of the position of the war. Clearly, there was an opportunity to propagandise occupied countries, and their occupiers, as a form of psychological warfare, but it was not clear until 1942 what role the BBC should play in this, if any.

The propaganda conducted by Lord Northcliffe against enemy countries at the end of the First World War had been considered by many to have been successful in undermining morale. Broadcasting offered greater scope to propagandists, but any early planning was beset by quarrels over responsibilities, particularly with the Foreign Office. The appointment of Bracken coincided with the creation of the Political Warfare Executive (PWE) which had responsibility for coordinating foreign policy aims and propaganda abroad. The BBC input came from Kirkpatrick, who took control of the European output of the Corporation the following year. While the BBC presented 'white' propaganda to Germany through its news and talks service, PWE staff presented 'black' propaganda, or misleading information, on transmitters which appeared to be situated on the continent. There was much discussion at the time, and later, about the efficacy of the operation, and some complaint within the BBC at the time that they interfered with the 'legitimate' broadcasting.

There is no doubt that under the aegis of the PWE the tone and presentation of news was orientated towards the British viewpoint, but that was a matter of opinion, not fact. In the context of the war in 1942 and 1943 both forms of broadcasting had a place in the war effort, but the insistently accurate reporting by the BBC of events as the tide turned for the Allies reinforced its reputation for reliability, which was to be of importance in the post-war period.

As the European war went into its fourth year there were many in Britain who were contemplating the future. This whole question raised problems for the Ministry of Information. The consensus which had been created to fight a war might be undermined by the encouragement of debate about the future policies. The publication of the Beveridge Report on Social Security, in December 1942, was a case in point. Bracken recognised the importance of the blueprint for those engaged in the war effort, and as a general statement about the nature of a liberal democratic society for which they were fighting. It was given wide publicity, but Churchill had no wish to be bound by such a statement of policy, and discussion was closed down. However, the theme of war aims and reconstruction was one taken up by documentary film-makers working for the Crown Film Unit.

The war witnessed the highpoint of documentary film-making in Britain, although in the first year the ministry had no coherent film policy. In August 1940 the Crown Film Unit was formed out of the old GPO unit, and began making morale-boosting films during the Blitz, moving into longer feature-length movies such as *Target for*

Tonight. Other documentary-makers took advantage of the need for a range of explanatory and exhortatory films which had a guaranteed exhibition in cinemas. Newsreels offered visual images of the war but with little real explanation of the meaning behind the action. In the finest documentaries, such as the work of Humphrey Jennings, the relationship of the war to wider issues of British culture and ideological outlooks was established through a subtle use of picture and soundtrack. The effect on the audience was difficult to judge, but the possibilities of film as a medium of democratic education were being explored to the full.

In the last two years of the conflict men like the Boulting brothers, who were to make their name in the feature film industry, began to examine the future. They looked forward to the social reconstruction of Britain on more equitable lines, and premeditated the appearance of a Labour government committed to social reform, yet the images they presented looked back to a golden age rather than forward to an uncertain future.

The commercial film industry was stimulated by the war as larger numbers of people had little else to do with their time. The result was a number of films which represented the predicament of the British people in wartime, and their qualities of perseverance and honesty. Many clearly showed the influence of the documentary film-makers. The commercial cinema had created a clear relationship with the audience before the war, and recognised that entertainment was the key to successful selling. Successful collaboration was achieved with the Ministry of Information on certain projects, but given the general role of the British Board of Film Censors no direction need be given to producers, since they knew their audience rather better than the ministry did. One aspect of the success of the Ministry of Information after 1941 lay in recognising that it functioned best by expediting and coordinating the activities of who could do the task well. It truly represented the best aspects of a pluralist society.

One may place against this the experience of Germany. The parallels with Britain should not be drawn too sharply, but one can recognise similarities in the question of political support for the Propaganda Ministry; the competition with other departments, particularly the military; and the relationship with channels of information, especially newspapers. The conflict in Britain over the organisation of propaganda might be seen as an important manifestation of political struggle in a democratic society; however, the conflict in National Socialist Germany clearly represented a struggle for power in a state which claimed to be unified in purpose and spirit.

Goebbels gave a clear lead to his own departmental staff within the Propaganda Ministry by presiding over a daily conference where the main themes and issues were laid down. However, his own control over the preparation and presentation of war news was soon undermined by the High Command of the Wehrmacht (*OKW*), the activities of the Reich Press Chief, Otto Dietrich, and the Führer himself. The *OKW* had supreme command over all three services with its own propaganda section which prepared daily communiqués. These were shown to Hitler before being sent to *DNB*, the government newsagency. Any alterations by the Führer were to stand, irrespective of the general propaganda position being developed in the Ministry. Continually at his side was Dietrich, who was head of the Press Division in the ministry, but who acted increasingly as propaganda spokesman for Hitler, and bypassed Goebbels in communicating with the press.

In 1942 a form of arbitration was worked out between these protagonists which stopped the development of a separate Press Office in the Chancellery, but effectively placed control of press policy in the hands of Dietrich. This development coincided with the Battle of Stalingrad, the turning point in the European war, and as victories turned to losses the presentation of news became more difficult.

In the face of this challenge to his control Goebbels concentrated on broadcasting, which offered direct contact with the people. The *Reichsrundfunkgesellschaft* (German Broadcasting Company) had centralised responsibility for broadcasting under the general control of the Propaganda Ministry, and Goebbels was able to develop a programme structure by May 1941 which offered a variety of listening, similar to that available in Britain. After 1943 there was wider disruption of programmes because of bombing, but with an audience growing by over 50 per cent between 1939 and 1945 radio was of prime importance in the mobilisation of the country for total war after 1943. From the start of the war the Foreign Ministry, under Ribbentrop, sought to intervene in the preparation of propaganda aimed at foreign countries. They were incapable of constructing an integrated organisation, like the PWE in Britain, because inter-personal and inter-departmental rivalries were too great.

It was in the area of film that Goebbels was able to have most control, and be most flexible in the relationship between the Propaganda Ministry and the producers. As in other countries the domestic cinema audience increased during the war, and was a key target area for propaganda. This took two forms, the feature film, which might be overtly political, but often was conceived as purely entertainment, and the newsreel. Goebbels took a personal interest in both categories, but was particularly involved in the preparation of the weekly newsreel through which the course of the war was presented to the German people. The *Deutsche Wochenschau* has been recognised as a major element in domestic propaganda since it had the most proficient and courageous technical staff producing outstanding footage, and was able to illustrate in graphic detail the main aspects of National Socialist ideology.

Feature films were also intended to perform this function, and the control of scripts and production staff was refined still further during the war although the ministry rarely commissioned specific films. With the complete disappearance of American films in 1940 there was great pressure on producers to fill the gap, not only for distribution in Germany, but throughout occupied Europe. The reorganisation and nationalisation of the whole industry in 1942 enabled production to be rationalised, and in the light of public demand the ratio of entertainment films to political films rose to 4:1. While disruption and shortages caused problems in the last two years of war there was a continuing commitment to a film programme which was appreciated by a population with little else to enjoy. The extraordinary film *Kolberg*, showing the resistance of the Prussians under Gneisenau to the French in the Napoleonic period, was released in the last month of war and was shot entirely in colour with thousands of extras. It had little chance to stiffen resistance to the invaders.

Films had often used historical dramas as a way of presenting current issues; for instance, political and military leadership through an examination of the careers of Frederick the Great and Bismarck. In doing so they were continuing to construct an ideological view of the Germans in history, and the role of the Leader, reinforcing one of Goebbels' greatest achievements, the creation of the *Führer-myth*, the idealisation of Hitler.

Such an idea was more difficult to sustain during the course of the war. The magnetism of Hitler's personality which could be captured by broadcasting from rallies was lost when the Führer was confined to smaller occasions or the studios. After 1942 he appeared less in public, since there had been a deterioration in his physical condition, and less in the newsreels. There was no doubt of the power that he exercised, but the link with the people, the key to his popularity, was in danger of being broken since he could not, or was unwilling to, make use of the radio or cinema.

In essence Goebbels took his place. He could argue that while the Leader fought the war he was standing in for him at home, and as the military position deteriorated he coordinated a more coherent propaganda policy which recognised the failures and orientated the nation towards outright defence. In the last two years of war Goebbels mediated between the German government and the people, but never turned against the Führer publicly. The battle for national survival, which he orchestrated, was based upon the essential tenets of National Socialism, anti-Bolshevism and anti-Semitism. As Britain united around an ideological symbol of its nationhood in 1940 as an embattled democracy, so the struggle for Germany was constructed by Goebbels into the defence of a mythical past against the Communist menace. How far people fought to the bitter end for this idea is difficult to judge.

The contribution of government propaganda to the war effort of the United States is also difficult to evaluate. Roosevelt had utilised the radio networks and the press to publicise himself and his policies in the 1930s, but was wary of committing himself to the organisation of a government information service. The State Department was encouraged to develop pan-American relationships in 1939, and an Office of the Coordinator of Inter-American Affairs was established in 1941 to encourage cultural exchanges. In July of that year an Office of Coordinator of Information was set up 'to collect and analyse all information and data which may bear upon national security'; it was essentially a collector of intelligence data on the state of public opinion.

In October 1941 the President created the Office of Facts and Figures (OFF) which was concerned mainly with the dissemination of factual information on defence matters to the domestic audience. Clearly the issue of the response of the United States to the European war was of prime concern, but after the Japanese attack on Pearl Harbor on 7 December 1941 and the entry of the US into the war the question of censorship and propaganda became more urgent. On 16 December the Office of Censorship was created with Byron Price of the Associated Press news agency as Director.

The policy of the office was similar to the United Kingdom; that all censorship was to be voluntary. Price issued a code of practice for all newspapers and other media in the United States, but the Office had no means of enforcing the code, apart from the draconian penalties involved in contravention of the Espionage Act which had been passed in 1917. Freedom of the press was defined as the freedom to express opinions, not the freedom to disclose information, unless the opinions came within the area of sedition. The Office of Censorship was specifically concerned with domestic matters, but there were rigid compulsory controls exercised outside the country by the army and the navy on military questions.

In June 1942 the Office of War Information (OWI) was established with Elmer Davis, a news analyst with CBS, as Director, responsible directly to the President. It took on the work of the OFF, but was primarily concerned with the organisation of propaganda to foreign countries. For this purpose it commissioned films, published news-papers and magazines, and produced news broadcasts on short-wave transmissions in over thirty languages. The economic and technical resources available to the OWI far exceeded those of the Ministry of Information in Britain or Goebbels' Propaganda Ministry, not only because of the immense wealth of the United States, but also because there was no requirement to produce domestic propaganda. The OWI did have a responsibility on the home front acting mainly as the coordinator of priorities in allocating government department advertising on radio, and exhorting the film industry to present its subjects in a way which would help the war effort. Although it also operated as a news service, the voluntary censorship system and the quality of radio reporting made it redundant.

Americans were safe in their fortress, hardly touched by the war in Europe or Asia, except through the experiences of the military, or newspaper and radio reporting. They could be relied upon by the government to present a picture of the conflict which appealed to the ideas and values of most Americans. While the foreign-language press and radio stations became the subject of close scrutiny, the commercial networks had the opportunity to serve the nation, and make a profit. As newspapers suffered from shortage of newsprint, and government agencies sought to disseminate messages to the public, the advertising revenues of the networks increased. They were also helped by large firms diverting taxable income into 'institutional' advertising in order to keep their names in front of the public during the war.

While CBS had the strongest news service, and had the opportunity to develop this potential during the war, with key reporters like Ed Murrow, NBC was more prominent in entertainment. However, in 1941 the Federal Communications Commission decided, after three years work, that the Company, which controlled two complementary networks, red and blue, should divest itself of one of them. The decision demonstrates the normality of life in the United States when a major reorganisation of the broadcasting structure could be debated in the middle of a war. However, the discussions were not merely about broadcasting but covered the wider questions of government intervention in free enterprise and the question of un-American activities among officials of the FCC. James Fly, its chairman, was a strong advocate of the anti-trust outlook of the New Deal and was unimpressed by the opposition to the proposal. To many of his opponents this made him tantamount to being a Communist. The battle was fought long and hard, but in October 1943 the Blue Network was sold to Edward Noble, and became the American Broadcasting Company (ABC); the main divisions of network broadcasting in the United States for the next thirty years had been established.

The intervention of Martin Dies, chairman of the House Committee on Un-American Activities, in the affairs of the FCC is evidence of the underlying tensions in American society, faced with dangers from outside. Hollywood, with its apparent influence over American morals and outlooks, had often provoked criticism from people who saw themselves as native Americans whose position was liable to be undermined by the activities of second-generation immigrants. In 1940 Dies had attacked the Hollywood community in print, but to little effect. In October 1941, isolationists considered a range of films which it was argued were influencing public opinion towards intervention in Europe. However, when war was declared the film industry was offered a further opportunity to demonstrate its commitment to American ideals, constructing them for audiences at home and around the world.

The growth in cinema business kept pace with that of the economy, and while satisfying the declared needs of the government after 1941 for propagandistic films and allowing directors to work for the armed services, Hollywood also recognised the demands of the audience for entertainment, particularly a domestic audience little touched by the realities of war. Some films were made with the express intention of whipping up hatred of the enemy, be they German or Japanese, but it was impossible to deal adequately with the conduct of the war except in the form of documentaries. Many of the films made during this period sought to deal with the experience of a changing world and changing values. The war as an issue might intervene, but only to set off wider questions of personal and public values in society. It might be suggested that at a time when the British and German film industries were constructing a mythical image of societies unified in the face of the external threat, Hollywood began to examine the diversity and inner tensions of the society it served. It was to continue that investigation in the post-war period.

The war ended with the capitulation of Germany in May 1945, followed by that of Japan four months later. Germany as a political unit had been eradicated from the map, and Goebbels had gone to his death with the Führer in Berlin. The United States government dismantled the OWI in August 1945, but recognised the need to keep some machinery in existence in the State Department for the presentation of the American case abroad. The Ministry of Information transmuted in April 1946 into the Central Office of Information (COI), since a government enquiry had suggested that coordination of government information was still required. It had no power, could take few initiatives, and was effectively submerged by the public relations officials of the ministries it sought to serve. In 1951 the last link with the war was destroyed when the Crown Film Unit was disbanded. The organisations of state propaganda had been dismantled, but the debate would continue on their contribution to the war effort. Clearly the war had been won by force of arms, but societies had been mobilised to support the effort by means of the mass media. Questions were now posed in the democracies as to how this potential power might be utilised and developed in the post-war world. New sources of conflict began to emerge, both on the national and international stage, presenting new challenges for the mass media. Firstly, the ways in which the communication industries might be involved in material and psychological reconstruction. Secondly, how they were to respond to the ideological challenge from the USSR. These were new features of tasks already developed during the war, thus emphasising the continuity of experience. They were now to be undertaken outside the immediate direction of the state.

There are a number of aspects which emphasise continuity in the British film industry in the 1940s. One is the role of J. Arthur Rank, who as producer, distributor and exhibitor became a major influence not only in the domestic market, but in America as well. Another was the influence of documentary film-makers who contributed to the war effort in propaganda films, and subsequently used their expertise in feature film production. In a wider sense there was another aspect in which Rank, the documentarists, and other producers participated; the creation of the myth of what it meant to be British, which was not merely an important aspect of wartime film-making, but also a key aspect of dealing with the uncertainties of social and economic change in peacetime.

Two related problems for the British film industry which had been endemic since the 1920s were the domination by Hollywood and the chronic lack of finance for film production, and these continued to be underlying pressures throughout the post-war period. Hollywood studios, anxious to preserve their market position abroad, developed favourable exhibition arrangements with the two main cinema chains in Britain, ABC and Gaumont-Odeon. Between them they owned over 1000 cinemas, about a quarter of the total in the country, and a third of all seating capacity. More important for the producers was the proportion of prime-sites and first-run houses owned by the two major circuits, since they produced the highest returns. By 1946 ABC was controlled by Warner Brothers, and for two-thirds of the year showed MGM films, while the Gaumont and Odeon groups, nominally separate, but both controlled by Rank after 1942, had a similar arrangement with Twentieth-Century Fox.

American films had continued to be imported during the war, but the British feature film industry had developed sufficiently to warrant some optimism about developments in the post-war period. There was a continuing belief that film was a key element in the national culture, and with 30 million admissions every year, cinema was a major element in the general education of the population. The problem, as in the previous decades, was how to develop further the productive capacity of the British film industry to compete at a qualitative level with Hollywood films.

The 'quota' system still operated whereby a certain percentage of British-made films had to be exhibited, but these were often 'quota-quickies', cheap films, financed by American companies, to fulfil the terms of the legislation of 1927, which had been further amended to protect the industry in 1938. However, the protection had never been achieved because of the exigencies of wartime production, particularly the shortage of film stock. Films made in America were able to satisfy the demand.

Independent British producers also found it difficult to obtain distribution since J. Arthur Rank through control of General Film Distributors, the main agency in Britain, had a major stake in the distribution of British and American films to cinemas outside his own Odeon–Gaumont interests. There were in fact few film producers who did not have a financial or distribution arrangement with Rank by 1946, the most famous being Sir Alexander Korda, who had entered into a financing arrangement with MGM. However, the monopolistic structure developed by Rank, while causing dismay in some quarters, did not solve the problem of production finance, since not enough money returned from the box-office to film producers once other groups in the industry, and particularly the government, through an Entertainments Tax, had taken their share. Even if the number of American films distributed in Britain had been restricted it was unlikely that the industry had the capacity to fill the gap.

An opportunity to test this assumption arose in August 1947 when the Labour government, faced with a balance-of-payments crisis and a shortage of American dollars, appeared to attempt to solve two problems with one measure. By imposing a 75 per cent duty on all foreign films imported into Britain the government hoped to stem the flow of dollars out of the country through the distribution profits of American production companies, amounting in 1947 to $70 million. The restriction on trade, it was felt, would encourage British producers and offer opportunities for exhibition.

The weakness of the British government's position, and that of the film industry were demonstrated in the next few months as Hollywood studios held back new films, but continued to distribute old productions on which no tax was levied. At the same time Rank announced a substantial investment of over £9 million in 'first-feature' films which were intended not only to replace American productions in Britain but also to challenge Hollywood films in the

United States. It was a case of misplaced optimism since the domestic market was still dominated by American productions, and counter-measures could be taken to restrict the distribution of British films in America, irrespective of how popular they were likely to be.

In March 1948 the government lifted the punitive tax, imposing instead a 45 per cent quota of screen time for British films and within a year setting up the National Film Finance Corporation with a budget of £5 million. An industry producing something like fifty feature films in 1947 was asked to triple that number by 1949. It was quite incapable of meeting the demand and many cinemas gained exemption from the quota restrictions. The failure to produce quantity was matched by a decline in quality and subsequent disappointment for the exhibitors. The result were further economic losses for producers, and Rank was in serious trouble by 1949, while Korda was baled out to the tune of over £2 million by the National Film Finance Corporation. Both producers had staked the future of the British industry on high-budget productions which would find a market outside Britain. Unfortunately, as Korda found in the 1930s, the quality required could not be maintained, and the domestic market was not large enough to secure a return on the capital costs. Furthermore, the aggressive marketing characteristics of Hollywood, faced with their own major problems, made it virtually impossible for Rank and Korda to succeed.

Whereas the crisis in the American film industry had occurred because of external political pressures and internal restructuring which led to a general undermining of confidence, the problem in Britain arose out of the underlying financial weakness and the inability of politicians to create a viable industrial structure. In both cases they became even more vulnerable to the challenge from television as audiences were lost and revenues declined further. It would, however, be another decade before the two industries became virtually inseparable and British film production was essentially based upon finance from the United States.

It is important to remember that during the period of internal crisis in the late 1940s and early 1950s the industry in Britain produced some of its most creative and successful films. Independent producers under the aegis of the Rank Organisation were given the opportunity to develop subjects and particular styles: Carol Reed with *The Third Man*, David Lean with *Great Expectations* and *Oliver Twist*, Michael Powell with *A Matter of Life and Death* and *The Red*

Shoes. However, the most continuously successful producer, both critically and financially, was Michael Balcon, who made Ealing Studios a community of film-makers representing his ideal version of Britain in the post-war period; a group of people applying traditional creative strengths and outlooks to new problems.

Although it was necessary for Ealing to have a distribution and financing arrangement with Rank, Balcon rejected his expansionist outlooks, preferring to concentrate on satisfying the domestic audience with his necessarily small-scale studio organisation. The overseas success was a welcome bonus, apparently vindicating Balcon's view that any film must be rooted in specific 'national' values to be successful. It is in the output of Ealing in the late 1940s that one can recognise the continuity of outlook from war into peacetime. It was the construction of an idea of Britain and the British people, often utilising the talents of documentary-makers, but within the context of fictional films. Comedy and fantasy scenarios were placed in realistic settings of the post-war period allowing the release of present tensions in a form of escapism. Underlying the films was an attitude about the inherent virtues of the British, a view which emphasised aspects of the past, traditional and artisanal, rather than reflective of the present or looking to the future.

At a time when the economic and political power of Britain had declined the essential goodness of her people was allowed to shine through. As in the war, the homogeneity of the community appeared preferable to the disputes in other parts of the world. While ideological tensions appeared to be tearing the United States apart, the commonsense attitudes of the British allowed all groups to work together.

It might be argued that the popularity of the films demonstrated not only their quality, but also the way they engaged with deep feelings which had been engendered by the war, and encouraged by propaganda during the conflict. By the early 1950s reconstructions of the wartime experience were being produced in all the British studios; for instance, *The Cruel Sea* and *The Dambusters* emphasising the characteristics of the nation in fighting and winning the war, particularly the individual contribution to the common good.

In many ways the ideals of the British documentary film-makers of the 1930s had at last been taken up by the commercial cinema, but in a sentimental and essentially escapist form. The demand that film should be a key element in civic education was heard again in the aftermath of war, articulated particularly by those who had seen their work neglected before 1939. However, the structure of the industry offered little scope for the development of the factual film since production and distribution were geared to features, and the Labour government took little interest in developing the genre within the framework of the Central Office of Information.

The Crown Film Unit had been incorporated within the COI but there was no clear direction for its activities, since money and ideas for films had to come from separate ministries. Personnel moved into feature film production as it expanded in the late 1940s, reinforcing the influence of documentary techniques, but without the commitment to education which had been the hallmark of the purist. Documentaries could only be made successfully when sponsorship was available and access to distribution facilities assured; circumstances which only obtained during the war.

The spirit and outlook of documentary film-makers found its way into the medium which began to challenge the cinema, television. Within the context of public service broadcasting there was scope for the development of a documentary form which could attempt to investigate and explain contemporary issues to a wide audience. Those who argued for the factual film in the 1940s were still fighting the battles of the 1930s, but the terms of the struggle were changing rapidly. Nevertheless, the importance of film as a means of propaganda, and the idea of a continuity of experience from one decade to another, had been reinforced by a seminal work published in America by a German refugee.

In 1947 Siegfried Kracauer published a study of the German cinema during the Weimar and National Socialist period which was to stand as an exemplar of a particular form of film analysis. Kracauer had been an influential critic on the *Frankfurter Zeitung* but had emigrated to the United States from Germany in the 1930s and was particularly associated with the Frankfurt School of cultural criticism. In *From Caligari to Hitler*, he sought to investigate how films reflected 'psychological dispositions – those deep layers of collective mentality which extend more or less below the dimension of consciousness.' He believed that the study of films from the period would uncover a national mentality, with which the films engaged, and would make understandable the rise of Hitler and the National Socialists, as well as the failure of democracy in Germany, a concern of particular importance to those exiled by the National Socialist regime.

Kracauer's 'psychological history of the German cinema', the subtitle of his book, was intended not merely as an explanation of the past, but also as a key to the study of contemporary mass society in the United States. It had originated as a contribution to the study of psychological warfare against Germany and constructed a model of society around the 'anonymous mass' and the possibility of its manipulation by others. There was no reason, Kracauer argued, why the same analysis could not be applied to the United States, or to the cultural reorganisation of societies after the war.

Although the work can be studied for its influence on critical attitudes towards film and society over the next twenty years it stands as an intellectual indicator of the continuing belief in the United States about the political and social influence of the cinema industry in the 1940s. By emphasising the psychological dimension of the cinema and the ways in which particular needs, political and emotional, were gratified through the reiteration of specific themes, Kracauer offered ammunition to those who had less altruistic motives for considering the role of Hollywood films and film-makers in American society.

Studio owners, and their financial backers, had developed strategies over many years for dealing with pressure groups and lobbies who sought to control their product, while at the same time taking note of the reaction of the consumer at the box-office. This combination of political nous and business acumen had served them well during the war years. They were able to satisfy the desires of those, particularly in government circles, who looked for a patriotic commitment in the output from Hollywood and found it in the stereotypical Germans and Japanese, the external enemies of the United States. After 1942 there was a greater problem in representing another ideological enemy, but present ally, Soviet Russia. This was achieved by emphasising the personal bravery and humanitarian beliefs of individual Russians, illustrating their common bonds with the Americans.

While the number of films dealing in explicit propaganda was small, the war impinged on many of the productions in different ways, not least in the inflationary costs of film-making. Hollywood sought to satisfy the constant demand for entertainment from a domestic audience which was enjoying an increased standard of living as a result of the developing war economy. While musicals and romances continued to be produced, often with a war theme, one genre became particularly associated with 1940s Hollywood, *film noir*. Often based on detective stories and thrillers, and regularly directed by expatriate Europeans such as Fritz Lang and Billy Wilder, they had a distinctive style based upon lighting, sets and the presentation of character, particularly women. While partly the result of war economies in the studios, they also represented a different form of narrative presentation.

The emphasis in the films was on the crisis of the individual, trapped in a hostile world and uncertain of friends and enemies. They created and investigated the 'psychological dispositions' of the characters, offering few solutions for their predicaments, and portraying personal relationships in a pessimistic light. While not being the most popular box-office attractions in the 1940s they became bench-marks of film style, and represented a development in cinema which appeared to reflect at a personal level the underlying ideological tensions in society which on the international stage became known colloquially as the 'Cold War'.

The underlying ideological antagonism between Soviet Russia and the United States which had lain dormant for much of the previous thirty years was made manifest in the confrontation in Europe over the post-war settlement, particularly in Germany. It was a confrontation complicated by the preponderance of military and economic power held by the United States, and the need for that power to construct an international policy in the post-war world with little information from or about Russia. Given the overwhelming strength of the United States, it was felt by many people that the only real weapon available to the Soviets was the ideological undermining of American society. For this the Hollywood cinema appeared to be a key factor.

It is important to place the work of Kracauer and other determinist theorists of the mass media within this atmosphere of suspicion and doubt. They were establishing, within social scientific terms, the efficacy of the message in securing specific effects on an audience, even at the subconscious level. Questions about the possibility of brainwashing became more prevalent, particularly with reference to the cinema and its apparent psychological power. What had been assumed about the cinema by many people for decades appeared to be proved, but it now took on a wider political significance. Whereas in the 1930s there was discussion of Communist influence in the film industry, particularly in the period of the New Deal and during labour disputes, there was no widespread concern. The articulation of this came in 1940 with the inception of the House Committee on Un-American Affairs (HUAC) under its chairman, Martin Dies.

His enquiries into the activities of particular individuals in Hollywood marked the beginning of the legislature's specific interest in the industry, and particularly in the beliefs and outlooks of important artistic members of the community. During the war they were able to display their loyalty, but in the developing cold war period it was more difficult to be categorical when it came to motives and attitudes behind specific actions. It could be argued that *film noir* reflected as much the inner conflict inside an industry where, after 1945, it was difficult to decide who were enemies and who were friends.

The HUAC public hearings, in October 1947, on the extent of Communist influence in Hollywood had been well prepared by the chairman, Parnell Thomas. He had used the internal struggles among the unions, and disputes among actors and producers, both personal and professional, to assemble a range of witnesses who appeared to be 'friendly' to the aims of the investigation, which was the eradication of all Communist influence, in whatever form. In pre-hearing enquiries names of 'unfriendly' witnesses had been gathered, and they were subpoenaed to appear before the committee. Ten refused to answer the key question of whether at any time they had been members of the Communist Party and as a result were indicted for contempt of Congress. They took their stand on the symbol of the First Amendment and the right of free speech, but subsequently found themselves in prison, and blacklisted in the industry.

The unwillingness of the Hollywood Ten, as they became known, to testify signalled the end of the hearings, but not of the general campaign to root out supposed Communists in the industry. Faced with continuing scrutiny by anti-Communist groups, and aware of the danger of guilt by association, the major producers blacklisted those personnel who refused to answer questions about their past political affiliations. However, the climate of accusation and unsubstantiated innuendo passing for evidence lasted for many years, destroying careers and undermining the confidence of the industry as a whole.

The investigation of Hollywood was only one aspect of a general intention among some groups in the United States to 'weed out' Communist influence in all public institutions, particularly the State Department. It was not a campaign orchestrated by the administration, but reflected more the ways in which groups in a free society were able to utilise the institutions of government to further their aims and restrict other peoples' freedom of opinion. By focusing on Hollywood, and establishing what appeared to be clear cases of subversive influence, anti-Communist activists secured maximum publicity and further legitimisation for their activities.

The success of the film industry had been based upon a confidence to predict what would sell in the market, but now the new pressures of public scrutiny affected the choice of stories, writers, actors and treatments. Divisions in the industry, exacerbated by these tensions, only added to another fundamental change which affected its basic organisation.

Between 1947 and 1950 under anti-trust legislation the major studios were forced to sell their interests in cinemas, thus breaking the monopolistic structure which allowed a secure domestic market for their products. The fixed capital costs of the studio complexes required continuous production, but in the uncertain climate of the late 1940s this became more difficult to sustain. In 1946 the American film industry had achieved its highest penetration into a potential audience, and highest box-office returns: within four years there were clear signs that this predominant position in the field of entertainment would be difficult to maintain. In 1951 it was noted that in cities with television stations, cinema audiences had dropped by up to 40 per cent. In those without television, audience figures remained stable. Once the block on the proliferation of stations was lifted by the FCC the future of the industry would be in jeopardy.

While production in Hollywood was cut back in the face of these problems the development of television offered more secure employment for some actors, writers and technicians, thus draining-off further talent from the industry. However, not all the personnel made redundant by Hollywood were welcome in broadcasting, since the anti-Communist crusade began to target the network radio for closer investigation.

The attack on broadcasting is less well known than that on Hollywood, but was much more specific, with the publication, in 1950, of a book, *Red Channels*, which named 151 persons who had been associated with liberal, socialist or New Deal causes in the past. This, in the eyes of the author, was tantamount to Communist sympathy. Although many of the charges were ludicrous, the networks found it propitious to bow to such pressure in the future employment of named personnel, however prestigious their position in the broadcasting world.

The HUAC hearings had been conducted at a time when United States foreign policy was at its most assertive with the enunciation of the Truman Doctrine in March 1947, promising aid military or economic to countries threatened by Communist aggression. However, the 'revelations' of 1950 appeared at a time of the greatest national insecurity. China, the key to American foreign policy in the Far East, had been taken over by a Communist government in 1949 and in the same year the United States armaments superiority was undermined when the USSR exploded an atom bomb. The trial and conviction of Alger Hiss, a State Department official, appeared to justify claims of Communist subversion within the administration itself.

In February 1950, some months before the publication of *Red Channels*, Joseph McCarthy, a rather nondescript Senator from Wisconsin, started his meteoric rise to fame with the delivery of a speech in West Virginia, in which he claimed to know of 205 members of the Communist Party in the State Department, but he did not name names; *Red Channels* did. Its publication also coincided with the opening of the Korean War, which demonstrated to many Americans the overt threat of aggressive Communism in the world.

While many people disliked McCarthy as a person, and abhorred his methods of vilification and innuendo in investigating areas of public life, they sympathised with his declared motive of securing the national security of the United States, and the principles on which it was founded. In reality he negated ideas of rationality and freedom of expression, and utilised the forms of mass communication devoted to these democratic principles in order to further his career.

The attacks on broadcasting personnel contained in *Red Channels* clearly affected the attitudes of network executives towards the general phenomenon which became known as 'McCarthyism'. As had happened in Hollywood, internecine quarrels within the network organisations produced leaks to McCarthy's organisation. Fearful of the effect on audiences and advertisers of being branded as 'disloyal', let alone 'traitorous', the networks and advertising agencies sought to protect their organisations by discreetly compiling black-lists of individuals, and developing an editorial system of referral upwards for all forms of broadcast material.

The company which produced *Red Channels* had no particular links with McCarthy, apart from sharing a virulent anti-Communist stance. It published a weekly newsletter, *Counterattack*, which con-tinued to name individuals, including Raymond Gram Swing, a distinguished newspaper and radio journalist, after he had the courage publicly to debate the issue with T. C. Kirkpatrick, secretary-treasurer of American Business Consultants, which pro-duced both publications. Many people, including Swing, wondered why the doyen of liberal news commentators, Edward R. Murrow, declined to take on McCarthy, particularly since there was no other journalist in the United States who had proved his loyalty so clearly in the Second World War, and had such a secure position within a network.

By the 1950s Murrow had become the epitome of the committed radio journalist, not only to many Americans, through his reports from Britain and Europe during the Second World War, but also to many Europeans who had been impressed by his integrity, conviction and lucidity. Throughout the war Murrow had consistently argued the virtues of liberal democracy. He saw himself as more than a mere reporter and he used radio in wartime as a means of political education, particularly in his attitude towards the Axis powers. He brought the horror of the European war home to many Americans through the masterly use of language and a clear, commanding delivery. Murrow personified the CBS network, whose main strength during this period lay in its News Division, and he developed a strong personal relationship with the network founder, Bill Paley. Furthermore, Murrow's friendship with Allied statesmen and mili-tary leaders added a further cachet to the reputation of Paley's network.

A study of Murrow's broadcasting career in the 1940s and 1950s underlines the continuity between the Second World War and the Cold War period. He made use of the medium of radio at a time when it had become the primary source of news for the majority of the population in the United States and he made use of the opportunity to explore its power, and carried his expertise and authority into the post-war period. In his own case, to be distanced from the war effort inside the United States allowed him more

freedom post-war, since he had not been associated with organisations which had been attempts to create solidarity with the Soviet
Union, but in the late 1940s were seen by many, with a somewhat
prejudiced hindsight, as elements in a Communist conspiracy. Yet
he had to rethink his position as a broadcaster when faced with the
development of television and Paley's all-out attempt to make CBS
the primary entertainment network. It was during this period that
the McCarthy challenge was at its most virulent, and Murrow's
early reticence in dealing with the issue might have arisen from not
knowing how best to use the new medium, or how secure he was
with Paley.

The first problem was solved in collaboration with Fred Friendly,
who had worked with Murrow on transferring his radio documentaries, *Hear It Now*, to records, and from 1951 produced the
television version, *See It Now*. As a weekly half-hour programme it
offered an opportunity to stand back from the immediate news and
investigate specific topics. In October 1953, Murrow and Friendly
concentrated on the case of Milo Radulovich, who had been
dismissed from the airforce on the basis of innuendo. Soon after the
transmission Radulovich was reinstated.

In March 1954 *See It Now* dealt with the phenomenon of McCarthy.
It was a classic use of the new medium; editing together filmed
material of hearings chaired by the Senator, showing his rudeness
and bullying tactics. The champion of freedom was shown as a loud-
mouthed tyrant, full of bluster, but of little substance. Even in the
programme McCarthy made as a right-to-reply he was unable to
rebut the impression created by the Murrow programme. The visual
images of television were crucial in creating this reality, but *See It
Now* did not destroy McCarthy: it did, however, serve to undermine
his credibility, which was totally eroded by his performance in the
televised hearings against the army some months later.

While the end of McCarthy and Murrow's role in his demise may
be considered as an important aspect in the early history of television
it may also be seen as the end of an era in wartime journalism.
Murrow trod less securely in the uncertainties of the Cold War
period than he had between 1940 and 1945, and he found the
importance of informational broadcasting, in which he believed,
being undermined by the economic requirements of a network which
needed to compete in the expensive world of television. While Paley
and other CBS executives applauded the McCarthy programme

after its transmission, they had distanced themselves from the project beforehand, and within months investigative television journalism was given a lower priority in scheduling. If the worst excesses of the Cold War mentality had been extinguished with McCarthy, the political, economic and social uncertainties of the post-war world allowed little scope for others to follow Murrow's lead. The *See It Now* programme on McCarthy may be seen as the end of an era rather than a beginning.

McCarthy eventually fell because he was unable to control the publicity machine which had served him so well over four years. Not least of those who had prepared the ground for 'McCarthyism', and had been tardy in investigating its excesses, was the American press, particularly the newspapers of the Hearst organisation. In the 1930s Hearst himself had spearheaded campaigns against Communists, and encouraged the kind of tactics among his reporters which were refined to an art by McCarthy and his associates. Needless to say that in the atmosphere of the early 1950s the Senator from Wisconsin was able to secure favourable coverage, not only in these papers, but also in others which competed for an audience, and recognised McCarthy as news. News agencies were anxious to pick up quotes and accusations, and rush them on to the wires without checking their factual basis.

Henry Luce, the proprietor of *Time* magazine, had every reason to be sympathetic to McCarthy's aims since, as a conservative and an old China expert, he was appalled by the events of 1949, and had particular targets in the administration. He advocated 'subjective journalism', and 'fairness'; the creative use of facts in order to produce an understandable story. The question was how far 'fairness' would be allowed to intrude into Luce's own areas of prejudice. The answer was not at all.

The use by McCarthy and his associates of the press and broadcasting media to publicise their activities brought into focus once more the question of press responsibility, and its role in a democracy. The problem had been stated by the Hutchings Commission in 1947. Firstly, that few people had access to the press and could express an opinion; secondly, that the press as a whole provided a poor service for society; and thirdly, that the organisers of the press had sometimes engaged in activities inimical to the best interests of society. It is ironical that the initial suggestion for such a Commission, looking into the present state and future prospects of the freedom of the press, had come from Henry Luce in 1942, and the bulk of the money for the enquiry was donated by Time, Inc. The Commission, under the chairmanship of Robert Hutchings, the Chancellor of the University of Chicago, was completely independent, and had among its members Harold Lasswell, who had wide experience of propaganda; Arthur Schlesinger, the historian; and the theologian, Reinhold Niebuhr. Its foreign advisers included John Grierson. The result of their deliberations was a series of reports, published in 1946 and 1947, which covered not only the newspaper press but also radio broadcasting and the film industry.

The Commission's work was essentially concerned with the role of the mass media as public educators, an issue of particular relevance in wartime, and the reorganisation of societies in the post-war period. Although the Commission did recognise the importance of the effect of the mass media on culture, the concerns voiced by Lippmann in the aftermath of the First World War still held a predominant position in thinking about the media. They found it hard to reconcile the inalienable right of newspapers to report without prior restraint with the needs of liberal democratic society to be reliably informed.

The fact that Robert McCormick, publisher of the very successful *Chicago Tribune*, arch-conservative, anti-Communist and polemicist, was the chairman of the committee on the freedom of the press of the American Newspaper Publishers Association for over twenty years will give some idea of the difficulties which the Commission faced in providing a solution to this problem. Rather than a guide to future practice the reports stand as a comprehensive record of the economic, social and legal position of the mass media in the United States at a time when the issues of freedom and responsibility were to take on new relevance.

The role of the Commission as an independent fact-finding and policy-orientating agency was very similar to that of Political and Economic Planning (PEP) in Great Britain. This group had been responsible for the first major report on the British press in April 1938, and had voiced similar concerns to those developed by the Hutchings Commission, particularly the question of concentration of ownership, political influence, and journalistic responsibility. The question was how far a democratic government would feel it right or proper to intervene, except in the most extreme cases, in the organisation of the press. As we have noted, the Second World War raised specific problems, but with the peace, and a reorganisation of many aspects of social and economic life under a Labour government the question of the role and future of the British press once more became a political issue, particularly since the bulk of newspapers were against the government.

The result was the appointment of a Royal Commission (1948/49), set up by Parliament, to investigate the issues set out already in the PEP Report of 1938. While broadcasting in Britain had been the subject of a number of enquiries, and was to undergo yet another in 1949, there was no attempt to consider the general links between the two forms of media. The Royal Commission looked back rather than forwards, investigating, often from a position of ignorance, and with the active hostility of press proprietors, an industry endeavouring to recover from wartime controls. The only concrete result of its work was the eventual establishment of a Press Council, a tribunal from within the industry charged with policing the activities of journalists and newspapers. It was an attempt, within a democracy, to create a framework of 'responsible journalism' without the intervention of the state. Any success it might have had depended upon the willingness of publishers and owners to abide by certain rules of professional conduct and impress these upon their journalists. By the time the Press Council had begun its work in the middle 1950s the advent of commercial television had begun to change the character of the newspaper industry by challenging its commercial viability and assumptions about its future role in British society.

While the United States and Britain came to terms with the post-war world it was the defeated Germany which became a social laboratory in which liberal theories about the mass media in society could be tested. Unconditional surrender in May 1945 left the country in the hands of four powers: the United States, Britain, the USSR, and France. Germany was divided into four zones of occupation, to be ruled over and administered by each of the Allies through a military commander and his staff. Working through a joint Allied Control Council they were all committed to the continued existence of Germany as a unitary whole, although the political and administrative structure of the country was to be decentralised. The success of these general aims depended upon cooperation between the commanders, and their ability to cope with the catastrophic economic, social and political situation which faced them in central Europe.

The more immediate problems lay in the reconstruction of some form of civilised existence in a country which was economically exhausted, with a dislocated transport network, millions of displaced people, and shortages of all the necessities of life, particularly food and fuel. There was little time for reflection and consultation, and the requirement to utilise the human and physical resources in the country itself made nonsense of the directive issued by the United States government to its military commander, General Clay. On the basis of this document, the German people in the American zone were to continue to be treated as hostile enemies, and dealt with through a policy of non-fraternisation, de-Nazification and de-industrialisation.

None of these policies could be put into operation successfully since any rehabilitation depended on cooperation with the occupied people, but behind their formulation lay an image of Germany and the Germans which had been constructed during the war, and even earlier. They were perceived as a nation of pariahs, who deserved to be punished, a view which was reinforced by the evidence from the concentration camps. The question was how they might be incorporated again into the international community after experiencing the excesses of National Socialism? The answer lay in something called 're-education'.

It was a word which appears to have entered the vocabulary of diplomats and administrators during the war, suggesting that fundamental outlooks about the nature of society would be susceptible to change. It was argued by some that it would not be enough merely to alter the political structure of Germany, as had happened after the First World War. They believed that underlying cultural and political outlooks and beliefs from the nineteenth century had been allowed to exist in Weimar Germany, and had then been rearticulated in the nationalism and militarism of Hitler and his followers. It would require a more fundamental approach to the reconstruction of society to alter these attitudes; in effect, the rebuilding of minds. If, as many believed, Hitler had propagandised the German people into following him, it should be possible to reorientate them with a new kind of propaganda prepared by the Allies. They had, as Clay himself believed, to penetrate the German consciousness.

This general attitude was certainly shared and promulgated by British officials and politicians. They envisaged an opportunity to inculcate into German public life political and civic virtues which were inherently British, not least the idea of 'objective reporting'. It was a worthy aim, which in hindsight might appear patronising, but in the aftermath of war seemed to be absolutely necessary. The question in 1945 was how far there could be general agreement among the Allies on what was the 'objective' reality of the situation, and whether they too wished to put forward 'British' virtues? For instance, the French also had clear plans for their zone, which included cultural orientation towards France, and economic exploitation. The Russians, with a wholly different ideological outlook, were likely to agree on the need for 're-education', but within the context of a socialist society.

The main political aim of the USSR was to seek revenge on the Germans, while destroying the old economic structure of Germany and consolidating its own position in the future political organisation of the country. One example of the combination of these motives was the Russian claim for immediate reparations, which had been agreed at international conferences, but which was clearly detrimental to the economic rehabilitation of Germany. Machinery and goods were shipped out to Russia, not only from its own zone, but from those of Britain and the United States, under the agreements. It was an immediate source of friction in the Allied Control Council and by the spring of 1946 reparations payments to the Russians from the British and American zones had been stopped, and cooperation at all levels became even more difficult. A common industrial and economic policy was impossible to implement, and an *ad hoc* decentralisation of Germany began to take place, based upon the zonal organisations.

The problem of Germany became the touchstone of relationships in the Cold War. The developing division of the country exemplified in practical terms the ideological split in international society: the failure to reach agreement in Europe was blamed on the attitudes and policies of the other powers. It is within this context that one has to place the 're-education' of the German people; eventually it was to be part of the propaganda battle of the Cold War.

The mass media were only one element in the process of 're-education'. The first task was the process of de-Nazification, the identification of those who had actively worked for the regime, and their removal from public life. It was an almost impossible task considering the number of people involved at many levels in the organisation of the National Socialist state, but there was an immediate necessity to find personnel to provide an administrative infrastructure in the zones.

Another key area was the reorganisation of school and university education. Buildings had been destroyed, teachers had to be put through the de-Nazification procedures and textbooks rewritten. The French were particularly assiduous in these activities and were responsible for the foundation of a new university at Mainz. There was a clear belief that French *civilisation* would prove superior to any future manifestation of German *Kultur*.

The third element in the 're-education' process was the utilisation of the mass media, particularly press and radio. In the immediate aftermath of war the military forces established German-language newspapers which, in the case of the American Army, were originally produced by the Psychological Warfare Division. Few lasted after 1949, the honourable exception being *Die Welt* which attempted to present the best features of the British press, but was always regarded as an occupation paper by the Germans, and was eventually sold to Axel Springer in 1953. Irrespective of the policy of non-fraternisation it was considered imperative to involve Germans in press production as soon as possible, and on 31 July 1945 the *Frankfurter Rundschau* was licensed in the American zone.

In the western zones there were two interrelated aspects to any press policy, both of which were key elements in the protection of freedom of the press. Firstly, the need to produce an economic and journalistic infrastructure which could present 'objective' news. Secondly, to determine the relationship between this structure and the state. The model which they sought to remove for ever was of the state-orientated, monopolistic press of the National Socialist period and under the occupation the German press reverted to a regional and local structure, reflecting the decentralising policies of the Allies.

Licences to publish newspapers were offered to individuals and groups who could prove they had no association with the previous regime. It was a difficult task, but the Russians and Americans began immediately, and by July 1946 there were 38 licensed German newspapers in the US zone. The British were much slower, not giving their first licence until January 1946, but they initiated a somewhat different policy from the Americans, specifically attempting to create a balanced political press by licensing groups supporting the different political parties in each *Land*. This was not seen as the development of a political press, but rather as a way to increase political dialogue which would encourage debate and the genuine growth of democratic institutions from the grass roots.

Shortages of newsprint and distribution difficulties were recurrent problems for all newspapers, but since the occupation authorities took responsibility for solving these problems the commercial aspects were not pre-eminent. In 1948 the currency reform in the western zones posed some temporary problems since the cost of newsprint rose and demand fell, but with increased economic activity amounts of advertising increased. With the end of licensing restrictions it was clear that newspapers could once more become sources of profit. The licensing system in the western zones had restricted commercial competition, allowing newspapers and magazines to concentrate on their educational role. This was further encouraged by the scrutiny of newspapers by press officers after publication. The system of control did inhibit criticism of the occupying authorities, but not necessarily of those in another zone, as the British discovered from newspapers published in the Russian area.

Licensing of newspapers was seen as a temporary measure, to be continued until the reorganised *Land* legislatures passed suitable laws guaranteeing freedom of the press. There was no uniformity on this issue between the three western zones, or indeed between the *Länder* which they administered, and the question dragged on until 1949 when, with the establishment of the Federal Republic (FRG), freedom of opinion was embodied in the Basic Law. However, through the federal character of the state, responsiblity for the regulation of the press still lay with the *Land* within the general framework of the Basic Law.

The Federal Republic had only limited autonomy between 1949 and 1955 when it was declared a sovereign state, and until then the Allied High Commissioners, civilians who had replaced the military commanders, had the general right to protect freedom of opinion in the state. There had been a fear that delicensing of newspapers would allow new publishers to appear who represented older traditions in the German press. In fact the majority of licensed papers were able to withstand the competition, having established secure circulations. However, in the next few years there would be a growing concentration of ownership and a clearer pattern of large papers with local editions, giving the impression of independence, but with no editorial organisation of their own. Economic considerations would undermine the diversity of outlook which had been the aim of the western allies.

Diversity had also been allowed in the Soviet occupation zone after 1945, although only accredited politial parties had been given licences to produce newspapers. The amalgamation of the Communist and Socialist Parties into the Socialist Unity Party (SED) in April 1946 led to the publication of *Neues Deutschland*, which continues to be the main newspaper for the German Democratic Republic (GDR). Other papers found more difficulties in obtaining newsprint, and after the amalgamation of all parties in an anti-Fascist front in 1948 there was little need for any which followed a non-Socialist line although they continued to survive.

The growth of conformity was encouraged after the establishment of the GDR in 1949. The ruling SED group saw the need for a press which articulated more clearly the needs of the party, and the control of content and outlook became more rigid. As in other authoritarian societies the press was seen not as an area of debate but as a tool of government, and crucial in constructing a society which offered an alternative social and economic outlook to that in the West.

While the tangible and intellectual quality of newspapers seemed to give them a pre-eminence in the 're-education' of the German people after 1945, radio broadcasting had a more immediate impact, and was of more importance in presenting an accurate picture of conditions inside Germany as the occupation proceeded. Although faced with almost insuperable technical difficulties, since many studios and transmitters had been destroyed, the zonal military authorities had a workable service in operation within days of the capitulation. These broadcasts provided essential information to the population which still had radios.

The future organisation of broadcasting was now in the hands of the occupying powers, and as with the press there was no unified view among the Allies except the need to decentralise the structure. This precluded the transmission of an all-Germany service which would have had to be transmitted from Koenigs Westerhausen which lay in Soviet-occupied territory. As a result developments in each zone followed the inclinations of the authorities who set up stations on the model of their own domestic experience. In the case of the Americans this meant regionalising the service with four separate stations, while the British and French centralised activities with one main broadcasting organisation, *Nordwestdeutscher Rundfunk* (*NWDR*) in the British zone based on Hamburg and Cologne, and *Südwestfunk* in the French zone. *NWDR* was also responsible for a service in Berlin.

While there were different patterns of organisation in all three zones there was agreement over financing and the relationship with the state. The 'public-service' outlook of the BBC was taken as the model for new broadcasting organisations, a view of the function of broadcasting in society which admirably suited the idea of 're-education'. Finance was to come through licence fees collected by the Post Office, thus obviating the worst excesses of the commercial system, and state intervention was precluded by the institution of intermediary boards responsible, with the controller, for running the station. The *Länder* were given legal responsibility for broadcasting, so emphasising its decentralised character, and weakening any possible attempt by the future federal government to intervene in this area. Furthermore, it was hoped that the regional nature of broadcasting would encourage cultural outlooks which were more diverse, and representative of a pluralist society.

From 1946 to 1949 responsibility for broadcasting was gradually handed over to Germans, until with the foundation of the Federal Republic the three zonal structures came together. Only then was it possible to consider the diversity in size and organisation between the stations, and attempt to reconcile them within a structure which represented the needs of the new republic, rather than those of the occupation authorities. However, in the case of the GDR there was little real problem in the change-over of power, since the organisation of broadcasting had increasingly come under the aegis of the SED, a prelude to the centralisation in Berlin in the early 1950s. As with the press, broadcasting in the GDR truly had an educational function, in presenting a particular picture of the world to the population of the state; however, the technology of the medium allowed other voices to be heard, and made it more difficult for Germans in the Soviet zone to be isolated without resorting to jamming foreign broadcasts. Once again, Germany was in the front line of the Cold War.

Any attempt to 're-educate' a nation could only be undertaken with a belief in the efficacy of the methods and the malleability of the subjects. Preconceptions about the nature of the Germans and the power of propaganda were necessary starting points for that attempt in the 1940s, but irrespective of the ludicrous character of the proposition, Germany in the post-war period was not an ideal laboratory for practical experiments in social engineering. Germany had become a power vacuum, suffering a complete breakdown of all forms of social, economic and political activity, but the German people were not passive, and could recognise that they held the key to the future organisation of Europe. In the late 1940s, through their leaders, the German people negotiated for their future survival as a political grouping, but within the parameters allowed them by the Cold War. In the end 're-education' became the orientation of German public life towards the ideological outlook of the occupying power; accepted because they agreed, not because they had changed. The success of each system in the end depended less upon the propaganda than upon the forms of coercion and economic success.

Between 1939 and 1945 the mass media in Britain, Germany and the United States had been mobilised as part of the machinery of state to fight not only in an armed conflict but also an ideological struggle. The influence of the media was little understood, but a number of assumptions underlay their use by governments, notably the belief in the persuasive power of propaganda once it had entered the mind of the recipient. The control of information was clearly linked to the control of the institutions which acted as channels into society, and in the conditions of wartime the rights of governments to intervene were recognised, even in a democracy. However, the active proponents of propaganda were themselves experimenting with forms, and developing the role of the institutions during the war.

In its aftermath they were in a position to aid the task of reconstruction, not least in the field of psychological rebuilding. However, they were then part of an ideological war in which the mass media appeared to be the main battlefield, where the enemy was less clear, and the coherence of the home front less certain. One unifying element in the 1940s is that the United States and Britain created a propaganda machine to fight a war and then dismantled it, only to find themselves embroiled in a battle of ideologies with another authoritarian society. As the press and cinema learned to adjust to the new conditions of the post-war world they found another threat in the development of television.

8. The Age of Television

In the second half of the twentieth century television has become the primary focus of discussions about the role of the mass media in society. The reason lies in the specific character of the medium; its immediacy, universality, and placing within the domestic environment. It has also combined and developed other forms of cultural and social communication, particularly the popular cinema, journalism and advertising. Sound broadcasting acted as both a stimulus and a deterrent to this development. Observers in the 1920s recognised the potential power of a combination of pictures and sound transmitted into the home and in some cases they actively encouraged research. They were also aware of the technical and financial problems, particularly at a time when sound broadcasting still had to be established as a viable form of social communication.

As with other complex technologies, there was no one inventor of television, although in their more xenophobic moments nations have claimed a prime role for their own scientific pioneers. Many individuals conducting pure research in electrical and chemical engineering at the turn of the century were providing the elements required for the efficient transmission of visual images. While many individual researchers developed the mechanical system, using a scanning dish demonstrated by Paul Nipkow, a German, in 1884, others, including Boris Rosing in Russia and Campbell-Swinton in Britain, recognised the importance of the cathode-ray tube in the process of scanning an object electronically, offering, potentially, a high-definition picture quality.

None of them were close to devising a workable system of transmission before 1914, but in the aftermath of war individuals began to investigate more closely the potential of the technology. Two, in particular, concentrated on Nipkow's mechanical device: John Logie Baird, in Britain, and Charles Francis Jenkins in the United States. In 1925 both men, working with very little financial backing, demonstrated publicly the capabilities of the system, but found no sustained enthusiasm among radio manufacturers or broadcasting institutions.

While Jenkins hardly commands a footnote in broadcasting history, Baird figures prominently, largely because of his extraordinary flair for publicity, which he used in his battles to win financial and institutional support for his system. That he was ultimately unsuccessful was less to do with lack of support, than with the proved inferiority of the system itself. His lasting contribution to broadcasting lay in understanding the potential of the medium, encouraging others to respond to his vision and actively working towards its realisation.

Any development of television as a public system of communication required the active cooperation of those institutions primarily concerned with sound broadcasting, either in manufacturing or organisation. From 1926 to 1932 Baird was continually frustrated by the prevarication of the BBC which, faced with its own financial problems, was unwilling to produce transmission facilities for a medium with few receivers and little chance of immediate success.

In 1931 it was estimated that over the previous two years the German Reichspost had invested 200,000 Marks in television experiments based on the Nipkow system with little appreciable result. The main initiator of the scheme had been a Hungarian scientist, Denes von Mihály, who while working for AEG in 1924 had patented his own system. In 1928 he formed his own company, and received support from the *Reichs-Rundfunk-Gesellschaft* which organised the transmission facilities. However, enthusiasm for the system had evaporated by the end of 1930.

In March of that year, coinciding with an exhibition to mark the eightieth birthday of Nipkow, another German scientist, Manfred von Ardenne, had produced a television picture using an electrical scanning system. The more efficient alternative to Nipkow's scanning disc would soon be practically possible.

von Ardenne was one of many individual scientists seeking technical solutions to the problem of electronic scanning in the 1920s. Some were amateur enthusiasts, like Philo Farnsworth, living in California and funded by private investors, who by the end of the decade had perfected a system sufficiently reliable to arouse the interest of David Sarnoff, the head of RCA. That organisation already employed a Russian émigré, Vladimir K. Zworykin, who while at Westinghouse had been given permission to carry on studies he had started before the Revolution. By 1923 he had patented an electronic television camera. Six years later, on moving to RCA, he was given greater resources to develop his work, aided eventually by the buying out, by RCA, of Farnsworth's patents. Eventually the pioneering work at RCA would produce a technical system capable of becoming the basis of public television broadcasting in the United States and Britain, in the latter case as a result of the incorporation of a new company, Electric and Musical Industries (EMI) in 1931.

EMI was the result of the merger of two key organisations in the British music recording industry, the Gramophone Company and the Columbia Gramophone Company. The former was controlled by the American firm, the Victor Talking Machine Company, which in 1929 had merged with RCA. By this means EMI had direct access to American research in television, and would acquire further expertise in 1934 by forming a new business organisation with Marconi, concerned principally with transmitters and aerials. Thus Baird found himself confronted by a rival possessing infinitely larger technical and financial resources than himself, even though between 1932 and 1934 he held the advantage of an agreement with the BBC for so many test transmissions per day.

It became increasingly difficult for Baird to maintain his advantage. Fundamental doubts inside the Corporation about the quality of his results led Baird to experiment with Farnsworth's apparatus, and at the same time, to argue that approaches to the BBC from EMI, with its electronic scanner, signalled a potential take-over of the new medium by American financial interests. It was an argument appealing more to cultural chauvinism than economic policy and was vehemently denied by EMI which emphasised the wholly British character of the firm and its equipment.

With the end of Baird's agreement with the BBC in March 1934 the future of television, particularly as a public service, lay in the hands of the British government, since questions of finance and control had to be decided at the highest level. Kingsley Wood, who as Postmaster-General was the responsible government minister, set up a committee which reported in January 1935.

Even before the committee reached its final decision there was no doubt in the mind of the chairman, Lord Selsdon, that the BBC, with its monopoly of sound broadcasting, should be the only body responsible for the administration of a public television service.

Questions of technology and finance were not solved so easily. Although it was agreed that the future lay with electronic scanning and 'high-definition' television the committee did not make a choice between Baird's improved system and that of EMI, suggesting that both forms should be tested alternately by the new service. The costs were to be borne by the BBC out of its normal budget since, although advertising was ruled out as a source of revenue, there was no agreement on future funding. Decisions in both areas were to be considered by a Television Advisory Committee.

The response in the BBC was mixed. While reassured by the acceptance of its monopoly in broadcasting there was no whole-hearted acceptance of the need for, or capability of, providing a television service at a time when the Corporation was committed to the expansion of sound broadcasting in Britain and of services overseas, particularly to the empire. Reith was less convinced than others of the future of television, given its technical problems, and those men detailed to set up a service were assured that their future careers were still safe within sound broadcasting if the experiment failed.

The BBC television service began on 2 November 1936 and within three months the Advisory Committee came to the inevitable conclusion that the EMI system was superior to that of Baird. He remained an embittered man until his death in 1945, certain that he had never been given a fair chance. Visionaries may look too far ahead, and be unable to cope with immediate problems. Television, in Britain in the late 1930s, was in the hands of more pragmatic individuals, concerned more with survival than the future.

Pragmatism and survival were the hallmarks of many concerned with the future of television in Germany. In 1930 Hans Bredow, the Reichspost official who essentially controlled broadcasting policy through the RRG, had argued that financially and technically there was no immediate likelihood of a television service, but with the takeover of power by the National Socialists in 1933, political pressures necessitated some urgent rethinking. The Reichspost, still committed to television experiments, had had its fundamental interest in sound broadcasting undermined by the resignation of Bredow in January 1933, and the subsequent takeover of the organisation of broadcasting by Propaganda Ministry personnel in the spring of that year. Both the RRG, now under the control of Eugen Hadamovsky, and the Reichspost vied for a pre-eminent position in the development of television, with the latter mainly concerned with control of transmission facilities and the RRG concentrating on amplifiers and studio equipment. The result was an agreement to work together, leading in March 1935 to what was claimed to be the first regular public television service.

While preceding the BBC service by eighteen months it used mechanical cameras and the content mainly consisted of films and newsreels. Furthermore there were no individual domestic receivers, the audience congregating in special auditoria in Berlin. The purpose of the service was mainly to activate interest in the National Socialist Party and state. Hadamovsky, at the first television congress in Berlin in May 1935, emphasised the potential importance of television to propaganda work, and in private argued that Goebbels' ministry should control the medium, including all technical facilities.

The decision lay with Hitler and was embodied in a decree of 12 July 1935 which delegated ultimate responsibility for television, not to the Propaganda Ministry, but to the Air Ministry under Goering. This reflected not only the internecine rivalry inside the government and the particular influence of the Luftwaffe Minister, but also the military importance of television technology, especially in the field of radar and air defence. It has been suggested that such considerations influenced the willingness of the British government to encourage television experiments in Britain and accelerate the organisation of a public service, but such motives are clearer in the case of Germany.

Goebbels' refusal to accept the decision precipitated further discussions over the summer and autumn until a further decree was promulgated in December 1935 by which were determined the prime responsibilities of the Air Ministry for defence requirements and the Reichspost for technical equipment. The Propaganda Ministry merely had an interest in the organisation of programmes. With a clearer division of responsibility the Reichspost and RRG could work in closer cooperation to improve technical standards and determine a policy for the wider dissemination of television broadcasting.

Any expansion into a domestic market was bound to be slow, given the problems of transmission and manufacture of receivers, as well as the more basic issue of how a service could be financed. In 1936 the RRG estimated that only 36,000 households in the Reich were likely to be able to afford a television set and by 1939 there were only about 350 privately-owned receivers, mainly in Berlin;

the majority of those who did see television continued to watch in public viewing rooms.

It is worth comparing this with Britain where the manufacturers were extensively involved in attracting viewers, and where it has been estimated that, by August 1939, 20,000 to 25,000 sets were in use in the London area. The quality of reception and variety of the programmes, as well as the cheapness of receivers, produced this result, although it is worth remembering that in 1938 nearly 9 million radio licences were sold in the United Kingdom: television was still a minority interest.

It is clear, nevertheless, that a credible and creditable public service did exist in Britain well before any other country in Europe, and before any service was feasible in the United States. Since the latter was in the forefront of research in the early 1930s this may seem strange; American tardiness was the result of patent disputes, problems of agreeing technical standards with the Federal Communications Commission (FCC) and the unwillingness of RCA and the networks to rush into a development which had no clear commercial potential and which might affect the lucrative returns from radio.

David Sarnoff was as visionary about television as he had been about radio in the 1920s and continued experiments with RCA equipment through the middle 1930s. NBC, its associated network, began experimental outside broadcasts in 1937, but Sarnoff held back a regularly transmitted service until 30 April 1939, when it was inaugurated with the opening of the New York World Fair by Franklin Roosevelt, the first President of the United States to appear on television.

CBS conducted experiments throughout 1939 and 1940, and by May that year there were 26 stations in the US, but these were all classed as 'experimental' since there was no uniform technical standard until the FCC adjudicated early in 1941, allowing commercial transmissions to begin on 1 July. Five months later the United States was at war and although the next four years saw important technical developments, the organisation of television as a public service was drastically curtailed.

Not in fact as drastically as in Britain where, fearing the possibility of the television transmitter acting as a directional beacon for bombers in the case of war, the service closed at noon on 1 September 1939. The German Wehrmacht had ordered the closure of the Berlin transmitter on 24 August, and although the service was resumed on

15 October it continued to be restricted by disputes between the competent ministries over the control of technology and programming, by the scarcity of receiving outlets, and by increasing Allied bombing raids, culminating on 23 November 1943 with the destruction of the Berlin transmitter. The reorganisation of German television would be part of the wider reconstruction of German society after the war; as, indeed, the development of television in the US and Britain would be dependent on the social and economic changes affecting those societies in the post-war period, although continuing to work within the organisational frameworks established in the 1930s.

As part of the wider discussions about the role of the BBC in Britain after the war a committee, under Lord Hankey, reported on the future of television in March 1945. There was no doubt, as the Report stated, that 'television was here to stay', and it proposed the extension of the service to large areas of population, and eventually, colour transmissions.

The committee, irrespective of the attitude towards commercial sound broadcasting in Britain, did not dismiss sponsorship of television programmes out of hand, but recognised that no commercial groups would be interested until a television service had been established. While there was still agreement that the BBC should be responsible for broadcasting in sound and vision the 'logicality' of this decision was questioned rather more than it had been a decade earlier. For the immediate future extra finance would be provided by a combined sound and television licence for receivers.

For many of the technical members of the committee expansion of the service was linked inextricably to the manufacture of equipment and future export potential, particularly to the United States. Hopes were to be dashed as the networks, particularly NBC, invested heavily in the medium after the war. Both major networks conducted colour experiments, and in the spring of 1947 the FCC adopted a system of compatible, if crude, monochrome and colour transmission and reception developed by NBC. As with radio after the First World War, while the technical potential and personnel were available for the expansion of the medium, the problem was one of finance.

Whereas in Britain the proposed expansion would take place in a period of post-war austerity which was to last into the 1950s, in the United States there was an immediate increase in real wealth and domestic consumption. The increase in the ownership of television receivers would reflect this fact, while the growth of the consumer market made advertisers anxious to sell goods through the most efficient and all-embracing broadcasting channel. Throughout the 1940s this continued to be radio, which became the milch cow for the expansion of television by the networks.

By 1948, when the FCC for a variety of reasons, both technical and political, froze new franchise applications for four years, there were only 108 television stations in operation. New York and Los Angeles had seven each, but other large cities had only one, and many none at all. The primacy of radio as a domestic entertainment medium had yet to be challenged, but as networks sought continuing and increasing profits from radio in order to finance their television operations the character of programming began to change. Non-sponsored and educational output gave way almost completely to quiz shows and recorded programmes which were cheaper and gained larger audiences. Established entertainers on one network found their popularity plummeting when scheduled in direct competition with the new phenomenon of give-away shows. This did not stop CBS inveigling many of the NBC top performers, including Jack Benny, to join the network. They had good tax reasons for doing so, but the initiative was indicative of Paley's aim to make CBS the premier network, and those stars would be invaluable in television programming in the 1950s.

Critical observers on both sides of the Atlantic found their worst fears about commercial broadcasting realised as the consumer orientation of society was apparently reflected in the get-rich-quick outlook of game shows. It was a portent for the future, when television, not radio, would provide the crock of gold for the networks, and audience ratings would totally determine programme scheduling.

The FCC were made aware of such fears by educationalists who sought the right to have some television channels exclusively under their control and the success of their lobbying was shown in 1952 when, as the freeze on applications came to an end, 242 channels were reserved for educational use. At the same time 700 commercial applicants awaited approval for their licences: in July 1952 the moratorium was lifted, just as a presidential election campaign began in earnest.

While the FCC may have temporarily retarded the expansion of television coverage in the United States there was evidence of a phenomenal growth of interest among the general public and commercial organisations. There was no doubt that both were attracted by television, and radio would very quickly be of secondary importance to the networks. There is little evidence that such clarity of thinking existed in Britain.

The reasons were both financial and historical. The amount of capital available to the BBC for the expansion of its television operation was restricted by the post-war Labour government, which had not only to cope with balance-of-payments problems, but also the restructuring of much of Britain's social and economic infrastructure. Added to this, the cost of domestic receivers was high at a time when prices were rising ahead of wages. Without the immediate expansion of transmission areas there would be no call for the mass production of sets, even if this were possible in the economic climate.

Meanwhile radio, as a source of entertainment and news, continued to feed off the reputation it had achieved during the war. The television service was of peripheral interest to many decision-makers in the BBC administration. Furthermore, the whole future of broadcasting was to come under scrutiny once more, and the monopolistic position of the BBC likely to be challenged.

The Charter of the BBC was due for renewal in 1946, but owing to the peculiar circumstances of wartime, the government decided to extend it for another five years. Fundamental questions about the role of the BBC, its funding and the future of television were left for a committee of enquiry which began meeting in 1949 under the chairmanship of Lord Beveridge.

Beveridge had not been the government's first choice, but he had wide experience of public affairs, producing, in 1942, an important report on the future development of social security in Britain. In very real terms, the report on broadcasting which was published in January 1951 was Beveridge's. He laid out the issues and the intellectual framework in which they should be considered. While recognising that the 'public service' element should be the pre-eminent principle in British broadcasting, as an old style liberal Beveridge sought more diversity and a greater role for the individual listener. In his view, and that of the committee, the bureaucratic complacency of the BBC needed to be challenged, but not to the extent of producing an alternative service funded by the commercial sector. Competition, it was argued, would lower standards.

It was a view which was not shared by one member of the committee, a Conservative politician, Selwyn Lloyd. In a minority report he advocated the establishment of commercial radio and television as the best way to challenge the monopoly of the BBC. His own experience of broadcasting in the US suggested that it would be possible to safeguard standards while finding whole new sources of finance. He did not seek to challenge the continuing contribution of the BBC to national life, but articulated more clearly than some had previously, alternative opportunities within the same broad canvas of 'public service broadcasting'.

The Beveridge Report had clearly identified areas of general unrest about the organisation of the BBC, but the key factor in the development of television was the return of a Conservative government in October 1951 under Winston Churchill. The previous Labour administration had had little time to implement the findings of the committee, and it was not until May 1952 that the new government outlined its broadcasting policy. While continuing to support the BBC's role in sound broadcasting it opened up the possibility of competition in television based upon commercial funding. The BBC Charter was renewed in July 1952, but a chink had been opened up in its monopoly which was to widen over the next two years as the debate over commercial television extended into all areas of public life.

Eventually, a Television Act was passed in July 1954 which provided for a competitive service, administered by an Independent Television Authority (ITA), but with programmes provided by companies based in different regions of the United Kingdom. The eventual shape of commercial television was not as envisaged by many of its proponents in the early 1950s. It was essentially a compromise between those who sought to break the monopoly, those who sought new sources of profit, and those who feared the worst excesses of American television. The ITA would act as a public watchdog, monitoring the output of the companies, and representing the aspects of 'public service' which had been built into the Act.

Although known as 'independent television', its independence only lay in standing outside the organisation of the BBC. Having been established by parliamentary statute its relationship with the government was more restricted and less ambiguous than the Corporation with its Royal Charter. Furthermore, the relationship with advertisers and the requirement to maximise audiences were bound to affect programming policies.

Over many years in fighting for its position the BBC had perfected its style of lobbying inside the governing circles of the British establishment. It was virtually incapable of mobilising popular support, the result of years of complacency and subscription to an essentially patronising view of the audience. The activists for commercial television had conducted their campaign not only in the lobbies but in public as well, and one fundamental result of their success was to make the BBC more aware of its public image. By September 1957, when Independent Television (ITV) had captured three-quarters of the audience who could receive both channels, the role of the BBC as a publicly-funded service came into question.

Only four years earlier BBC television had reached the apogee of its post-war history in televising the coronation of Elizabeth II. All available resources were mobilised to broadcast the occasion, not only in the United Kingdom, but by telerecordings throughout the world. The national role of the BBC established from the time of the General Strike in 1926 had been reasserted, and its reputation for taste and decorum could not have been higher, particularly when compared with the NBC coverage of the coronation in the United States, which featured the appearance of J. Fred Muggs, the well-known chimpanzee, in the middle of the Communion Service.

While supposedly heralding the start of a new Elizabethan era, the coronation harked back to the certainties of a glorious past; of empire, deference, and political stability, with television providing the evidence for their existence. H. V. Kaltenborn, the American commentator, sardonically suggested that perhaps the show was put on by the British as 'a psychological boost to their somewhat shaky Empire'. If so it was short-lived, but the role of television in the political process, both as a bearer of cultural meanings and a reporter of political events was becoming greater every year.

Irrespective of the comparatively restricted television coverage in the United States both major parties used the medium extensively in the 1952 presidential election. The image of Dwight D. Eisenhower as a popular war hero was exploited by the Republican Party and its advertising agents to counter the intellectualism of Adlai Stevenson, who fought the election on television as if he was still on radio. Lessons were learnt by both parties, but particularly by the Republican vice-presidential candidate, Richard Nixon, who used the medium to rebut charges of financial corruption and emphasise his essential honesty. It was the start of his love–hate relationship which was to last for twenty years.

Politicians, in the main, were wary of the new medium. They understood the role of the press, and had come to terms with radio and newsreels, but television required different skills, particularly in presentation. It was an intimate medium which could emphasise personal characteristics less obvious in a large public meeting. Most still thought of the audience as essentially passive, liable to be easily swayed by what was presented to them, and in Britain this encouraged a defensive attitude among politicians, and also in the BBC, anxious to demonstrate its impartiality, particularly in a period of institutional uncertainty.

The sterility in political debate applied equally to radio under the 'Fourteen-day Rule', agreed with the political parties in 1944, by which no issue to be debated in Parliament within the next fourteen days was open to discussion. It was to last until November 1956, undermined eventually by the development of television news coverage, and the challenge of the independent channel.

The presentation of news by the Corporation had always been seen as the acid test of its impartiality. Television required pictures, but these came in the form of a newsreel and were distinct from news bulletins which were in sound only. Departmental rivalries in the BBC, as well as a general fear of the personalisation of news, retarded progress. The coming of ITV with its own news-reporting organisation provoked the necessary response.

Independent Television News (ITN), began with the problem of attracting an audience accustomed to the news values and practices of the BBC. Unburdened by years of tradition, but concerned with its public service role, ITN looked elsewhere for a different model of news presentation. The United States provided some, but not all of the answers.

Both NBC and CBS had fifteen-minute, early evening news programmes, which according to Erik Barnouw were the 'schizophrenic offspring of the theater newsreel and the radio newscast', a description which might have been applied to the BBC in the early 1950s. The difference lay in the style, the emphasis on entertainment, on capturing the interest of the viewer through the personality of the newsreader. The role of news 'anchorman', linking the material, was developed by John Cameron Swayze for NBC and

Douglas Edwards for CBS who were more concerned for their ratings and their sponsors, Camel cigarettes and Oldsmobile, than for veracity and balance. News values were determined also by the requirements of the medium with its emphasis on pictures and action, rather than explanation and discussion. With improvements in the technology of television news gathering, immediacy also became of prime value. Speed and brevity were of the essence in a medium where time was money.

ITN, which was funded by the programme-making companies, did not have the problem of attracting sponsors, but allowed its 'newscasters' to establish their own personalities by writing, as well as reading, the news. Many came from professions other than journalism, but all were young and politically aware. Their first test was the Suez Crisis of October/November 1956.

Suez was also of major importance to the BBC, which asserted its impartiality by voicing criticisms in the country against government action in Egypt, much to the chagrin of the Prime Minister, Anthony Eden, who in viewing the conflict in terms of the Second World War, saw the BBC action as nothing less than treasonable. ITN's interview with Nasser, transmitted while the two countries were still in a state of war, could well have been viewed in the same way.

The right of the state to intervene in broadcasting in the national interest had been established in Britain from the earliest days of the BBC. The question of when and how intervention should take place was less easy to determine when two competing channels vied for a television audience, which was growing at an amazing rate. By March 1956 the sale of combined sound and television licences had reached nearly 6 million, giving a potential audience of 16 million, and the BBC estimated that 3 million people were able to watch ITV. It is within this context that changes in the relationship between broadcasters and politicians must be placed.

When radio had provided access to large audiences politicians had been aware of the problem of the control exercised by the BBC. Television, which was believed to be an infinitely more powerful medium, posed the same problem, but with the complication of requiring new techniques of presentation. Politicians who had gained some experience in the medium were seen as dangerous by colleagues who lacked both access and expertise. Furthermore, interviewers on both channels, in current affairs and news, took on the role of arbiters, acting as representatives of the audience, and framing the terms of the debate in which politicians might take part.

British television was coming to terms with how it might reflect politics, but the political parties recognised the need to come to terms with the medium itself. The general election of 1959 was the first occasion in which television played a considerable part in the electoral process and in which the political role of television could be judged in Britain. Even then, the examination, conducted in a seminal work by Trenaman and McQuail, concentrated on the immediate effect of television on the voting performance of the electorate. While calling upon sophisticated statistical techniques it lay within the mainstream view of the 'hypodermic' effect of the medium, since, as the authors argued, the 'television screen compels attention'. The results, while inconclusive, emphasised one particular aspect of the campaign, summed up in the title of the book, *Television and the Political Image*, the role of personality. It was now possible to see future political leaders in immediate close-up, to be aware of their idiosyncrasies, and from these to make political judgements. Successful politicians had always been aware of the importance of their image, and would now make full use of television techniques in party political broadcasts to create a managed picture. As always the United States was in the forefront of this development.

By 1956 Republican and Democratic Party conventions were television spectaculars, crucial in establishing the unity of the party behind the presidential candidate. Stage-managed for the cameras, they still had, in Eisenhower and Stevenson, men who had little liking or understanding of the medium. Four years later it was to be argued that John F. Kennedy secured the presidency because of his use of television, and the television debates with Richard Nixon, captured on telerecordings, have taken on the role of myth.

There is no doubt that Kennedy, whose youth, inexperience, Catholicism and wealth could have counted heavily against him, would not have been elected without television. He cultivated the journalists, recognising that through them he could determine the nature of the issues. He was also important to the networks in retrieving their public image after the scandals of quiz-show rigging and disc-jockey bribery in 1958 and 1959. The public service element in American broadcasting was to be reasserted through an emphasis on news coverage, and the campaign of 1960 provided the occasion. The medium and the candidate needed each other to confirm their respectability.

Writing two years later, Daniel Boorstin, in his pessimistically critical study of American image-making, brilliantly noted that the debates with Nixon might have been called the '$400,000 Question', since they followed the format of the discredited game shows, emphasising the contrived situation of confrontation rather than offering information, and giving $100,000 a year for four years to the successful competitor.

Irrespective of his jaundice, Boorstin had isolated the relationship between television practice and political presentation. There was no such thing as 'political television', only television, whose forms dictated the nature of the experience to the viewer. Politicians in the United States would be packaged within existing television genres, particularly soap opera, and linked inextricably to the world of entertainment. Kennedy had shown what might be achieved when the politicians and television acted in unison; the question to be answered in the 1960s was how far other groups in American society would be able to mobilise support through a medium which entered the homes of 85 per cent of the people of the United States. Executive power over broadcasting still lay with the administration, but how would that power be exercised in the face of growing domestic and international instability?

With hindsight it often appears that the emergence of television as the primary source of information and entertainment in western industrialised societies heralded and encouraged a decade or more of domestic conflict. What is clearer, however, is the effect on the cinema and newspapers.

In Britain the increase in the number of television licences to over 10 million by 1960 and the success of a second channel were paralleled by a catastrophic decline in cinema attendances with concomitant effects upon the whole cinema industry. We have already noted the failure of post-war attempts to consolidate British film production in the face of American competition and the emergence of television. Hollywood studios, undermined by anti-trust legislation, political pressure and the popularity of the new medium had cut production and sought salvation in new film technologies unavailable to television, notably widescreen presentation and stereophonic sound.

The real problem was the general shortage of films, leading to the demise of independent exhibitors unable to compete with the larger chains and their booking power. In 1958 there was a rationalisation of the Rank circuits, leading either to the closure of cinemas and the selling of sites for property development or a change to other leisure activities, particularly, with a relaxation in social and legislative attitudes towards gambling, to bingo halls. These fundamental changes in the infrastructure of the industry were further factors in the demise of the cinema in Britain as a medium of mass entertainment, but secured its future as an artistic form aiming at more specific audiences, particularly those aged under thirty. By the early 1960s they comprised 50 per cent of those going to the cinema regularly, and that figure would drop over the next two decades. Simultaneously British feature film production declined to under 80 a year, many aiming at the youngest members of the family group.

This marked the decline of new voices in cinema who had found a market in the late 1950s, commenting upon, albeit in a rather constrained fashion, changes in the social and cultural outlooks of the working class. Unshackled by the need to be popular with large audiences and helped by changes in the censorship system the British cinema appeared to shake off irrelevance and take on a more positive role, reflecting more clearly a mood of irreverence and challenge among the youth of the country. Films such as *Look Back in Anger, Saturday Night and Sunday Morning,* and *Room at the Top* were successful examples of a more 'naturalistic' method of film-making, but stylistically betrayed their origins in plays and novels. By the early 1960s their critical stance had been taken over by television, and there was greater emphasis on the more overtly neutral escapism of James Bond, and horror movies. Cinema could still offer a range of experiences not available on the small domestic screen, but at a cost, and by the middle 1960s, 80 per cent of film production costs in Britain were met by American capital.

The reasons were purely commercial. The break-up of the studio system in the United States had spawned numbers of production companies which sought out the cheapest site for their activities. Britain offered many advantages, not least the subsidy from the British Film Fund to productions which could be deemed as British if they used only British technical facilities. The advantage to British producers was access to the Hollywood distribution organisation, and a guaranteed return on investment, as well as the financial backing to make more expensive, and internationally orientated, films. The challenging social outlook of some film-makers in the late

1950s was submerged beneath the weight of American investment, and the requirement to produce for the American and international markets. At the same time an important part of the European market was secured for products of the American film industry.

The development of television had accelerated the further demise of the British film industry, but had also presented new opportunities for cooperation between the media. Film producers, having failed to seize the opportunity to influence the development of television in the 1940s, bought their way into the new commercial stations. Diversification was a key element in their economic strategy when faced with the decline of the traditional industry.

At a creative level, directors such as Ken Russell and John Schlesinger, trained in using film on television in documentaries and commercials, had the opportunity, later, to make feature films. There was also a wider diffusion of film culture with larger numbers of recent films being shown as a staple element in television programming, after the initial refusal to sell film libraries to broadcasters.

This parasitical aspect of television, utilising the products of other forms of popular culture, was most obvious in the United States after 1955 when the major studios and distributors made their film libraries available to television stations. Rather than stand out against the medium the film companies were able to provide cheap reliable programming using material which was essentially unusable in the commercial cinema. Live television was expensive to produce, and programmes could only be retained and replayed by a form of telerecording which was inferior in quality to film. The percipient film companies did not stand aside from television for long. As feature film production declined studios became available, and in 1954 Warner's concluded an agreement with ABC for the production of 40 one-hour programmes, twelve of which were to be repeated, based on story lines owned as properties by Warner. The result was the western series *Cheyenne*, which was an enormous success, encouraging other studios which were turning to television film production. By 1957 there were over 100 series on American television, using the staple cinematic genres of detective, spy and war stories. The most popular continued to be the Western.

Although there had been a few successful examples of live television drama productions transferring to the large screen, notably *Marty* and *Twelve Angry Men*, the predominant movement was the other way. At the point where the potential of live dramatic form on television was being realised the stations turned to the cheapness and predictability of filmed series. They secured the future for Hollywood as the major production area for television, not only in the United States, but throughout the world, as other television systems, seeking programmes, turned to those which were easily accessible and relatively cheap. Independent television companies in Britain not only bought American series, but other programme formats, particularly quiz and game shows, which were adapted for the British audience. Companies which had struggled for over a year to survive, while they built up an audience and attracted advertising, began to secure nearly 75 per cent of the possible television audience. Critical voices were raised about cultural standards and the predominance of commercial interests above those of 'public service' on ITV. Debates about broadcasting, going back to the 1920s, were reopened, fuelled by the emerging scandal of quiz-show rigging in the United States and statements that ownership of a commercial station in Britain was 'like having a licence to print your own money'.

It had been made by Roy Thomson, a Canadian newspaper publisher and businessman, after the inauguration, in August 1957, of the main commercial television company in Scotland of which he was the chief shareholder. He had bought *The Scotsman*, an ailing Edinburgh newspaper in 1954, adding it to his Canadian press empire, and moved to Great Britain in the same year. In his view the function of any commercial enterprise was to make money, and that applied as much to newspapers and television companies. He brought a trans-Atlantic entrepreneurial style to the media industries, and an honesty of purpose which affronted many suscepti- bilities, particularly, in 1959, when he acquired Kemsley News- papers, including the prestigious *Sunday Times*, on the basis of his profits from Scottish Television. The Kemsley Group was largely made up of provincial daily newspapers and gave Thomson a foothold in the profitable area of local advertising which he was able to develop over the next decade.

The rules governing commercial television in Britain precluded a television company taking over a newspaper but publishing groups had been heavily involved in the initial organisation of many of the companies themselves. Competition between newspapers had been restricted by the post-war rationing of newsprint which was not lifted until 1955. It was a profitable period with substantial advertising competing for space in small newspapers sold at a normal retail price.

Derestriction pointed up the vulnerability of some newspapers because, as they expanded in size, spiralling costs of production were not met by revenue, particularly from advertising. Commercial television was not totally to blame for this, although by 1958 its advertising revenue had already surpassed that of all national newspapers. Advertisers and agencies were more selective, and with decreases in sales among the medium-circulation dailies they became most vulnerable. The demise of the *News Chronicle* in 1960 was the most important casualty, but other famous titles continued to incur large debts. Economic survival meant finding a clear market and a product which would guarantee circulation and advertising. The position was complicated by the emergence of television news, offering pictures and up-to-date information.

The result was an increasing conformity in the press, with newspapers acting in two ways as complementary aspects of television. The quality press sought out the expanding quality consumer market for its advertising while providing the in-depth analysis on news which television rarely attempted. The tabloid mass-circulation press concentrated on human interest stories increasingly related to events and personalities on television.

These changes in content were to be most pronounced through the 1960s, and were preceded by further mergers and amalgamations of publishers, notably the organisation of the International Publishing Corporation (IPC), which had not only the Mirror Group of newspapers, but also magazines, and a large stake in the paper-making group, Reed. IPC, like Thomson, had a major stake in a commercial television company (ATV), an important source of finance for its expansion in the 1960s.

The juxtaposition of competition in television with increased competition in the press had a clear effect on the content of the latter, and exposed the weakness of management and lack of cost-effectiveness in many newspapers. Television, while important, was only one factor affecting newspapers, the most important being the increase in costs of production which could only be reduced by increasing economies of scale, a monopoly position in particular centres, and the use of new transmission and printing technologies.

These were also features of newspaper production in the United

States in the 1950s and 1960s. Large cities were left with only one morning or evening paper, many owned by the large groups, including those which had developed earlier in the century, notably Hearst and Scripps-Howard. By 1966, New York had only three general-circulation dailies, the *Times*, *Daily News*, and *Post*. Strikes by newspaper workers, aimed at restricting changes in work practices, further undermined the financial viability of newspapers, and failed to halt the introduction of new technologies, all of which required the capital which was only available from large economic units. It could be argued that television as a medium of news hardly impinged upon the performance and content of metropolitan dailies. They responded to demographic and economic changes in their own immediate environment, providing through innumerable supplements services for all sections of the large urban community. As in Britain, newspapers would survive by identifying and providing for specific markets, with an emphasis less upon hard, immediate news, a function which would be taken over eventually in the 1960s by television.

It was a prospect which was difficult to appreciate in Britain or America at the turn of the decade. The freedom of the press was an inherent part of the theory of democracy, and that freedom depended upon the existence of numbers of newspapers offering a range of opinions. The demise of any paper raised pertinent questions about the nature and future of democratic society.

In Britain two major enquiries addressed themselves to some of these questions. Since the BBC Charter and the Television Act were to be renewed in 1964 the Conservative government set up, in 1960, a Committee of Enquiry into broadcasting under Sir Harry Pilkington. It was the first to take account of the changes in structure and content which had occurred over the previous ten years, and looked in particular at the performance of independent television. One of the guiding forces on the committee was Richard Hoggart, an academic who was highly critical of the content of the commercial network and its effect on cultural standards. His influence might be seen in the Report, published in 1962, which castigated independent television, suggested that a third television channel should be given to the BBC, and that the independent system should be reorganised.

In making such economic and technical suggestions the report was based upon social and moral outlooks about the role of broadcasting in society. It was responding to fears occasioned by the remark of Roy Thomson, the possible effects on young people of the violence in popular film series, the spurious excitement and ease of gaining wealth in game shows, and the conviction that television had become the most effective force for changing the outlooks of people in society.

Reactions to the apparent effect of television on politics, and the political behaviour of the electorate in Britain and America raised serious questions about the role of television as an agency of information, and how it should be funded. At the widest level it argued against the stratification of content for specific audiences as determined by the needs of advertisers, and for the widest presentation of all cultural forms for the population at large. It was almost Reithian in arguing that broadcasting should be a positive force for good in a democratic society. The conformism inherent in the predictable and unimaginative commercial sector needed to be stripped away. The BBC was hardly tainted by this criticism, and the result was a flowering of confidence within the Corporation which allowed, over the next few years, a reflection of the social and economic changes occurring in Britain.

While the Pilkington Committee considered the problems of competition in television broadcasting a Royal Commission on the Press reported, in 1962, on the growing monopoly structures in the newspaper industry. The mergers and takeovers undertaken by Thomson and IPC, among others, posed a different set of problems from those considered fifteen years before. Then the question had been the relationship between power and responsibility, and how the press might be effectively policed in order to carry out its democratic function. In 1962 it was how the diversity of the press might be maintained within the changed economic conditions. The answer was that it could not, without a radical restructuring of the industry, even to the extent of the state providing printing facilities for those papers which were not economically viable.

The separation of printing and publishing drew upon an analogy with the role of the ITA which acted as the provider of transmission facilities for commercial television companies. The deliberations of Pilkington suggested that this separation did not always produce the desired results. Questions of who should receive this facility, and on what criteria, posed wider questions of censorship.

The importance of both enquiries lies in the underlying assumptions that inform their conclusions. The press, in Britain, was still deemed a major element in the organisation of political opinion, while television appeared to have a predominantly cultural role with less specific social and political effects. They pinpointed the perceived social roles of the main forms of mass communication in Britain at a moment of political and social change. In the next decade the nature of the debate would change quite radically.

The late 1950s in the United States and Britain have been characterised as a period of economic expansion and political quiescence. President Eisenhower and Harold Macmillan, Prime Minister in Britain after 1957, presented themselves as figures of stability. So too, did Konrad Adenauer, the Chancellor of the Federal Republic of Germany since its inception in 1949, but the debate about the contemporary role of the media was bound to be more pointed in that country.

The post-war establishment of press and broadcasting by the Allies had been intended to reflect the democratic, pluralist society which was being constructed in political and social institutions. While freedom of opinion, the essential constituent of a democratic society, was embodied in the Basic Law of the FRG, implementation in the media was complicated not only by the economic factors affecting other western democracies, but also the precarious position of the state itself.

A diversity of newspapers had been encouraged by the occupying authorities, and these were essentially local and regional in outlook. There were newspapers which gained an international reputation in the 1950s, particularly the *Frankfurter Allgemeine Zeitung*, but no national daily newspaper, unless one accepts the tabloid *Bild-Zeitung*. The diversity was more apparent than real, and in 1954, although 1500 papers were published in the FRG they were serviced by 225 editorial staffs; by 1963 this had shrunk to 183. As in the 1920s and 1930s small-circulation newspapers became part of larger organisations which guaranteed their existence, but which provided a uniformity of news and comment.

In the 1950s and 1960s the problem of press concentration centred on the role of Axel Springer and his publishing empire. It was founded upon the success of *Bild-Zeitung*, an old style *Boulevardblatt* which he established in 1952, and contained all the worst excesses of the 'yellow press' early in the century. There was no doubting its popularity across the whole of the FRG, and after adding the serious Hamburg paper, *Die Welt*, to his collection of magazines and papers in 1953 Springer began to move into book publishing and other ventures. The style and content of *Bild* caused the most concern to observers, since it offered little more than titillation and ill-informed comment. Springer's papers were uniform in their conservative outlook, emphasising the dangers to the new republic from within and without. Rather than opening up discussion, he was concerned with closing it down and reiterating the 'national' outlook of the FRG. Ever watchful of historical parallels, some Germans remembered the career of Hugenberg, and his eventual support for National Socialism. There is no doubt that the ruling conservative Christian-Democrat grouping under Konrad Adenauer welcomed the support of the populist publisher in confronting the enemies of the state. It was difficult to see how support for the Federal Government could be established in the field of broadcasting since the organisation of radio and television was firmly centred in individual *Länder*.

The setting up in 1950 of the *Arbeitsgemeinschaft der öffentlich-rechtlichen Rundfunkanstalten der Bundesrepublik Deutschland (ARD)* to coordinate the activities of the nine separate broadcasting authorities provided the essential administrative framework for their development. The advantage of pooling the resources of large and small *Länder* became clear in 1953 when the general development was started throughout the FRG. The *ARD* became the organisation whereby programmes and finance could be coordinated, leading to the setting up, in 1954, of a network administered by *ARD*, calling upon all the regions for programmes. This was, and continues to be, financed, by a combination of licence fees and commercials, a form of mixed economy which was intended to preclude too much interference from the area of advertising. The question of interference from the Federal Government was raised in discussions about the opening of a second television channel in the late 1950s.

Under Adenauer the Federal Government had considered various schemes for the reorganisation of broadcasting, and the application by the *ARD* for permission to start a new television channel offered a new opportunity. While delaying a decision on the *ARD* proposal the Federal Government supported the establishment, in 1959, of a private company representing publishing and advertising interests, whose aim was to provide a second channel. In 1960 public money was allocated to the company, and the decision taken to start the service in 1961, which was, as many pointed out, an important election year. A number of *Länder*, led by Hamburg, took the issue to the Constitutional Court, on the basis of an infringement of their rights by the Federal Government. In February 1961 the Court found in their favour, arguing further, that the involvement of the Federal Government in broadcasting would violate the right of freedom of opinion.

Responsibility for setting up a second channel, the *Zweites Deutches Fernsehen* (*ZDF*), lay with the *Länder*, who undertook to provide a service which complemented the other channel and did not compete for audiences. Financed in the same way as the first channel, *ZDF* programmes were intended to reflect more clearly the totality of the German experience, but the problems of 'coordinated contrast' between the channels raised major headaches for programme planners.

The Constitutional Court decision effectively determined the future organisation of television in the FRG and re-emphasised the basic provisions for freedom of opinion in the state. It was a timely reaffirmation since the state itself appeared under threat from the USSR and the pressure it was applying on Berlin. The building of the wall between the Russian and Western sectors in August 1961 was seen as provocation at the time, and contributed to the immediate tension. In the long term it established a *de facto* relationship between both Germanies and Russia which stabilised the political situation and allowed a greater fluidity of discussion about the future. Television in the FRG was to play a crucial part in the organisation and development of that debate, but within the parameters of the need to uphold the constitutional framework of society.

The greatest danger to this appeared to come from the German Democratic Republic where there was little debate about the role of the media in society. Their function was, and continues to be, to uphold and proselytise the socialist organisation of the state, and to consolidate the position of the ruling group of the Socialist Unity Party. During the 1950s and 1960s a system of control and coordination was set up which allowed no diversity of approach or outlook in newspapers and magazines. This was achieved through a system of state licensing, a monopolistic state news agency, and regular directives on the correct selection and presentation of news.

Radio and television, while performing the same political and social function, did so within the context of competing programmes emanating from outside the state, particularly from the FRG. There were two ways in which the authorities tried to deal with this problem. Firstly, they tried to prohibit the reception of foreign stations, although this was almost impossible to carry out short of jamming them. Secondly, they tried to provide a service which was technically sophisticated and which could bear comparison with western programming. One programme, *Der schwarze Kanal*, 'The Black Channel', created a form of counter-propaganda, replaying parts of West German programmes which were available in the GDR, and emphasising elements which redounded to the credit of the socialist bloc and to the discredit of the West.

Political uncertainty in the 1950s had not restricted the development of the press and broadcasting in both parts of Germany, and both forms of media played crucial roles in developing a political consciousness which reflected the changed conditions of the country after the war. The limits of journalistic freedom, which were clearly drawn in the GDR, were still to be defined in its western counterpart. The *Spiegel* affair became the most important test case in the 1960s, leading to another judicial defeat for the government, and the resignation of the Defence Minister, Franz-Joseph Strauss. The weekly news magazine, *Der Spiegel*, had been founded in 1946 by Rudolf Augstein on the pattern of *Time* in the United States. In a country without a national press it provided not only an important digest of national and international news, but also in-depth political and cultural coverage. By the middle 1950s it had established itself as a profitable journal, politically influential, and a continuous thorn in the flesh of the Federal Government through its investigative journalism. The genesis of the affair lay in a series of articles published in October 1962 which critically examined the defence capability of the Federal Republic. The response of the government was to arrest the author of the articles and the editor of the magazine, to search its offices and confiscate materials, and to accuse them of treason.

The memory of the National Socialist past was invoked, and the actions of the government condemned in many quarters, not least the Constitutional Court when the case was finally settled in 1965. The *Spiegel* affair emphasised the abnormal political situation in West Germany and the tenuous definition of freedom of opinion even in peacetime. It also represented the changing character of the political structure of West Germany, as the post-war leaders came under attack for their obduracy and complacency. As the challenge grew television and the press would amplify, distribute and channel the protest, not only in West Germany, but in other western industrialised countries.

9. Mass Communication and the Modern World

THIS study will conclude at the point when developments in the transmission and reception of information through satellite technology appeared to presage a revolution in national and international communications. At the same time television sets became not only the receivers of broadcast visual entertainment and news but were also connected to video-recorders and computers, becoming a new source of domestic entertainment. These developments would pose new challenges to commercial entrepreneurs, media institutions and governments, but around the same issues with which this book has been concerned. The deciding factor will be the social use of the technology, the character of the institutions in which it is placed, and the political organisation of the states of which they are part.

One major theme of this book has been the relationship between the state, however politically organised, and forms of mass communication. Control of the latter was assumed to be the key to the holding of power in any society. The dilemma was how this might be achieved in a pluralist, democratic society. The experience of Richard Nixon will provide an illustration of that dilemma, and draw this work to a conclusion at the point where governments began to find new strategies to cope with the problems of information control.

In a speech on 13 November 1969 in Des Moines, Iowa, Vice-President Spiro T. Agnew initiated a campaign to undermine the credibility of the press and television news media in the United States. It was not merely an opportunity for someone normally known as 'Spiro Who?' to establish a personal reputation, but the beginning of a concerted attempt by the Nixon administration to articulate and mobilise genuine fears in society about the power of the media in order to exercise influence over individuals and institutions in network television and the press. Although conducted by Agnew, the campaign was orchestrated by the White House, and while it represented another stage in the continuing battle between the executive and the media over control of information, it owed as much to Richard Nixon's paranoic hatred of journalists, nurtured during his years in the political wilderness.

In his initial speech Agnew reflected on the way in which television network news set the agenda of political debate, and the terms in which the domestic audience understood the policies of the administration. In essence, he argued, the picture of society which Americans were given was that decided by a small, unrepresentative and unelected group of men with responsibility only to the network which employed them. While the speech concentrated on the way in which a presidential broadcast had been presented by the networks, this was but one aspect of wider concerns. It was a populist message, addressed to sections of society increasingly worried by the demonstrations and riots which seemed to dominate domestic news. The institutions of the media were being blamed for concentrating on the manifestations of social and political discontent associated with the Civil Rights Movement and opposition to the Vietnam War. By arguing that such coverage encouraged discontent and distorted the true picture of American life, Agnew was to strike a chord with individuals who had no party political interest, but were concerned about the apparent power of television to undermine basic values in society.

In the early 1920s Walter Lippmann, who would become an influential commentator on political affairs, had explored the problem of news selection and argued that a 'pseudo-environment' was created by newspapers: an unreal world created by those who chose news stories. As we have noted, it was a view reiterated with some force by Daniel Boorstin forty years later, faced with the growth of public relations, advertising and television as a political tool. It was, however, a Canadian academic, Marshall McLuhan, who in a series of works published through the 1960s, provided a series of aphorisms which acted as a framework for the analysis of television in society. 'The medium is the message', 'a "cool" medium', 'the global village' became terms which emphasised the power of television as a medium to change feelings, perception and spatial understanding.

As a cultural critic McLuhan was concerned with the undermining of the print medium as the main source of communication, but he also sought to understand the nature of the psychic effect of new forms of transmission upon individuals in society. Whereas, he argued, literacy had allowed apparent involvement in the social world but encouraged personal detachment, the new electronic media, acting as technological extensions of their nervous systems, brought people together in one large involved and involving community.

McLuhan was a philosopher, not a sociologist. His interest in the media arose from a need to understand the individual as a knowledgeable being within the cosmos. His method was to set up a series of postulations, or 'probes', which sought to provoke a response. Accepted by many as scientific statements, such aphorisms as television being a 'cool' medium were really theoretical concepts which could only be explored on McLuhan's terms. His intellectual brilliance and ability to utilise television in order to popularise his ideas gave him a credibility as a coherent thinker which he did not deserve. His main contribution to the debate about the role of the media in society was to look more closely at the relationship between the medium and the audience, and how the medium itself constructed meaning. This, fundamentally, was how 'the medium was the message'.

Semiologists and structuralists would provide a more 'scientific' basis for this fundamental idea, breaking down messages into their constituent elements, following the example of European linguistic pioneers such as Ferdinand de Saussure and Roland Barthes. Others would provide theoretical frameworks which incorporated Freudian and other psychological perspectives about the relationship between the message and the audience. While crucially important in the academic debate they have lacked the wide popular appeal which McLuhan was able to command. In the 1960s he did appear to provide new perspectives on the nature of communication in the television age.

He was certainly taken seriously by Richard Nixon's closest advisers in the 1968 presidential campaign. Extracts from McLuhan's *Understanding Media* were circulated to Nixon's staff with an analysis of their importance to the presentation of the candidate on television. The success of the campaign appeared not only to vindicate the theory, but also to convince Nixon that all his future appearances on the medium, which he disliked, should be subject to effective control. The image constructed in 1968 had to be perpetuated, and that meant some influence over the way he was presented on television; hence the development of the attack on the networks.

Although Nixon's own performance had contributed to his success in 1968, the comparative failure of his opponents was no less significant. They had been undermined particularly by the live pictures of riots at the Democratic Convention in Chicago. To many people the scenes typified all that seemed wrong with a divided America, but they provided intensely exciting television. Coverage of civil disorders posed a difficult problem for television reporters and executives. How far was the mirror which reflected society actively encouraging anti-social behaviour by amplifying the scale and nature of the opposition?

Many groups in American society had already recognised the importance of gaining access to the medium, and this could best be achieved by 'making' news and staging events. It has been argued that the development of a Civil Rights Movement in the United States would have been impossible without television. The medium not only raised the consciousness of black and white populations to the magnitude of the problem, but also presented the growth of support and the strength of the leadership through news reports and features. Marches and demonstrations reflected the popular character of the movement and appeared to be in opposition to the authority of the state in the form of the police or National Guard, who were continually on the defensive. The coverage of riots in the inner cities further emphasised the social and economic divisions which existed in the country.

The television coverage of the war in Vietnam was a continuous backdrop to disturbances at home. It has been called the first 'television' war, provoking discussion about the effects of such coverage. Some have argued that the nightly reports from the battle fronts produced boredom: others, that the pictures of carnage and destruction encouraged opposition to the war. Whatever the effect on the audience, television allowed the opposition to be heard and brought into focus for the first time the problems, for both government and networks, in providing extensive immediate and detailed reporting of the action.

The most important aspect was the dichotomy between the official outlook of the government and the reports which began to appear on the news. Increasingly, the stated political objectives seemed at odds with the actual character of the war as portrayed on television.

They also exposed, through the televising of Congress hearings of the Fulbright Committee in 1965–6, the lack of clear direction in American foreign policy. There was no machinery whereby the government could control the coverage except by threats to the networks, and their executives held the view that the pictures from Vietnam, accompanied by critical reporting, were of vital importance in informing the American public of the 'true' state of affairs.

They certainly made it impossible for Lyndon Johnson to contemplate another four years in office, mainly because he was seen not to have the situation under control. His successor, Richard Nixon, had good reason to learn from this example. If he was to offer a sense of purpose and unity to the nation he required the active assistance of network television. His method was to question the loyalty of employees, and to encourage affiliate stations to put pressure on the networks. Increasingly they fell into line.

Opposition to American involvement in Vietnam became the key political issue in the second half of the decade, not only in the United States, but throughout the developed world. It was as if McLuhan's 'global village' was in existence as populations in other countries shared the pictures from Vietnam. The fallacy of this view was that they could not share the experience of either the American people or the Vietnamese people. Nevertheless opposition to the war offered a focus for a range of groupings in west European countries, centred around the activities of youth groups, particularly university students.

Youth, which as a consumer group had been cultivated by commercial music entrepreneurs as a growing market throughout the 1960s, was a political factor in the internal affairs of France and West Germany in 1967 and 1968. As in the United States, television offered access to the political arena to groups who made news. By identifying with ideas of freedom and self-determination articulated with reference to Vietnam, but applied to their own country, they called into question the outlook and competence of ruling groups who found it difficult to cope with this new phenomenon. In May 1968 it appeared that France itself would succumb to a new revolution inspired by urban workers and students. It was a chimera; within weeks de Gaulle had reasserted his own power, and more effectively tied French television to the state.

Even Harold Wilson, who had cultivated an image as the leader of a new dynamic Britain in 1964, found his government under pressure in October 1968 as student demonstrators challenged British support for the American position in Vietnam. Of more importance to the future relationship of the government to the media in the United Kingdom was a civil rights march in Londonderry, Northern Ireland, in the same month. Catholics in the province used the tactics of civil rights campaigners in the United States to highlight their economic and political position. They achieved their objective when television cameras portrayed police violence in dealing with marchers, and the attention of the British government was forcibly drawn to a long-standing and insoluble problem.

The issue of Northern Ireland has become a microcosm of the wider questions about the role of the media in society, particularly the relationship of the broadcasting organisations to the state in a period of civil disorder, their role as information gatherers and disseminators in a democracy, the appropriateness of the concept of a national culture and the role of the media in its construction. At a time when Britain committed itself to joining the European community it was engaged in the process of redefining itself as a nation through the agencies of the media.

Yet the very nature of the technology which made the idea of a 'global village' feasible also brought into question the control which could be exercised over broadcasting in the future. The first satellite had been successfully launched by the USSR in 1957 and within a decade satellites were key elements in the transmission of information around the world. Just as wireless telegraphy and telephony had transcended physical frontiers, and had been developed for their military uses, so communications satellites, costing so much to build and launch, were developed as part of the national defence capability of the two major states, the USA and USSR. The development of any public communications network depended upon the cooperation of either power. Following legislation in 1962, a commercial consortium, COMSAT, was formed in the United States. It could make use of a network of satellites, and any nation could subscribe to the consortium if it could afford the contributions. Large corporations also recognised the commercial potential of the satellites since they were capable of reaching transnational audiences and effectively creating an international advertising market. The development of satellite technology for the transmission and reception of information raised fundamental questions of media policy for national states. Direct broadcasting by satellite offered speed and immediacy of communication; it had, for instance, provided the means whereby television pictures could be relayed from Vietnam to the United States with the minimum delay. At the same time it raised issues of access, control, finance, and the determination of content as well as providing new rivals for national broadcasting organisations using surface transmission, whether by aerial or cable.

Satellites offer a range of transmission facilities, not least those of words and speech, but the ability to process this information has depended upon the concurrent development of computers. They have been developed to store, analyse and reassemble material, and were a major factor in the reorganisation of newspaper industries in the 1970s. Computer technology allowed the whole process of newspaper production to be simplified: journalists could set pages ready for printing: editorial offices and printing works could be physically separated, and new editions prepared at a minimum cost. Newspaper industries began the slow change from being labour-intensive to capital-intensive, securing the survival of small-circulation newspapers as production costs fell. The imminent demise of the press as a major form of communication had been continually forecast with the development of television as the primary news medium, but it became clear that the newspaper would survive in a multiplicity of forms, although less certain that the trend towards monopoly structures of ownership would be halted.

It was clear, too, that newspapers and broadcasting organisations would continue to offer challenges, in their own way, to governments concerned with the control of information in a democratic society. In some cases newspapers were able to challenge more effectively than the broadcasting media. In June 1971 the *New York Times* began to publish the 'Pentagon Papers', edited extracts of a comprehensive history of American involvement in Indo-China prepared by a team of experts for Secretary of Defence Robert McNamara in 1967–8. They had been presented to the *Times* by Daniel Ellsberg, a career official in the Defence Department who was concerned about the character of American foreign policy-making and how it was being presented in the early 1970s. As soon as the *Times* began publishing the papers the administration attempted to obtain a restraining order. Eventually the Supreme Court ruled in favour of the *Times* on the basis of the First Amendment. The role of the free press to inform the public had been vindicated, and attempts by the Nixon administration to stifle criticism foiled. The result was further attempts to control the leaking of information from government sources, and the recruitment of a group of 'plumbers'; their activities in the Watergate building in June 1972 brought about the downfall of Nixon, but only through the dogged persistence of two newspaper reporters and the courage of the editor and publisher of the *Washington Post*. The investigation of the involvement of the White House in the Watergate burglary could have only been achieved and published as newspaper journalism. It can also be argued that it could only happen in the United States of America.

It would be rather neat to argue that this book has now come full circle, starting with challenges to the freedom of the press, and ending in a glorious victory. Such a 'progressive' view would be at odds with the main aim which has been to emphasise the dilemmas and compromises which have been part of the relationship between technology, industry, commerce, culture and the state in the last century and a half. All these elements have been combined in the development of channels of communication, the mass media. The exact relationship between the elements has not been constant, neither has that between the channels themselves. Essentially a comparative study of the mass media in any society is a study of power, and the means whereby it is held and legitimised without recourse to coercion. While concentrating on the growth of institutions I have attempted to emphasise that their key function was to present texts to an audience which constructed the known world with its structure of domination and control.

The modern world may be defined as the coming together of the industrial and political revolutions. The former provided the means for greater inequalities in society, the latter claimed the rights of all to be equal. Forms of mass communication were the sinews that bound the revolutions together, the nerves that produced the sense of meaning whereby individuals could understand the nature and character of the modern world. Channels of mass communications were the means whereby the contradictions in the growth of the centralised bureaucratic, industrialised state might be related to ideas of freedom and democracy. This was the fundamental dilemma of the modern world which could only be solved through forms of mass communication.

Bibliography

THERE are no specific references throughout the book, but the main sources for each chapter are listed below. The general section comprises works consulted extensively. The rest of the bibliography has been laid out under the chapter headings, but in many cases a single work will be relevant for more than one chapter. In some cases individual articles have been selected from edited collections, which in themselves have general relevance

GENERAL

Press

G. Boyce, J. Curran and P. Wingate (eds), *Newspaper History: from the 17th Century to the Present Day* (London, 1978)
E. Emery and M. Emery, *The Press and America* (New Jersey, 1978)
Stephen Koss, *The Rise and Fall of the Political Press in Britain*, vol. I, *The Nineteenth Century*, vol. II, *The Twentieth Century* (London, 1981, 1984)
Kurt Koszyk, *Deutsche Presse im 19 Jahrhundert* (Berlin, 1966)
Kurt Koszyk, *Deutsche Pressepolitik im Ersten Weltkrieg* (Duesseldorf, 1968)
Kurt Koszyk, *Deutsche Presse 1914–1945* (Berlin, 1972)
Alfred Lee, *The Daily Newspaper in America* (New York, 1937)

Cinema

Roy Armes, *A Critical History of British Cinema* (New York, 1978)
J. Curran and V. Porter (eds), *British Cinema History* (London, 1983)
S. Kracauer, *From Caligari to Hitler* (Princeton, NJ, 1947)
Eric Rhode, *A History of the Cinema from its Origins to 1970* (Harmondsworth, 1978)
Robert Sklar, *Movie-made America* (New York, 1975)
B. Wright, *The Long View* (London, 1974)

Broadcasting

Erik Barnouw, *A History of Broadcasting in the United States*, vol. I, *A Tower in Babel*, vol. II, *The Golden Web*, vol. III, *The Image Empire* (New York, 1966, 1968, 1970)
Hans Bausch (ed.), *Rundfunk in Deutschland*, 5 vols (Munich, 1980):
  1, Winfried B. Lerg, *Rundfunk in der Weimarer Republik*
  2, Ansgar Diller, *Rundfunkpolitik im Dritten Reich*

3, Hans Bausch, *Rundfunk nach 1945, Erster Teil*
4, Hans Bausch, *Rundfunk nach 1945, Zweiter Teil*
5, Hansjoerg Bessler, *Hoerer- und Zuschauerforschung*
Asa Briggs, *The History of Broadcasting in the United Kingdom*, vol. I, *The Birth of Broadcasting*, vol. II, *The Golden Age of Wireless*, vol. III, *The War of Words*, vol. IV, *Sound and Vision* (Oxford, 1961, 1965, 1970, 1979)
Burton Paulu, *Television and Radio in the United Kingdom* (London, 1981)
Anthony Smith, *The Shadow in the Cave – the Broadcaster, the Audience and the State* (London, 1973)

Journals

These are of particular importance for the wide range of articles on all aspects of the history of the mass media.

Media, Culture and Society
Historical Journal of Film, Radio and Television

APPROACHES TO THE STUDY OF THE MEDIA

R. Barthes, *Mythologies* (London, 1973)
D. G. Boyce, 'Public opinion and historians', *History*, 63 (1978), 214–28
Roger Brown, 'Approaches to the historical development of mass media studies', in J. Tunstall, *Media Sociology* (London, 1970)
J. Culler, *Saussure* (London, 1976)
J. Curran and J. Seaton, *Power without Responsibility* (London, 1985)
T. S. Eliot, *Notes Towards a Definition of Culture* (London, 1962)
M. Gurevitch, T. Bennett, J. Curran and J. Woolacott, *Culture, Society and the Media* (London, 1982)
S. Hall, D. Hobson, A. Lowe and P. Willis, *Culture, Media, Language* (London, 1980)
Stuart Hall, 'Cultural studies: two paradigms', in T. Bennett, G. Martin, C. Mercer and J. Woolacott, *Culture, Ideology and Social Process* (London, 1981)
R. Hoggart, *The Uses of Literacy* (Harmondsworth, 1958)
Joseph T. Klapper, *The Effects of Mass Communication* (New York, 1960)
H. Lasswell and R. D. Casey, *Propaganda, Communication, and Public Opinion* (Princeton, NJ, 1946)
F. R. Leavis and D. Thompson, *Culture and the Environment* (London, 1933)
Denis McQuail (ed.), *The Sociology of Mass Communications* (Harmondsworth, 1972)
Denis McQuail, 'The influence and effects of mass media', in J. Curran, M. Gurevitch and J. Woolacott, *Mass Communication and Society* (London, 1977)
Denis McQuail, *Mass Communication Theory: An Introduction*, 2nd edn (London, 1987)
C. Seymour-Ure, *The Press, Politics and the Public* (London, 1968)
C. Seymour-Ure, *The Political Impact of the Mass Media* (London, 1974)
Paul Smith (ed.), *The Historian and Film* (Cambridge, 1976)
A. Swingewood, *The Myth of Mass Culture* (London, 1977)
D. Thompson (ed.), *Discrimination and Popular Culture*, 2nd edn (Harmondsworth, 1973)
J. Tunstall, *The Media are American* (London, 1977)

Raymond Williams, *Culture and Society, 1780–1950* (Harmondsworth, 1963)
Raymond Williams, *Television: Technology and Cultural Form* (London, 1974)
Raymond Williams, *Communications*, 3rd edn (Harmondsworth, 1976)
Raymond Williams, *Keywords* (London, 1976)
Raymond Williams, *Culture* (London, 1981)

THE DEVELOPMENT OF THE PRESS

J. H. Altschull, 'Chronicle of a democratic press in Germany before the Hitler takeover', *Journalism Quarterly*, 52 (1975), 229–38
O. Boyd-Barrett, 'Market control and wholesale news, the case of Reuters', in G. Boyce, J. Curran and P. Wingate, *Newspaper History* (London, 1978)
O. Boyd-Barrett, *The International News Agencies* (London, 1980)
C. Chapman, *Russell of 'The Times'* (London, 1984)
G. Cranfield, *The Press and Society: From Caxton to Northcliffe* (London, 1978)
M. Eksteins, *The Limits of Reason* (Oxford, 1975)
I. Fischer-Frauendienst, *Bismarcks Pressepolitik* (Münster, 1963)
William H. Hale, *Horace Greely* (New York, 1961)
Alex Hall, *Scandal, Sensation and Social Democracy. The SDP Press and Wilhelmine Germany 1890–1914* (Cambridge, 1977)
Alan Lee, *The Origins of the Popular Press* (London, 1976)
F. L. Mott, *American Journalism* (New York, 1941)
E. Naujoks, 'Bismarck und die Organisation der Regierungspresse', *Historische Zeitschrift*, 205 (1967), 46–80
L. O'Boyle, 'The image of the journalist in France, Germany and England, 1815–1848', *Comparative Studies in Society and History*, 10 (1967–8), 290–317
R. Pound and G. Harmsworth, *Northcliffe* (London, 1959)
Don S. Seitz, *Joseph Pulitzer* (New York, 1924)
Fritz Stern, *Gold and Iron* (Harmondsworth, 1987)
G. Storey, *Reuter's Century* (London, 1951)
W. A. Swanberg, *Citizen Hearst* (London, 1962)
A. J. P. Taylor, *Beaverbrook* (London, 1972)
F. Williams, *Dangerous Estate* (London, 1957)
R. Williams, 'The growth of the popular press', in *The Long Revolution* (London, 1961)

THE EMERGENCE OF THE CINEMA

E. Barnouw, *Documentary, A History of the Non-Fiction Film* (London, 1974)
W. Bredow and R. Zurek (eds), *Film und Gesellschaft in Deutschland, Dokumente und Materialien* (Hamburg, 1975)
K. Brownlow, *The Parade's Gone By* (London, 1968)
M. Chanan, *The Dream That Kicks* (London, 1980)
Thorold Dickinson, *A Discovery of Cinema* (London, 1971)
A. Field, *Picture Palace* (London, 1974)
Robert M. Henderson, *D. W. Griffith. His Life and Work* (New York, 1972)
Cecil Hepworth, *Came the Dawn* (London, 1951)
Lewis Jacobs, *The Rise of the American Film* (New York, 1969)
I. C. Jarvie, *Towards a Sociology of the Cinema* (London, 1970)

E. Lindgren, *The Art of Film*, 2nd edn (London, 1963)
R. Low, *The History of the British Film*, vol. i, *1896–1906* (with Roger Manvell), vol. ii, *1906–1914* (London, 1948, 1949)
Lary May, *Screening out the Past* (New York, 1980)
Terry Ramsaye, *A Million and One Nights* (London, 1964)
G. Sadoul, *Histoire du cinéma mondial des origines à nos jours* (Paris, 1949)
D. J. Wenden, *The Birth of the Movies* (London, 1975)

PROPAGANDA 1914–1918

Kevin Brownlow, *The War, the West, and the Wilderness* (London, 1979)
George Creel, *How we Advertised America* (New York, 1920)
Klaus Epstein, *Matthias Erzberger and the Dilemma of German Democracy* (Princeton, NJ, 1959)
Cate Haste, *Keep the Home Fires Burning* (London, 1977)
D. Hopkin, 'Domestic censorship in the First World War', *Journal of Contemporary History*, 5, No. 4 (1970), 151–69
P. Knightley, *The First Casualty: The War Correspondent as Hero, Propagandist and Myth Maker from the Crimea to Vietnam* (London, 1975)
H. D. Lasswell, *Propaganda Technique in the World War* (London, 1927)
R. Low, *The History of the British Film*, vol. iii, *1914–1918* (London, 1950)
Alice Marquis, 'Words as weapons: propaganda in Britain and Germany during the First World War', *Journal of Contemporary History*, 13 (1978), 467–98
N. Reeves, 'Film propaganda and its audience: the example of Britain's official films during the First World War', *Journal of Contemporary History*, 18 (1983), 463–94
M. L. Sanders, 'Wellington House and British propaganda in the First World War', *Historical Journal*, 18 (1975), 119–46
M. L. Sanders and P. M. Taylor, *British Propaganda during the First World War* (London, 1982)
J. D. Squires, *British Propaganda at Home and in the United States from 1914 to 1917* (Cambridge, Mass., 1935)
Sir Campbell Stuart, *Secrets of Crewe House: the story of a famous campaign* (London, 1920)
P. M. Taylor, 'The Foreign Office and British propaganda during the First World War', *Historical Journal*, 23 (1980), 875–98
D. G. Wright, 'The Great War, government propaganda and English "Men of Letters", 1914–1916', *Literature and History* (1978), no. 7, 70–100.

CONSOLIDATION

A. Briggs, *Governing the BBC* (London, 1979)
D. Cardiff, 'Time, money and culture: BBC programme finances 1927–1939', *Media, Culture and Society*, 5 (1983), 373–93
M. Eksteins, *The Limits of Reason. The German Democratic Press and the Collapse of Weimar Democracy* (London, 1975)
R. Elson, *The Intimate History of a Publishing Enterprise*, 2 vols (New York, 1968, 1973)
Peter Gay, *Weimar Culture* (London, 1968)
D. Halberstam, *The Powers that Be* (New York, 1979)

206   BIBLIOGRAPHY

A. Hitler, *Mein Kampf*, reprint (London, 1969)

John A. Leopold, *Alfred Hugenberg. The Radical Nationalist Campaign against the Weimar Republic* (New Haven, 1977)

W. Lippmann, *Public Opinion* (New York, 1922)

W. Lippmann, *The Phantom Public* (New York, 1925)

R. Low, *The History of the British Film*, vol. IV, *1918–1929* (London, 1971)

Robert Metz, *CBS. Reflections in a Bloodshot Eye* (New York, 1975)

William S. Paley, *As it Happened* (New York, 1979)

Robert E. Peck, 'Policy and control – a case study: German broadcasting 1923–1933', *Media, Culture and Society*, 5 (1983), 349–72

Mark Pegg, *Broadcasting and Society* (London, 1983)

Lord Reith, *Into the Wind* (London, 1949)

Ronald Steel, *Walter Lippmann and the American Century* (London, 1980)

Charles Stuart (ed.), *The Reith Diaries* (London, 1975)

Philip M. Taylor, *The Projection of Britain* (Cambridge, 1981)

THE MEDIA AND THE STATE IN THE 1930s

A. Aldgate, *Cinema and History: British Newsreels and the Spanish Civil War* (London, 1979)

J. Baxter, *Hollywood in the Thirties* (London, 1968)

A. Bergman, *We're in the Money* (New York, 1971)

E. K. Bramsted, *Goebbels and National Socialist Propaganda 1925–1945* (London, 1965)

Commission on Educational and Cultural Films, *The Film in National Life* (London, 1932)

M. Dickinson and S. Street, *Cinema and the State: The Film and the British Government* (London, 1985)

P. French, *The Movie Moguls* (London, 1969)

O. J. Hale, *The Captive Press in the Third Reich* (Princeton, NJ, 1964)

Forsyth Hardy, *John Grierson: A Documentary Biography* (London, 1979)

Ian Kershaw, 'The Führer image and political integration', in G. Hirschfeld and Lothar Kettenacker, *The 'Führer State': Myth and Reality* (Stuttgart, 1981)

A. Kuhn, 'British documentary in the 1930s and "Independence"', in Don MacPherson, *Traditions of Independence: British Cinema in the Thirties* (London, 1980)

R. Low, *The History of the British Film*, vol. I, *Documentary and Educational Films*, vol. II, *Films of Comment and Persuasion*, vol. III, *Film-making in 1930s Britain* (1979, 1979, 1985)

J. Petley, *Capital and Culture: German Cinema 1933–1945* (London, 1979)

M. S. Phillips, 'The Nazi control of the German film industry', *Journal of European Studies*, 1 (1971), 37–68

Political and Economic Planning (PEP), *Report on the British Press* (London, 1938)

J. Richards, 'The British Board of Film Censors and content control in the 1930s: images of Britain', *Historical Journal of Film, Radio and Television*, 1, No. 2 (1981), 95–116

J. Richards, 'The British Board of Film Censors and content control in the 1930s: foreign affairs', *Historical Journal of Film, Radio and Television* (1982)

P. Scannell and D. Cardiff, 'Serving the nation: public service broadcasting before the war', in B. Waites, T. Bennett and G. Martin (eds), *Popular Culture: Past and Present* (London, 1982)

J. P. Stern, *Hitler, The Führer and the People* (London, 1975)

S. Street, 'The Hays Office and the defence of the British market in the 1930s', *Historical Journal of Film, Radio and Television*, 5, No. 1 (1985), 37–56

T. Streeter, 'Policy discourse and broadcast practice: the FCC, the US broadcast networks and the discourse of the marketplace', *Media, Culture and Society*, 5 (1983), 247–62

Philip M. Taylor, 'British official attitudes towards propaganda abroad 1918–1939', in N. Pronay and D. W. Spring, *Propaganda, Politics and Film* (London, 1982)

Richard Taylor, *Film Propaganda: Soviet Russia and Nazi Germany* (London, 1979)

David Weinberg, 'Approaches to the study of film in the Third Reich: A critical appraisal', *Journal of Contemporary History*, 19 (1984), 105–26

David Welch, *Propaganda and the German Cinema, 1933–1945* (Oxford, 1981)

Z. A. B. Zeman, *Nazi Propaganda*, 2nd edn (London, 1973)

PROPAGANDA IN WAR AND PEACE

M. Balfour, *Propaganda in War 1939–1945* (London, 1979)

C. Barr, *Ealing Studios* (Newton Abbot, 1977)

A. Calder, *The People's War* (London, 1969)

Z. Chafee Jr., *Government and Mass Communications* (Chicago, 1947)

C. Cruickshank, *The Fourth Arm: Psychological Warfare 1938–1945* (London, 1977)

Robert E. Herzstein, *The War that Hitler Won* (London, 1979)

W. E. Hocking, *Freedom of the Press* (Chicago, 1947)

A. Kendrick, *Prime Time: The Life of Edward R. Murrow* (Boston, 1969)

K. Koszyk, 'The Press in the British Zone of Germany', in N. Pronay and K. Wilson (eds), *The Political Re-education of Germany and her Allies after World War II* (London, 1985)

Daniel J. Leab, '"See it Now": a legend reassessed', in J. E. O'Connor (ed.), *American History/American Television* (New York, 1985)

L. Lochner, *The Goebbels Diaries* (London, 1948)

Charles Lysaght, *Brendan Bracken* (London, 1979)

R. Maltby, 'Made for each other: the melodrama of Hollywood and the House Committee on Un-American Activities 1947', in P. Davies and B. Neve (eds), *Cinema, Politics and Society in America* (Manchester, 1981)

I. McLaine, *Ministry of Morale* (London, 1979)

C. Shindler, *Hollywood Goes to War* (London, 1979)

F. Taylor (ed.), *The Goebbels Diaries 1939–1941* (London, 1982)

Philip M. Taylor, 'Propaganda in international politics 1919–1939', in K. R. M. Short (ed.), *Film and Radio Propaganda in World War II* (London, 1983)

Parker Tyler, *Magic and Myth of the Movies*, British edn (London, 1971)

T. Wildy, 'From MOI to COI – publicity and propaganda in Britain 1945–1951', *Historical Journal of Film, Radio and Television*, 6, No. 1 (1986), 3–18

THE AGE OF TELEVISION

E. Barnouw, *Tube of Plenty: The Evolution of American Television* (New York, 1975)

208   BIBLIOGRAPHY

D. Boorstin, *The Image* (Harmondsworth, 1963)

R. Braddon, *Roy Thomson of Fleet Street* (London, 1965)

Lt. Col. Chetwode Crawley, *From Telegraphy to Television* (London, 1931)

John Hill, *Sex, Class and Realism: British Cinema 1956–63* (London, 1986)

R. Manvell, *The Film and the Public* (Harmondsworth, 1955)

J. Margach, *The Abuse of Power* (London, 1978)

M. Mayer, *About Television* (New York, 1972)

H. Newcomb, *Television: A Critical View*, 3rd edn (New York, 1982)

J. Sandford, *The Mass Media of the German-speaking Countries* (London, 1976)

B. Sendall, *Independent Television in Britain*, vol. I, *Origins and Foundation 1946–62*, vol. II, *Expansion and Change 1958–68* (London, 1982, 1983)

A. Smith, *The Politics of Information* (London, 1978)

J. Trenaman and D. McQuail, *Television and the Political Image* (London, 1961)

J. Tunstall, *The Media in Britain* (London, 1983)

A. Walker, *Hollywood, England* (London, 1974)

Theodore White, *The Making of the President: 1960* (New York, 1961)

A. Williams, *Broadcasting and Democracy in West Germany* (London, 1976)

G. Wyndham Goldie, *Facing the Nation: Television and Politics 1936–1976* (London, 1977)

MASS COMMUNICATION AND THE MODERN WORLD

S. Cohen and J. Young (eds), *The Manufacture of News* (London, 1973)

P. Conrad, *Television, The Medium and its Manners* (London, 1982)

Muriel G. Cantor, *Prime-time Television* (New York, 1980)

Liz Curtis, *Ireland: The Propaganda War* (London, 1984)

D. Dayan and E. Katz, 'Performing media events', in J. Curran, A. Smith and P. Wingate (eds), *Impacts and Influences: Essays on Media Power in the Twentieth Century* (London, 1987)

J. Ellis, *Visible Fictions: Cinema, Television, Video* (London, 1982)

Edward J. Epstein, *News from Nowhere: Television and the News* (New York, 1973)

N. Garnham, *Structures of Television*, revised edn (London, 1978)

J. D. Halloran, P. Elliott and G. Murdock, *Demonstrations and Communications* (Harmondsworth, 1970)

J. McGinnis, *The Selling of the President* (Harmondsworth, 1970)

Marshall McLuhan, *Understanding Media* (London, 1964)

A. Smith, *Goodbye Gutenberg: The Newspaper Revolution of the 1980s* (New York, 1980)

A. Smith, *Newspapers and Democracy* (Cambridge, Mass., 1980)

B. Woodward and C. Bernstein, *All the President's Men* (London, 1974)

Index